STRATEGY AND ETHNOCENTRISM

KEN BOOTH

CROOM HELM LONDON

© 1979 Ken Booth

Croom Helm Ltd, 2-10 St John's Road, London SW11

British Library Cataloguing in Publication Data
Booth, Ken
   Strategy and ethnocentrism.
   1. Strategy   2. Ethnocentrism
   I. Title
   355.4'3   U163
   ISBN 0-85664-528-1

Printed in Great Britain by
Biddles Ltd, Guildford, Surrey

CONTENTS

TO EURWEN

my daily reminder that there are other than
English, strategic, and masculine ways
of thinking

PREFACE

As far as strategy is concerned, we have seen the past and it did not work particularly well. Unfortunately the future is not what it was either. Perhaps it never was, but Armageddon is now an overnight possibility, not merely a distant Biblical prophesy. Of all the threats facing civilisation those posed by military technology and strategic doctrine are of particular concern, because they are the most instantaneous. Survival in these circumstances will be because of, not despite the theory and practice of strategy. However, some individuals reject the strategic paradigm, and argue that even to think about these matters is to condone and perpetuate a potentially catastrophic war system. Others, myself included, believe that because armed forces exist, and cannot be wished away, and because they can be the instrument of worthy as well as ignoble purposes, they are deserving of serious scholarly attention. Strategy is certainly brutal, but it is also concerned with profound moral questions. These questions are more important than simply life and death: they are also concerned with individual and group values, including definitions of freedom and aspirations for justice. Ultimately strategy is a continuation of philosophy with an admixture of firepower.

The overriding aim for those involved in strategic studies is to develop more incisive analysis and (either explicitly or as a by-product) better prescriptions, so that enough short terms can be cobbled together to enable the world to continue travelling, more or less hopefully, until it arrives at something better, or until it finally disappears. This book is concerned with one area of the subject where there is clear room for improvement, namely that area where what might be called the fog of culture has interfered with the theory and practice of strategy. In particular, the book is concerned with that phenomenon inelegantly known as 'ethnocentrism'. Cultural distortions, like other perceptual mechanisms, are important because there is no clear dividing line between image and reality: the reality of our strategic world is inextricably interconnected with our manner of conceiving it.

When I began thinking about ethnocentrism and strategy my attention had been attracted by a handful of intriguing episodes in recent history. On further examination, however, the scope of the relationship just grew and grew, and not in a limited and preordained fashion like that precocious *cliché*, Topsy, but in a pervasive fashion, like escaping gas filling a room. This was surprising, partly because academics expect there to be a direct relationship between the importance of a subject and the weightiness of its associated literature. On this occasion, however, the opposite was true: what appeared to be a major problem in strategy had virtually nothing written about it. The main aim of this book is therefore to provide the first extensive examination of the relationship between ethnocentrism and strategy, to demonstrate by wide illustration its importance in all areas of the subject, to follow through its implications, and to suggest ways of dealing with the different problems it poses for teachers, theorists and planners.

Essentially, this book is a consciousness-raising exercise. The audience to which it is addressed is varied. It is for those who have not thought about the relationship between ethnocentrism and strategy. It is for those for whom the idea of the relationship is not novel, but who have not had the time or inclination to speculate about its implications themselves. More particularly, it is for those who complacently think that they are aware of the relationship and its problems, but who have either misconceived it, or have failed to let it affect the way they approach or carry out their work: a sizeable group of strategists profess to recognise that the strategic world is multicultural, but they behave as if it is not. Most important of all, however, this book is addressed to the new students of strategic studies, in the hope that their sensitivity may be raised before it is too late, before what Charles Manning has called a 'hardening of the categories' sets in, and they become as culture-bound as their unliberated teachers.

The seed for this book was a paper which I presented to the Annual Convention of the International Studies Association in Toronto in March 1976. The subsequent completion of the book was made possible by the Advanced Research Program of the United States Naval War College, which gave me the opportunity, in the autumn of 1977, to be the Scholar-in-Residence at the College. I greatly appreciate the support of Vice-Admiral Julien LeBourgeois USN (Ret.), Rear Admiral Huntington Hardisty USN, Vice-Admiral James B. Stockdale USN and Captain William A. Platte USN — the three Presidents and Deputy-President of the War College who authorised support of my study under the terms of the Naval War College Advanced Research Program. I am especially indebted to two people who know how to make an academic feel both at home and yet completely independent in a War College atmosphere: I refer to Professor Hugh G. Nott, the Director of the Center for Advanced Research and Professor James E. King, former Director of

Research at the Center; Hugh Nott created excellent conditions for work, and at the same time provided a degree of general support which went far beyond that which I had a right to expect. James E. King is an inestimable mentor and critic, whose own painstaking work shows us all how strategy and scholarship can be compatible bedfellows. Needless to say, my views are my own and do not necessarily reflect those of anyone associated with the Naval War College.

Several individuals gave detailed criticisms of my original paper, and provided suggestions for further thought. For their help in this respect I wish to thank Masood Hyder, John Garnett, James King, James Piscatori, Bryan Ranft, Elizabeth Saxon and Harvey Starr. Jane Davis, as ever, was an invaluable support, at the same time a keen research assistant, careful editor and proof-reader, and compiler of the index. John Morse did useful early editorial work at the Center for Advanced Research, and Kathleen Ashook was an efficient research assistant at the Naval War College Library. Indeed, the whole library staff at the NWC were exceptional in their efficiency and helpfulness. For typing the various drafts I wish to thank Chris Anderson, Doreen Hamer, Debbie Tavares and Marian Weston. Finally, it gives me pleasure to record a special note of appreciation for Major Gerald Keller USMC for ensuring that all the needs of a Scholar-in-Residence were not only quickly and cheerfully met, but were, in true Marine fashion, anticipated and dealt with before they became problems.

Strategy books are concerned with the darker side of human behaviour. But this behaviour, unpleasant as it is, does have as its objective the creation of conditions in which cherished values can survive. In this respect I want simply to mention the Notts and the Kellers, two families who offered their support to strangers when the latter needed it. My appreciation of their friendship has nothing to do with the usual debts incurred in writing a strategy book, but ultimately it has everything to do with why we should think about 'better' strategy, why we should worry about strategy with a human face, and why the security of liberal societies is so important.

Ken Booth
Aberystwyth
June 1978

1 CONCEPTS AND PROPOSITIONS

The socio-psychological map of the world may be thought of as largely reducible to a cultural map. *Charles A. Manning*

If triangles had a god, he would have three sides. *Montesquieu*

Whether or not God created the world in his own image, men certainly create the social universe in their own images. Ethnocentrism is one cultural variant of this universal socio-psychological phenomenon: societies look at the world with their own group as the centre, they perceive and interpret other societies within their own frames of reference, and they invariably judge them inferior. Ethnocentrism is a phenomenon which has ramifications in most if not all areas of inter-group relations. Not the least of its ramifications is in that area, military strategy, where those groups called states deal with each other in the most brutal way.

Strategists as a professional body have not concerned themselves with the problem of ethnocentrism. There is only a very occasional reference to the problem in strategic literature. Even the best analyses of the state of the discipline apparently do not think ethnocentrism sufficiently important to deserve consideration.[1] Writers about ethnicity have not helped: their interest in violence has been restricted to the ethnic causes of intranational or international conflict.[2] Even psychologists interested in international relations, or international theorists concerned with problems of perception and misperception, have generally skirted the problem and have certainly ignored its military manifestations.[3] Despite this lack of attention, it will be shown that ethnocentrism is indeed a pervasive problem in the theory and practice of strategy. The questions to be addressed are not simple, nor are the attempted answers: and neither the questions nor the answers can be confined to the narrow bounds of what conventionally constitutes strategic studies.

Concepts

At the outset, it is important to clarify the two concepts, 'ethnocentrism' and 'culture', which underpin the whole argument of the book, and to introduce two related concepts, 'cultural relativism' and 'national character'.

Culture

Like Hermann Goering, strategists may be apt to reach for their revolvers

13

at the sound of the word culture. However, if students are to be serious anthropologists of *Homo Strategicus,* a relevant concept has to be delineated.

Culture is a notoriously nebulous concept: why else would there be over two hundred definitions? For present purposes, however, the following is a useful beginning: 'A culture is a set of patterns, of and for behaviour, prevalent among a group of human beings at a specified time period and which . . . presents . . . observable and sharp discontinuities.'[4] Within the sense of this definition culture embraces different modes of thought, implicit and explicit behavioural patterns and social habits, identifiable symbols and signals for acquiring and transmitting knowledge, distinctive achievements, well-established ideas and values, particular ways of adapting to the environment and solving problems, and significant discontinuities in all these respects as between one group and another. Culture is one of the key factors determining *who* is *whom* in the social universe.

Cultural thoughtways — myths as well as reason — form the core of societies and play a central role in the affairs of men. Culture is a basic concept in politics and history, and therefore inevitably plays an important role in strategy, which is concerned with the military relations between groups. The map of the world across which strategists are wont to draw their arrows is more than a politico-military map made up of state boundaries, physical features, transportation systems and deployed forces. It is also a cultural map, for those fighting units called nation-states are identifiable socio-psychologically, as well as politically. If culture is a major factor in strategy, it therefore follows that cultural appraisals (and distortions) will also be of great significance. This is where ethnocentrism enters the discussion.

Ethnocentrism

Like other important terms in international politics, ethnocentrism is often defined more easily than it is recognised. Although some may object to the term as a piece of unnecessary jargon, it has been persevered with because it is a relatively unfamiliar word in strategic studies and therefore calls attention with greater force than would otherwise be the case to the precise thesis, or set of problems, with which this book is concerned. Until our consciousness is raised, there is some advantage in having a word which we use self-consciously. This would not be the case with such a familiar phrase as 'national bias'. Ethnocentrism is used in the following closely related senses:

(1) *As a term to describe feelings of group centrality and superiority.*

This was the original meaning when the term was introduced by W. G. Sumner in 1906: ethnocentrism is the 'view of things in which one's own group is the centre of everything, and all others are scaled and rated with reference to it'.[5] This original meaning has been retained. The characteristic features of ethnocentrism in this sense include: strong identification with one's own group and its culture, the tendency to see one's own group as the centre of the universe, the tendency to perceive events in terms of one's own interests, the tendency to prefer one's own way of life (culture) over all others (seeing it as involving the best and right ways of acting, with an associated bias against other groups and their ways of acting), and a general suspicion of foreigners, their modes of thought, action and motives.[6] In these senses, ethnocentrism has been a universal social phenomenon.

(2) *As a technical term to describe a faulty methodology in the social sciences.* In attempting to understand other societies, social scientists, like all other social groups, tend to 'privilege' their own conceptual systems, and so distort their picture of what other groups may actually be doing. In this technical sense ethnocentrism involves the projection of one's own frame of reference onto others. It is: 'the tendency to assess aspects of other cultures in terms of one's own culture, and thus in social science research to apply in a biased and improper fashion the standards and values of one's own culture in the study and analysis of other cultures. Such bias is often caused by an implicit or explicit belief in the superiority of one's own culture.'[7] Such ethnocentric perceptions will clearly have considerable theoretical and practical significance in international relations. 'Cultural relativism' is the technical term used to describe the effort to overcome ethnocentric bias.

(3) *As a synonym for being 'culture-bound'.* Being culture-bound is a necessary condition for ethnocentric perception, and sometimes the terms are used synonymously. Being culture-bound refers to the inability of an individual or group to see the world through the eyes of a different national or ethnic group: it is the inability to put aside one's own cultural attitudes and imaginatively recreate the world from the perspective of those belonging to a different group. This means that it is almost impossible to empathise with foreigners. In this sense, again, ethnocentrism is a virtually universal phenomenon.

Cultural Relativism

If ethnocentrism is 'the natural condition of mankind',[8] it is evident that 'cultural relativism', which is the opposite tendency, will be in rather short supply. Cultural relativism is the approach whereby social and cultural phenomena 'are perceived and described in terms of scientific detachment as, ideally, from the perspective of participants in or adherents of a given culture'.[9] The observer attempts to be on guard against his own ethnocentric bias, and at least tries to transcend or eliminate it for the period of his observation. If the principle of cultural relativism is to be reasonably attained it requires a difficult exercise of imagination and empathy on the part of the observer 'so that he can see others as they see themselves or as they wish to be seen'. In practice, however, an observer cannot completely eradicate his own cultural conditioning, and the structure of ideas and values which it passes on to him.

To 'know the enemy' has always been a cardinal tenet of strategy. If this goal is to be achieved in the future with more regularity than it has been achieved in the past, then cultural relativism should take its place in the strategist's lexicon. Knowing the enemy is the bedrock of the business of strategy: strategic theories, in comparison, are second order problems. To concentrate on doctrines before enemies is to put the theoretical cart before the actual horse – a double error.

National Character

In discussing ethnocentrism in relation to groups as big as nations, as well as in relation to individuals, it is necessary to associate, albeit briefly, with the unpopular and contentious problem of 'national character'. It is probably true that we still do not know enough about national character to know whether it really exists or not.[10] Nevertheless, it is assumed in this book that one can reasonably talk about probabilities and tendencies as long as one does not attempt to explain every individual in terms of national character, or use the concept as a mono-causal explanation of international events. Few are likely to deny that 'certain qualities of intellect and character occur more frequently and are more highly valued in one nation than in another'.[11] What is usually wrong is not the concept, but the use to which it is put.

As national character is associated in some minds with extreme stereotyping, some writers prefer to talk about 'national styles' as a useful if again simplifying intellectual tool to create some order in our thinking about the behaviour of those responsible for foreign policy.[12] Other writers would object to this construct also. But even if one were entirely to reject both these approaches, the fact cannot be overlooked that many individuals and groups, including sophisticated analysts, do think in these terms. Such thinking may be misbegotten, but the illusions which emerge are politically and strategically significant, and require our close attention. Our mistaken beliefs form an integral part of our social universe (cynics and idealists might unite to say the largest part). Indeed, much more significant than any one nation's illusion of omnipotence in international politics is the omnipotence of illusion which grips the society of states as a whole.

Propositions

Some of the propositions below may be familiar in a general sense: what this book is concerned with, however, is their cultural dimension, an aspect which so far has been largely ignored by the strategic community. The chief interrelated propositions to be discussed are as follows:

(a) Ethnocentrism is one of the factors which can seriously interfere with rational strategic planning.

(b) Together with other mechanisms (psychological, historical and bureaucratic) ethnocentrism can distort important aspects of strategic thinking, especially where problems of perception and prediction are involved.

(c) Strategists as a body are remarkably incurious about the character of their enemies and allies. Ethnocentrism is one way in which individuals and groups consciously and subconsciously evade reality.

(d) Ethnocentrism is an inadequate and dangerous basis for strategic studies, but it has been neglected as a source of misperception in strategy and has not been the cause of much methodological anguish.

(e) Ethnocentrism in recent history has been a source of mistakes in strategic practice and misconceptions in theorising about strategy. This is disconcerting in a policy science such as strategy where the costs of mistakes are always high.

(f) From a narrow military viewpoint, ethnocentrism is not always dysfunctional.

(g) Ethnocentrism interacts with the irreducible predicaments, of international security, and intensifies them.

(h) Threat assessment is not concerned just with 'capabilities' and 'intentions', but also with the ways in which capabilities and intentions are perceived and misperceived. Images are the source of politico-military behaviour. Threat assessment is therefore seriously vulnerable to ethnocentric distortion.

(i) Strategic studies have become very inbred. The subject needs a more interdisciplinary approach, to the extent of abolishing 'academic strategists' as they have developed in the last twenty years.

(j) The construct of rational Strategic Man as a tool for thinking about the world is a dangerous distortion. It needs replacing by a move towards 'strategy with a human face'.

(k) Civilian strategists and policy planners need to 'retool' in order to take account of ethnocentric bias.

(l) Strategists as a profession have not accommodated, in deed or word, to the problems of conflict and stability in a multicultural world.

(m) The pursuit of cultural and strategic relativism is a liberating experience; it is a useful antidote to the grip of ethnocentrism, ignorance and megalogic.

(n) Strategy is a vital but misunderstood activity: it is too significant to be left in the hands of any narrow professional group.

(o) Better strategic studies are not necessarily synonymous with better strategic practice, nor is better strategic theory and practice synonymous with peace.

Whatever its origins,[13] ethnocentrism will be shown to be an important source of mistakes in the theory and practice of strategy. In particular cases it will not be the sole cause, but rather a contributory one. Too often, we simply will not know enough about individual or group psychology to determine the extent to which a particular thought or act was a manifestation of ethnocentrism or of any of the other large number of psychological mechanisms that screen information and distort perception.[14] However, in the illustrations which form the bulk of Chapters 3 and 4 below care has been taken to choose examples in which there seems little doubt that the problem stemmed at least in part from cultural factors, whatever other distorting mechanisms were also present. If successful, the discussion will not only help increase sensitivity towards the fact of ethnocentric bias, but will also help to undermine any complacency which strategists may have about their discipline or business. It is well for strategists to be reminded that misreading the future has always been one of their traditional callings.

It is not the contention of this book that all outbreaks of violence are the result of misperception, or that all misperception in strategy is caused by ethnocentrism. While the aim of the book is to show the importance of ethnocentrism, its thesis is neither a reductionist one nor one which seeks to 'over-psychologise'. It is important to avoid the temptation of exaggerating the role which misunderstanding and misperception play, and thereby tending to overlook the real clashes of interest and the brutal power relationships which actually exist. Sometimes conflicts do result from a lack of understanding, but sometimes they result from one nation or another understanding only too well and having an uncompromising determination to have things done in their own way.

Notes

1. See Hedley Bull, 'Strategic Studies and Its Critics', *World Politics*, XX (July 1968), pp. 593-605; C. S. Gray, 'Strategists: Some Views Critical of the Profession', *International Journal*, 1970-1, pp. 771-90.

2. See, for example, the extensive reader edited by Nathan Glazer and Daniel P. Moynihan, *Ethnicity: Theory and Experience* (Cambridge, Mass.: Harvard University Press, 1975).

3. The most substantial contribution to thinking about problems of perception and misperception is Robert Jervis, *Perception and Misperception in International Politics* (Princeton, NJ: Princeton University Press, 1976).

4. C. Levi-Strauss, 'Social Structure' in A. L. Kroeber (ed.), *Anthropology Today* (Chicago: University of Chicago Press, 1953), p. 536, quoted in Julius Gould and William L. Kolb, *A Dictionary of the Social Sciences* (London: Tavistock Publications, 1964), p. 165.

5. W. G. Sumner, *Folkways* (Boston: Ginn, 1906), p. 13.

6. The preceding list of characteristics is based on various definitions of ethnocentrism: Jerome D. Frank, *Sanity and Survival: Psychological Aspects of War and Peace* (New York: Random House, 1967), p. 104; E. Adamson Hoebel, 'Ethnocentrism' in Gould and Kolb, p. 245; Otto Klineberg, *The Human Dimension in International Relations* (New York: Holt, Rinehart and Winston, 1964), pp. 95-6; Ross Stagner, *Psychological Aspects of International Conflict* (Belmont, Calif.: Brooks/Cole, 1967), p. 25; Ralph K. White, *Nobody Wanted War: Misperception in Vietnam and Other Wars* (Garden City, N.Y.: Doubleday, 1968), p. 287.

7. Geoffrey K. Roberts, *A Dictionary of Political Analysis* (London: Longman, 1971), p. 76.

8. I. M. Lewis, *Social Anthropology in Perspective* (Harmondsworth, Middx: Penguin Books, 1976), p. 13.

9. David Bindey, 'Cultural Relativism' in *International Encyclopedia of the Social Sciences*, vol. 3 (New York: Macmillan and Free Press, 1968), pp. 543-7. The rest of the paragraph is based on this source and R. M. MacIver and C. Page, *Society: An Introductory Analysis* (London: Macmillan, 1949), p. 167.

10. Klineberg, *Human Dimension*, pp. 140-63.

11. Hans J. Morgenthau, *Politics among Nations: The Struggle for Power and Peace* (New York: Knopf, 1964), p. 126.

12. See Stanley Hoffmann, *Gulliver's Troubles: or, The Setting of American Foreign Policy* (New York: McGraw-Hill, 1968), pp. 87ff.

13. The origins of ethnocentrism, a very important subject in its own right, is beyond the scope of this book. Post-war theorists stressed social and environmental conditioning: see T. W. Adorno *et al. The Authoritarian Personality* (New York: Harper and Brothers, 1950); G. W. Allport, *The Nature of Prejudice* (Reading Mass.: Addison-Wesley Publishing Co., 1954). More recently, it has been argued by some theorists that ethnocentrism may have a biological basis: see the discussion on the sociobiology of nationalism in *New Society*, 22, 29 July 1976; 5, 12, 19 August 1976.

14. Note, for example, the select bibliography in Jervis, *Perception and Misperception* pp. 425-31.

2 THE STRATEGIC PARADIGM

My mother, drunk or sober. *G. K. Chesterton*

Grey is the colour of truth. *André Gide*

Strategy is a universal preoccupation of governments. Those responsible for the security of political units cannot opt out of it, for the threat and use of force as instruments of policy will not go away simply as a result of wishing or hoping. But to note that governments are interested in security, and hence strategy, does not get us far. Strategy itself might be characterised as a universal preoccupation, but that does not mean that it is conceived in universal terms. Whether the phenomenon is strategy or a mountain, what we see depends upon where we stand. In an operational sense strategy is more nationalistic in its nature than most other aspects of social behaviour. Some humour and some music can have immediate appeal to almost everybody, but strategic performances are not cultural universals. Strategy is a contextual phenomenon. The antics of Charlie Chaplin and the symphonies of Beethoven have been described as 'universal' in the way that they can have meaning to people who have been widely separated in time or space: the same cannot be said about the mental feats of Herman Kahn or the solemn incantations of Marshal Sokolovsky.

The Assumptions of an Ethnocentric Profession

Strategy is a peculiarly ethnocentric business. However, neither strategists themselves, nor non-strategists, have joined together to worry about the fact. Those professionally involved, and those on the periphery, have found the problem easy to ignore.

The oversight of non-strategists is not surprising. Strategy is a morbid and unfashionable subject, even to many in closely associated fields. Military policy might consume fabulous sums of money, its opportunity costs might mean that tantalising social possibilities are forgone, it might threaten life and society with unprecedented dangers — nevertheless, there remains a body of opinion which believes that strategy is not really something which a scholar and gentleman should spend his time studying, and still less practising. Strategy and all its attendant problems tend to be ignored or rejected by the majority of trained minds in the community. Despite the democratic impulses of the age, the deadly subject of war is thought to be too serious to be left to anybody but the experts.

The ostensible experts themselves, academic strategists and their official counterparts, have also ignored the problem of ethnocentrism. There are various explanations. One possibility is that strategic thinking has become so advanced that ethnocentrism does not arise as a problem. It would be a tribute to the founders of strategic studies if this were so, for no other area of international studies has been able to free itself. Obviously, this book would not have been written if strategic studies had achieved such a position. An alternative explanation might be that strategists simply accept the problem, and quietly live with it. This is not likely, for in strategic studies, as in the whole of the social sciences, if a problem is identified it is thought worth writing about, and if it is thought worth writing about it is thought worth writing about in over-abundance. There is no such literature about ethnocentrism. A third alternative is more likely. It is that strategists have simply ignored the impact of ethnocentrism. They have ignored it because they were not aware that it was a problem, or because they found it congenial (and easy) to ignore it. This explanation is the one which some of the critics of strategists would hold against them. By failing to think and talk about the problem, strategists show how ethnocentric they are: they are so ethnocentric that they do not recognise it in themselves.

The general reasons why strategy is pervaded by ethnocentrism will be readily apparent. If ethnocentrism is a universal socio-psychological phenomenon, it is hardly surprising that strategy and strategists are no freer of the tendency than are other toilers in human affairs. Why should strategists eschew some of the 'needs' allegedly satisfied by the feelings of identity and superiority which are part of the ethnocentric perspective? Furthermore, since strategic practice is always based on a nationalistic view of the world (and involves relations of the most brutish type), it is only to be expected that negative stereotypes, intense antipathies and inflated loyalties will reach a pitch. But by no means all strategists are dominated by ethnocentric perceptions. Indeed, as well as worrying about ethnocentrism in strategic studies, we might also ask ourselves why it is that some individual strategists have been able to avoid becoming as nationalistic and ethnocentric as their professional conditioning might have been expected to make them. Military history can show that some of the great commanders have been very successful at getting inside the minds of their adversaries, and so guessing what was happening 'on the other side of the hill'.[1] Indeed, individual strategists may be no more ethnocentric than the next man, and may sometimes be less.

But for the most part strategy and ethnocentrism are comfortable bedfellows. The most important reason for the special grip which ethnocentrism exercises on strategy lies in the very nature of the activity. By its very nature the theory and practice of strategy adopts a nationalistic view of the world. It is full of the concomitant value judgements of the traditional society of states. Perhaps above all activities, strategy is based on and devoted to an ethnocentric and nationalistic conception of international politics.

Strategy is premised on a clear conception of the nation-state (billiard-ball) model of international relations: governments are seen as the chief actors; defence is conceived to be the primary duty of the authorities; national stereotypes are seen at their clearest; so-called realism is the prevailing philosophy; relations between groups are conceived in terms of power; conflict and war are seen to be necessary and normal because of the struggle for power which determines the major clash of interests. Above all, National Interest is King. There is a different view. Businessmen and others are living and creating a new (cobweb) model of world politics, characterised by multiple non-governmental transactions. Those who embrace this trend, and extrapolate growing interdependencies into a more optimistic future, believe that the national interest doctrine is both anachronistic and dangerous: from this perspective it appears that in the kingdom of the one-eyed, the blind man is still King. Those responsible for the security of nation-states do not see it this way however: they see no alternative but to operate within the framework of an older set of loyalties and perceptions.

Strategic planners working within a government cannot distance themselves from the older assumptions, even if academic strategists sometimes can. But be they 'insiders' or 'outsiders', the majority of contemporary strategists in the West do share common outlooks. Peace and security are seen as primary goals, and thinking is directed towards promoting them through a mixture of deterrence, arms control, limited war and crisis management.[2] At the base of these assumptions is the belief that the present world is the best of all possible worlds. This is an almost uncontested view amongst contemporary Western strategists. However, it is a view which such grandiose strategists as Alexander the Great and Napoleon would have regarded as strange indeed. In the past even the best worlds seemed possible, and achievable by means of the successful wielding of military force. The *status quo* mentality of Western strategists is also out of touch with the assumptions of the theologians and popularisers of revolutionary warfare and their guerrilla practitioners. Through the Western world, however, and through most of the nation-state establishments it helped to create elsewhere, the premium is on perpetuating the system, maintaining its national units and attempting to prevent the erosion of national ways of life. Mainstream international politics has been described as an 'ideology' of the nation-state system:[3] this is also true of its sub-discipline, strategic studies. To paraphrase a well-known definition of ideology, Anglo-American strategic theory is a coherent set of interrelated beliefs about international order and its preservation.

Some of the assumptions of strategy have been reinforced by the way the subject has been studied. The conceptual framework of most strategists has been dominated by the 'rational policy model'. From this perspective foreign countries are conceived as 'black boxes', producing rational, value-maximising decisions and policies.

Criticism of this approach has been made at great length and with equal effectiveness by the students of bureaucratic politics, and does not require elaborating.[4] The rational policy model has stood hand in hand with the 'action-reaction' phenomenon. This is the idea that an action by one nation, or even a realistically potential action, necessarily triggers reactions by other nations. This idea is simple and intuitively satisfying, but too often it is used as an unconscious device for not thinking any deeper. According to the action-reaction model, nations in confrontation are Pavlovian dogs, responding mechanically to military stimuli. It is enough to know that one has an enemy: it is not necessary to worry overmuch what he is actually *like*.

The action-reaction concept is not altogether without meaning. States often do have real clashes of interest. Governments do conceive themselves to be locked into strategic competitions and do sometimes respond directly to each other's actions and potential actions. But they do not *necessarily* respond to military stimuli and they do not respond in any mechanical way. If they respond at all, they respond according to national styles and personal idiosyncrasies. The dogs of war, when unleashed, may sometimes exhibit Pavlovian behaviour, but they also have a pedigree.

The way we label our adversaries is usually no help. The Soviet use of the term 'imperialists' to cover a motley of Western powers, and the American habit of describing their adversaries as 'the Soviets', are both misguided and mischievous. The imperialists of Lenin's youth have long since decayed, and they were always more divided amongst themselves than even the brotherhood of Marxism—Leninism. Similarly, the 'Soviets' as such have long since ceased to have any real significance in decision-making in the USSR. The inaccuracies are important, but there is another point. Such language is often devoid of human content. 'The

Soviets' is a phrase which conjures up no human images. It stereotypes by designation. The British habit of calling these same decision-makers 'the Russians' is equally inaccurate in a formal sense, but at least it reminds us that they are *people*.

The world seen through strategic lenses is a relatively simple world: it is not the complex world as seen by statesmen or diplomatic historians. Indeed, it is hardly going too far to say that strategy as it has been narrowly and traditionally conceived is international relations with many of the complexities taken out. On the other hand, perhaps more serious in its consequences has been the tendency of some so-called statesmen and some so-called diplomatic historians to make the opposite mistake: they have conceived international relations with the military factor largely taken out. This is dangerous, because to a greater extent than many of us like to admit, the business of international politics is very much about the manipulation of military force, the clash of interests and the identification of enemies.

Strategists and Enemy Images

Strategy, like nature, abhors a vacuum: the field of strategy, be it a map, actual terrain, a sheet of paper or a mind (or set of minds), must be filled with enemies. Without enemies strategy is shapeless: it is like a house without walls. Strategy is in part a simplifying activity because strategists needs enemies. Strategists are most comfortable when relationships are polarising or polarised. Sometimes the enemies will be explicit; sometimes they will be implicit. Sometimes the assumption of an enemy relationship will be justified; sometimes it will be misperceived. Sometimes the enemies will be real; sometimes they will be imagined. But enemies there must be: theory requires it while it gives purpose to day-to-day practice. Both the theory and practice of strategy are simplified if an 'enemy' is assumed, rather than any of the more complicated relationships which exist between the poles of amity and enmity. Ethnocentric outlooks are significant in this respect because they exacerbate enemy images, whether these images are real or imaginary. Enemy images and ethnocentric outlooks separate the kaleidoscope of greys in international life into sharper blacks and whites: they help shape, simplify and give meaning to a strategist's world view, his priorities and his modes of action.

The sources and functions of enemy images are manifold. For both individuals and groups, identifiable villains ('diabolical enemy images') perform standard psychological, sociological and political functions.[5]
(i) Psychologically, enemy images may help sublimate frustration, justify

otherwise improper behaviour, serve as a focus for aggressiveness, divert attention from other problems, and provide a contrast by which to measure or inflate one's own worth or value. (ii) Sociologically, enemy images may help to foster in-group solidarity and cohesion, improve the definition of objectives, bring forth new goals, and make it easier for individuals to accept training and socialisation in group norms. (iii) Politically, enemy images may have a variety of effects in decision-making, the socialisation of citizens and the maintenance of values or ideology; they help in the identification of interests, the definition of goals and the planning of action programmes; and by polarising good and evil they intensify orthodoxy and dogmatism and so help create heightened nationalism, unity and consensus.

The psychological, sociological and political effects of enemy images are negative as well as positive.[6] They are familiar throughout politics. Furthermore, enemy images do not necessarily have anything to do with ethnocentrism. Ethnocentrism is just one of the mechanisms which combine to create and sustain our pictures of other nations. Among the other mechanisms the two most relevant are the 'intolerance of ambiguity'[7] and 'cognitive dissonance'.[8] Intolerance of ambiguity is the idea that individuals are unable to recognise the contradictory characteristics of a situation, and are reluctant to suspend judgement while examining the evidence. Intolerant of ambiguity, the individual tends to construct an interpretation of a situation based not on the balance of diverse evidence, but on the basis of existing beliefs or hopes. Cognitive dissonance is closely related. It is concerned with the ways in which we try to increase our comfort with the decisions we have taken. Individuals do not like the psychological discomfort which comes from having 'dissonant' thoughts, images or attitudes. Consequently they employ a range of techniques to reject or avoid discrepant 'cognitions'. Both these mechanisms can lead to misperception and self-delusion. They are rooted in our conscious and unconscious desire to reduce or avoid ambiguity in thoughts and action. They may be intensified by professional conditioning and outlooks, what Anatol Rapoport has called 'the blindness of involvement'.[9] Together, these mechanisms may interact with ethnocentrism to exacerbate enemy images, both while they are being formed and after they have been created. These are the ways in which we tend to construct our strategic 'realities'. They have little to do with rational processes of thinking and, needless to say, they may have little to do with Reality.

Strategists need enemies. Not only does the prosecution of a strategist's professional expertise depend upon their presence, either physically or in theory, but enemies reduce ambiguity and ambivalence, and make for psychological comfort. Because of this, and because it is easier to recognise an enemy than a friend, it is not surprising that strategists are usually most comfortable when dealing with adversaries. Henry Kissinger was by no means unique in this respect.[10] However, although the idea of an enemy or enemies plays such a crucial role in strategy, it is one of the main themes of this book that strategists do not worry overmuch what their enemies are actually like. There is little attempt to correct the crude images which are held. Attempts to set military policy in a foreign policy framework are usually quite perfunctory. One indicator of the limited interest of mainstream strategists in foreign countries is their generally low attendance at conferences concerned with a particular area, even if that area is as important as the Soviet Union. If a mainstream strategist does attend such a conference, he will often depart after having given his paper. He will vote with his feet on the significance of non-military developments in the country concerned. In Soviet studies there is often a sharp contrast between the images of the country which are projected by different specialists. The picture which emerges is a complex one, but mainstream strategists invariably cut themselves off from the ambiguous evidence and instead nurture their own cognitive consistency. To the extent that individual strategists do not make any effort to avail themselves of the full range of specialist studies, one is entitled to conclude that they do not want to be confused by evidence.

Many strategists, in fact, appear to have what T. E. Lawrence called 'a fundamental crippling incuriousness' about their adversaries.[11] Indeed, a 'record of incuriousness' has been exhibited by British policy-makers towards their enemies.[12] Whatever the roots of this incuriosity, it is a very noteworthy characteristic in an activity in which the ostensible aim is to produce rational policy. This record has by no means been confined to Britain. Stalin was but one major world leader whose lack of knowledge of the outside world has been well attested. If statesmen and academics are susceptible to incuriosity it is not surprising that military organisations often see ambiguous knowledge as a problem.[13] In most professions it is not difficult to brush aside alternative viewpoints and accumulations of contradictory knowledge. In the case of strategy, its practitioners have more than enough to think about, what with the speed of change in technology, the convolutions of strategic doctrine, the need to grapple with the problems of core concepts, and the burden of trying to keep abreast of current developments. Under such pressures it is only human that some corners are cut.

The problem, and possible tragedy, is that the corner is cut where strategists can least afford to engage in underthink.

The incuriosity is widespread. In addition to the tendency just described, few strategists spend time enquiring into the causes and consequences of the conflicts they involve themselves with: these are taken as givens. Strategists are mainly interested in 'playing the game'.[14] Or thinking about it. Practitioners are primarily interested in the skilful manipulation of the instruments of force, while theorists are primarily interested in the construction of sophisticated conceptual frameworks. When this is the case strategists can hardly claim to be little more than technicians: they cannot claim to be Clausewitzians in any rounded sense.

Enemy images help to clear up ambiguities. Intolerance of ambiguity is particularly strong for strategists, for the absence of an enemy undermines his professional *raison d'etre,* perhaps in his own mind and certainly in the minds of unsophisticated critics and overburdened taxpayers. If strategists do not have enemies, they must invent them. And they can often get away with it, for few are happy without someone to fear, and a satisfying illusion is often preferable to an uncertain and complicated reality. Everyone is the more susceptible to such arguments because in international politics prudence is a primary virtue and the costs of error are great. In the early 1920s the US Navy nursed the idea of a British naval threat, while the Royal Air Force nursed the idea of a French threat from the blue. Political relations between both pairs of countries ruled out war, but the naval and air staffs worked on programmes and plans. Bureaucratic politics played a part, but there was also an implicit desire to create a familiar operating framework. One suspects from these and other examples that once military planners have decided upon a particular posture there is a strong tendency for the image of the enemy to be moulded to fit the strategy every bit as much as the strategy is adapted to the behaviour of the enemy. Because strategists need enemies it is no wonder that they flourish and are energised during crises, but are listless and apologetic during periods of detente and still more entente. Vicarious pleasure – there is a voyeur element in all academic strategists – is no doubt part of the explanation for the plethora of books on the great international crises. When strategists lack enemies *anomie* strikes. Some firemen are sometimes tempted to become arsonists. Some strategists are tempted, if not to start fires, at least to sound the alarm.

Professional Predispositions

Ethnocentrism has never metamorphosed into an 'issue' in strategic studies. Until they become issues many objective difficulties, uncertainties and perplexities are ignored or lived with. If something is 'natural' people tend to think there is little point worrying about it. By this process, for centuries, infant mortality was tolerated and accepted as normal. The change came when people began to believe that infant mortality was not necessarily 'the will of God'. It was not natural: it was, in fact, an attitude of mind. Similar tendencies have affected thinking about the relationship between ethnocentrism and strategy. It has been neglected not *despite* the fact that it has been so pervasive a feature of the theory and practice of strategy, but *because* it has been so pervasive. The strategic paradigm contains an in-built ethnocentric perspective arising out of the nature of its practical aspects and because of the assumptions and ideology which inform its analytical and theoretical approaches. The grip of ethnocentrism is strengthened by a range of other factors, which affect individuals to a greater or lesser extent. Amongst the main factors are the psychological make-up or disposition of those who are part of the profession, the training received by strategists, and the climate of opinion in which most if not all strategists work and think. Together these factors mean that strategy as an activity attracts ethnocentric attitudes, as a discipline it fails to make newcomers aware of the problem, and as a profession it is pervaded by above-average pressures towards conformity. Not surprisingly, therefore, ethnocentrism is the natural condition of strategy.

Critics always argue that strategists are a hard-nosed group, narrowly nationalistic, conservative and possessing a very short-term conception of 'realism'. Indeed, critics would continue, would individuals have chosen to become strategists were they not of such a disposition? Critics further argue that strategists are generally naive about world affairs, and that their much-vaunted realism is no more than a brand of dehumanised cynicism.[15] Whether this is valid on an individual level is an open question. However, taking the so-called community as a whole, it can be argued with some validity that those strategists who are not academics in the 'purest' and traditional sense are all *professional* ethnocentrics.[16] They are professionally committed to preserving and promoting a particular national posture. By this process strategic reasoning becomes the servant of nationalistic passion.

Institutional factors shape an individual's thinking in a number of ways. Strategy is made in groups, and groups have pressures towards conformity. Professional socialisation therefore might be expected to increase individual tendencies towards ethnocentrism. Promotion within a department of defence or a political hierarchy will depend upon political reliability. Organisations value group homogeneity and individual commitment. Ironically, and most importantly, while ethno-centrism will seriously interfere with a strategist's professional task of getting to know the enemy, at the same time his ethnocentric preferences and certainties may well endear him to his superiors. As in other organi-sations, those who rise to the top decision-making positions are not always those with the most expertise. Studies of US policy-making have shown that substantive experts on a policy area are usually in relatively junior positions in a hierarchy, while the most senior players are selected for reasons other than their substantive expertise and previous professional training: 'This leads to the perverse result that as an issue is perceived to be increasingly critical, it passes from the scrutiny of experts up to the politically appointed generalists.'[17] There is nothing wrong with generalists; indeed, they are very necessary: however, they should be specialised generalists. To see oneself as a generalist should not be used as an excuse for not becoming a specialist in anything. A jack-of-all-trades who has at least mastered one will have something of a feel for what being a specialist entails, and that is an important learning experience. But these are not problems which are peculiar to strategy: these are faults of administration and the education of public figures.

Individual personality factors may well increase the predisposition of strategy in the direction of ethnocentric bias. There seems little doubt that the character and upbringing of the 'strategic community' in the West can be described for the most part as conformist and conservative. Strategists do not like disorder: they prefer a calculable environment, rational processes and 'reasonable' conceptual and operational frame-works. The members of the strategic community tend to be as security-conscious in their private lives as they are in their professional thinking, and this may well reflect the lower-middle-class social group into which they were born and/or in which they work. As Bertrand Russell said about philosophers, few strategists would be genuinely happy as pirates or burglars.[18]

The theme of this chapter has been that the strategic paradigm is rooted in ethnocentrism and that strategists are professional ethnocentrics. One should not rush to draw any premature conclusions from this regarding the integrity or competence of strategists. Ethnocentric out-looks exist in virtually all disciplines, and it does happen that strategy in its practical aspects is peculiarly rooted in a nationalistic approach to international relations. Ultimately, however, the problem of the relationship between ethnocentrism and strategy is not really the problem of strategy: essentially it is the problem of the world community and of organising it without military power, and hence of the need for strategists.

Notes

1. Norman Dixon has discussed some of the great commanders who have been free from ethnocentric tendencies. See *On the Psychology of Military Incompetence* (New York: Basic Books Inc., 1976), Ch. 27.

2. See John C. Garnett, 'Strategic Studies and Its Assumptions', Ch. 1 in John Baylis *et al., Contemporary Strategy: Theories and Policies* (London: Croom Helm, 1975).

3. G. Modelski, *Principles of World Politics* (New York: Free Press, 1972), pp. 8-9. See also the relevant comments of Colin S. Gray, 'The Practice of Theory in International Relations', *Political Studies*, vol. XXII, no. 2 (June 1974), esp. pp. 130-1.

4. See especially Graham T. Allison, *Essence of Decision: Explaining the Cuban Missile Crisis* (Boston: Little, Brown and Co., 1971) and Morton H. Halperin, *Bureaucratic Politics and Foreign Policy* (Washington, D.C.: Brookings Institute, 1974).

5. This paragraph is based on David Finlay, Ole Holsti and Richard Fagen, *Enemies in Politics* (Chicago: Rand McNally, 1967), pp. 6-24.

6. See Ch. 5 below.

7. Else Frenkel-Brunswick, 'Intolerance of Ambiguity as an Emotional and Perceptual Personality Variable', *Journal of Personality*, vol. XCIII (September 1949), pp. 108-43.

8. Leon Festinger, *A Theory of Cognitive Dissonance* (Stanford, Calif.: Stanford University Press, 1957).

9. Anatol Rapoport, *Fights, Games and Debates* (Ann Arbor, Mich.: University of Michigan Press, 1960), Ch. 16.

10. On Kissinger's preference for dealing with enemies rather than friends see Bruce Mazlish, *Kissinger. The European Mind in American Policy* (New York: Basic Books Inc., 1976), p. 272.

11. Quoted by Dixon, *Psychology*, p. 339.

12. Ibid., pp. 293-5.

13. On the anti-intellectual tendencies of military organisations, see William Eckhardt and Alan G. Newcombe, 'Militarism, Personality, and Other Social Attitudes', *Journal of Conflict Resolution*, 13 (1969), pp. 210-19, esp. pp. 214-15.

14. Anatol Rapoport, *Conflict in a Man-Made Environment* (Harmondsworth, Middx; Penguin Books, 1974), p. 172.

15. For elaborations of this theme see Anatol Rapoport, 'Critique of Strategic Thinking', Ch. 2 in Roger Fisher (ed.), *International Conflict and Behavioural Science* (New York: Basic Books Inc., 1964) and Rapoport's Introduction to *Clausewitz: On War* (Harmondsworth, Middx: Penguin Books, 1968).

16. 'Pure' motivations certainly do not free academics of the problem of ethnocentric thinking. The case for the traditional academic approach, untrammelled by pressures of practicality and relevancy, can be found in Kenneth R. Minogue, *The Concept of a University* (London: Weidenfeld and Nicolson, 1973).

17. Morton H. Halperin and Arnold Kanter, *Readings in American Foreign Policy. A Bureaucratic Perspective* (Boston: Little, Brown and Co., 1973), pp.

98-9. See also the essay by James C. Thompson, 'How Could Vietnam Happen: An Autopsy' in Halperin and Kanter, pp. 98-110.

18.Bertrand Russell, *Unpopular Essays* (London: Allen and Unwin, 1951), p. 74.

3 FAILURES IN STRATEGY

Strategic doctrine . . . is the mode of survival of a society.
Henry A. Kissinger

Nothing except a battle lost can be half so melancholy as a battle won. *The Duke of Wellington*

Everyone is a loser in the practice of strategy, only some lose less badly than others. Even successes in strategy represent a failure of one kind or another, and are always costly. Failures in strategy may directly result in the loss of lives, cherished values and wealth: but there are also indirect costs. Too often it goes unthought that the loss should also be counted in terms of opportunities foregone, from the wasted potential of individual lives to the unachieved development of whole societies. In its various guises, ethnocentrism has contributed to many strategic failures, both great and small, historical and contemporary.

Curiosity about ethnocentrism arises from an interest in the pathology of strategy. In this chapter a variety of illustrations are discussed which indicate some of the ways in which the phenomenon has adversely affected the processes, development, and consequences of strategic practice. In the following chapter the focus turns to the deleterious impact of ethnocentrism on some theoretical aspects of the subject. The record of misperception and misconception discussed in these chapters is the best indicator of the importance and pervasiveness of the problem. It is especially appropriate that these are the longest chapters in the book: after all, the consequences of strategic failure are also one of the longest chapters in world history.

Strategic History

It is not necessary to delve far into the development of strategic doctrine or the evolution of military history to appreciate the enormous significance of the various elements of ethnocentric perception for the way nations carry out their military business.

The Idea of Superiority

In strategy, pride is literally a deadly sin. Belief in national superiority has contributed to some spectacular military failures. Such beliefs have infected the military thinking of most if not all the major powers. Self-confidence is important for effective military behaviour, but too often it has been inflated into foolish over-confidence as a result of the interplay between the psychological needs of those involved, the pressures of the moment and ethnocentric predispositions. The result of this tendency has been a depressing and unedifying list of military commanders and planners who have seriously underestimated the qualities of those facing them.

Crude generalisations based on the idea of national character and how it manifests itself in 'fighting qualities' have caused some of the biggest mistakes in military history. Familiar British illustrations include the underestimation of the Russians in the Crimea and the equally serious dismissal of the Boers in South Africa. The British have frequently disparaged the Arabs, to the ludicrous extent of arguing in 1956 that Egyptian pilots would not be able to navigate the Suez Canal. More serious in its consequences was the blatant underestimation of the military skills of the Japanese before World War II. Among other weaknesses, the Japanese were credited with having 'slow brains' and 'overtired minds' by what passed as authoritative British opinion.[1] Such thinking contributed to the dramatic denouement on 15 February 1941: it took those 'thoroughly overtired' Japanese less than two-and-a-half months to capture Malaya and the 'impregnable' fortress at Singapore. Similar racial biases also affected US thinking about the Japanese before World War II. Such modes of thinking have not been unusual in US history, either before or since that time. Racial biases affected American policy-makers in the Caribbean and China at the turn of the century,[2] and persisted with disheartening virulence into the most important failure of American arms, the recent war in Vietnam.

The tendency to seek cultural and racial explanations of behaviour – based on the idea that 'inferior' nations lack military skill and spirit – have always been very popular. Simple explanations invariably drive out the more complex. A satisfying explanation based on national stereotypes will always find readier general acceptance than one which involves a diligent examination of multiple causes. The poor showing of the Italian Army in World War II resulted in many swaggering assertions by British observers about the fragility of the Italian spirit. Even granting the general lack of Italian commitment to the Axis cause, who bothers even to mention that the Italian forces sometimes had obsolete equipment and poor support, or that their best divisions won the respect of Field-Marshal Rommel? In a similar fashion, after the Six Day War in 1967, many Israelis were so puffed up with their own success that they became scornful of the fighting qualities of their Egyptian opponents. Objective studies later showed, and the October 1973 War confirmed, that Egyptian soldiers did not necessarily lack basic skills or bravery, though they did sometimes need better officers.[3]

Belief in national superiority naturally leads decision-makers to over-estimate their chances of military success.[4] But over-confidence is not always present. As Robert Jervis has argued, decision-makers in the past might have avoided war because they objectively underestimated their chances of victory. Nor does defeat in war necessarily mean that decision-makers were over-optimistic at the outset.[5] However, when decision-makers do underestimate their chances the likelihood is that they are deterred by their enemy's numbers and resources, rather than any belief in his inherently superior national characteristics. Decision-makers who have no faith in the inherent qualities of their own nation are not usually remarkable for their political longevity.

A belief in national superiority *à outrance* gripped French military thinking in the decades before 1914. It accompanied the so-called theory of the offensive, which resulted in the notoriously costly War Plan XVII. For a generation, ethnocentric perceptions fermented together with other psychological mechanisms, with old military traditions and preferences, and with developing social conditions and political pressures, to produce aberrant and disastrous military behaviour. The judgement of those responsible for French strategy and tactics became so distorted that they dismissed the significance of German material strength and the changes which technology was making on the battlefield. The French Army was seduced by a romantic conviction of the superiority of its thought and action. At the moment of truth in 1914 the French Army was ruthlessly cut to pieces. They had refused to acknowledge that in a decreasingly heroic world *élan* is not enough. Bernard Brodie's down-beat comment on this episode is fitting and could serve as the central text of this book. He wrote, 'This was neither the first nor the last time that bad anthropology contributed to bad strategy.'[6]

The Nation as the Centre of the Universe

Nations see themselves as the centre of the universe. They tend to worry about all manner of threats because they implicitly or explicitly see behaviour elsewhere being directed towards themselves. They interpret the actions of adversaries or potential adversaries in terms of their own problems and vulnerabilities. The sense of threat is intensified as policy-makers extrapolate all sources of aggression in their own direction. They see the world as a wheel, and themselves as the hub. They see a world full of dominoes, all of which might topple in their own direction.

The guardians of the British Empire were always prone to such attitudes. At the start of this century British policy-makers became concerned about the railways being built in southern Russia ('pointing to Afghanistan', as it appeared). This Russian enterprise seemed to involve great sacrifice. Although the potential military value of these rail links would have been just as great had they been built cheaply, the fact that they were costly seemed to imply to the British that they were inevitably being built for ulterior motives.[7] Together, the domino mentality of an island empire and the bourgeois values of a nation of shopkeepers combined to see Russian behaviour as meaning that the great game was once more afoot. Fifty years earlier the British had become anxious about other threats. Various invasion 'panics' exercised British opinion in the middle of the nineteenth century. When steam propulsion made the Channel into what Lord Palmerston called 'a river passable by a steam bridge', Britain's defensive moat seemed to have disappeared. The country became significantly more vulnerable to invasion, and some groups assumed that the French were bent on such a policy.[8] It was assumed that the old enemy *would* do what it *could* do. Arguments could be brought forward to support this 'worst case' forecast (mainly historical precedents and the beliefs of contemporary French military and naval men that they were turning the scales on the British). But in practice the British fears were misplaced. An even more misplaced fear of France exercised some British civil servants and service chiefs in the early 1920s. Again, the argument was based on the idea that France *might* do what it *could* do: in particular, it was argued that France had impressive capabilities in the air, and that its intentions could change overnight. This type of thinking places great emphasis on what intentions can do in theory (such as change for the worse) but contains little or no sense of proportion gained from an examination of how the nation concerned perceives its interests in reality. In a similar way there is a tendency to assume that what is 'aggressive' behaviour has no 'natural' limits. Some foreign ministries in Europe found it difficult to comprehend that Bismarck's military efforts were related to the aim of uniting Germany, and were not the product of an inexorable military ambition. But from the strategic perspective, which is both prudent and ethnocentric, all roads of aggression are seen as leading to one's own homeland. Defending San Francisco on the Mekong was a manifestation of such an attitude.

Such attitudes are not uncommon in international politics. Jervis has described the phenomenon as 'Overestimating One's Importance as Influence or Target'.[9] His basic thesis is that actors exaggerate the degree to which they play a central role in the policies of other nations. In terms of overestimating one's influence as a target, this means that an

actor is likely to see undesired behaviour on the part of others as being
derived from the latter's own internal drives (such as ambition or ideology) rather than as a response to his own actions: this means, for
example, that nation A will tend to believe that the actions of nation
B are primarily devised to do harm to A, rather than accept the possibility
that the 'threat' represented by B may be an unintended or at least
unavoidable side-effect of actions motivated by other considerations,
including defence against A's own security preparations. This attitude
is reinforced by the habit of ascribing greater coherence to the planning
and behaviour of opponents than is actually the case. The history of
the Cold War clearly shows how perceptions of hostility and duplicity
can drive out other explanations of adversary behaviour. The record,
as it has been steadily amassed by historians, shows that confusion,
factional struggles, bureaucratic politics and uncertainties about how
best to proceed all played important parts in policy-making in both
Washington and Moscow. All generalisations about politics have excep-
tions, but the least invalid is surely the following: policy-making (the
determination of aims and the fixing of tactics) is never as coherent
as it appears from the outside.

Related to the tendency to see all roads of aggression leading to one's
own homeland is the familiar failing of strategists to appreciate the
effects of their own behaviour on that of others. Governments chroni-
cally fail to appreciate that precautions which they take to defend the
interests of their own nation may well appear to other nations to be
threats directed against them. The idea that one man's security is often
another man's insecurity is a simple point to accept intellectually, but
history shows that it is extremely rare for this appreciation to inform
the thinking of strategists. When people believe that they are behaving
reasonably, as in preparing to defend their 'legitimate' interests, few
have the imagination to appreciate how dangerous and ugly their actions
may appear to others. The Soviet-American arms race gives abundant
evidence of this. There is little reason to suppose that the Kennedy
Administration agonised over the way the Soviet leaders would feel
about the (defensive) drive of the United States for strategic superiority,
just as there is little reason to suppose that Soviet policy-makers in
recent years agonised over the way US planners would feel about the
(defensive) build-up of their own war-fighting capability.

We impose order on complex data. To live with confusion is both
psychologically uncomfortable and intellectually unsatisfying. Pressures
of time and the need for action make these needs the more intense for
decision-makers. This results in giving in to the temptation to minimise

the number of causes operating on another's behaviour. For every international action there must be a well-laid plan: the image of the statesman as chess-player remains as stubborn as it is false. The idea of the nation as the centre of things tends to result in threats being exaggerated, while the idea of national superiority tends to lead to over-confidence in dealing with them. Together with other factors, therefore, these elements of ethnocentrism combine to produce a brew which stimulates simple feelings and fighting talk.

Faulty Methodology

The fallacy that 'our way is best' and 'what is good for us must be good for them' has been common in all branches of politics. It was evident in the unsuccessful efforts by British governments to implant the 'Whitehall model' on societies which were geographically and culturally remote from Britain. In strategic studies it was evident in the intellectual imperialism of the 'RAND mind' in the 1960s. Those who failed to conform with this limited and conceited outlook were seen to be perverse or foolish, no matter how geographically or culturally remote they were from Santa Monica. The history of strategy provides a number of illustrations of the way in which strategic ideas have been universalised, and thereby made to manifest the fallacy of the ethnocentrism.

It is important in this context to remember that the so-called makers of modern strategy were men of place as well as time. Clausewitz examined the nature of war and analysed theoretical aspects of strategy, but his roots were distinctively in the Prussia of the Napoleonic era.[10] While some of the things he said were of timeless significance, they were not of timeless truth. For example, operationally Clausewitz's direct approach to strategy was in a very different tradition from the indirect and long-haul strategies historically practised in Britain. Liddell Hart was one exponent of the latter, which has sometimes been called the 'maritime' approach, in distinction to Clausewitz's 'continental' outlook. Significantly, one of Liddell Hart's works was entitled *The British Way in Warfare*.[11] Equally significant is the fact that Liddell Hart, a masterly writer on military campaigns, and a strategist who was fully aware of the importance of 'looking over the other side of the hill' nevertheless wrote ethnocentric history. His *History of the Second World War* belies its title. The campaigns in Russia, which settled the issue, were virtually treated as a side-show.[12] Essentially it reads as a volume in the history of the British Army.

Strategic theorists cannot be understood apart from their national contexts. Guillio Douhet produced a famous theory of airpower, but with Italy's situation in mind.[13] Earlier, Admiral Mahan had produced voluminous works on naval strategy,[14] but his theory of command of the sea was relevant only to the United States and Britain. His theories have not been relevant to those states with neither the need nor the inclination to use the seas in ambitious ways. Nevertheless, alternative approaches to naval strategy have been deemed inferior by the classicists of the Mahanite school. The traditional monopolist maritime powers have seen their own doctrines to be 'right and best', and those who have not modelled themselves on Mahan have been discredited as 'not understanding seapower' (a concept, it should be added, over which there has been no little confusion amongst Western naval thinkers). This way of looking at things is mistaken. The Soviet Navy over the last decade has been said to be 'discovering' seapower. The implication of this attitude is that their approach has hitherto been inferior and backward, but that now it is moving out of the northern mists into the light of the only begotten Mahan. However, an open-minded investigation of Soviet naval history reveals that they have understood, within the limits of their own fallibility, why they have needed a navy at different periods in their history.[15] This has been related to their varying interests in using the sea (let us forget the mystique of 'seapower'). It should hardly be cause for surprise that the primary determinants of the Soviet Navy have been very different from those of an island empire such as Britain used to be, or of a maritime superpower such as the United States is now. Soviet naval behaviour, naturally enough, has been based on different interests in the use of the sea, different foreign and domestic policy objectives, different capabilities and different economic capacities. Nevertheless, Western commentators still tend to judge Soviet naval strategy against what they believe to be 'classical' Anglo-American approaches, rather than against the Soviet Union's own interests in and capabilities for using the sea. Doctrines which made sense for the United States and Royal Navies are not necessarily valid for all. In naval strategy, as in strategy in general, national tasks and priorities are more significant than what are sometimes supposed to be universalist theories.

Culture-Bound Thinking

The inability to recreate the world through another's eyes, to walk in his footsteps and to feel his hopes or his pain has been the cause of a plethora of strategic problems and failures. One can dip into the barrel of international history and pull out a sour plum almost at will:

It is difficult to appreciate another's problems. In 1917 the Western allies neither understood nor gave credit to the predicaments facing the Bolsheviks. In particular they could not see that defeating Germany was not as important for the Bolsheviks as it was for themselves. The Bolsheviks left the war. What the Bolsheviks saw as a matter of survival the allies saw as a case of treachery. Allied suspicion encouraged the slide into the military interventions which to the present day have been of decisive legendary significance in Soviet thinking and hostility to the West.

It is difficult to feel another's pain. In 1919 the Paris peace negotiations became bitter partly because President Wilson and the US delegates could not comprehend the French preoccupation with cast-iron security guarantees. Descending into the war like a fresh-faced *deus ex machina* the United States did not begin to comprehend the suffering which the French had endured.

It is difficult to understand another's ambitions. In the 1930s the British misconceived the extent of Hitler's ambitions and the risks he was willing to face. A society which was 'satisfied' and devoted to preserving the status quo could not appreciate the humiliation of a defeated great power, and the costs it would bear to achieve a better place in the sun.

It is difficult to internalise another's experience. At the end of World War II the Western allies were reluctant to accept Soviet demands for extensive reparations payments from Germany. Not only had the Western allies avoided suffering on the terrible scale of the Soviet Union, but they also failed to realise that the lessons which they had learned from post-World War I reparations had not been shared by the Soviet Union. The Western allies assumed that the Soviet leaders would see the situation in the same way as themselves. The ensuing Western opposition to the Soviet proposals on reparations was calculated to bring about acrimony, not primarily because of a clash of fundamental interests, but because a clash of different experiences translated into contradictory policies.

It is difficult to understand how our own actions appear to others. In 1948 Stalin failed to understand how the coup in Czechoslovakia would appear to the West. What was meant as the completion of a defensive glacis when looked at from Moscow appeared to be the extension of a spring-board when looked at from London or Paris. Similarly, the Western response, NATO, appeared to be an escalation of the Cold War from Moscow's viewpoint, and not the huddled defensive reaction it appeared to be from the West.

It is difficult to feel how threatened another may feel. In 1950 US policy-makers failed to comprehend how dangerous their advance to the Yalu would appear to the Chinese leaders. US policy-makers did not question the legitimacy of their attempt to prop up falling dominoes in Asia, but they failed to accept the legitimacy of China's attempt to prop up falling dominoes in its own backyard.

All the elements of ethnocentric perception were brought together in the Cold War. Belief in national superiority was a powerful one on both sides. Historically, Russian messianism has often produced haughty behaviour; Marxism carried on this tradition in a new guise. For their part, the Western powers had always regarded Russia as an inferior Asiatic country, not quite a proper member of the club of great powers. The feeling of centrality — overestimating one's importance as a target — resulted in both sides perceiving aggressive intent in actions which were primarily intended to be defensive or stabilising, such as the consolidation of Eastern Europe or the Marshall Plan. Faulty methodology resulted in both sides having expectations about the other determined by their own inappropriate frames of reference. The survivable Molotov looked for plots and cunning where there were none, while the hopeful Roosevelt had New World expectations for a state in which the word 'liberal' was a term of abuse. Finally, both sides were extremely ignorant of each other. Few policy-makers had the capacity to put themselves into the frame of mind of their counterparts. There was a general failure to understand the other's hopes and fears. A US–Soviet confrontation may have happened anyway — there were enough 'normal' suspicions and conflicting interests — but it is also very clear that acute ethnocentrism combined with the logic of events in a time of great upheaval to turn normal great power rivalry into a very dangerous Cold War.

The common thread running through all these examples was the lack of empathy and the general ignorance of other societies shared by many policy-makers. The lack of empathy has meant an absence of an intimate understanding of the feelings, thoughts and motives of others: this has prevented an accurate forecasting of likely responses. The lack of knowledge of other countries has meant that even when planners have gone through the motions of trying to think through an adversary's possible policy, they have only been able to project their own values and ideas of reasonableness. Strategic history shows that this has not been enough. It was not enough in the past and, as the illustrations in the rest of this chapter will show, it is not enough today.

US and Soviet Strategic Doctrines

The US–Soviet confrontation has been the central feature of post-war strategy. It has been significantly affected by ethnocentric perceptions. Both nations assumed an implicit and centrally directed enemy. Each believed its own approach to be both more rational and peaceable than its opponent's. Each failed to understand the other's points of reference. And each was unwilling to look at problems from the other's point of view, or even to become extensively knowledgeable about the other's society.[16] These attitudes confirmed already deeply held prejudices and inevitably helped to justify a predisposition towards over-insurance in strategic programmes. The illustrations which follow look at strategic doctrines as they appeared from a typical US standpoint. There is no reason to suppose that Soviet policy-makers have been any freer from cultural distortion. In fact, close observers argue that they have been worse.[17]

Strategic opinion in the West has been based overwhelmingly on the assumption that doctrine as it has evolved in the United States has been both right and best. It has been seen as sophisticated and professional, grappling more or less successfully with the complex issues of the day. Soviet strategic doctrine on the other hand has been generally regarded as unsophisticated, a crude and anachronistic response to the 'new' problems of a nuclear world. When dealing with such a backward and secretive opponent, the typical US strategist would argue that it is necessary to try and 'educate' the other nation in the finer points of the subject: more important still, it would be seen as necessary to 'make sure' in a practical sense. The strategic balance should never be allowed to become delicate, for bears are too unruly.

Deterrence theory is an important specific example of some of the problems caused by ethnocentric bias. As it evolved in the United States in the 1950s and 1960s deterrence theory was largely the product of civilians. Deterrence practice on the other hand was always less esoteric and was much more the province of military professionals. Theory and practice did not always meet, and certainly did not always clearly meet, but to those academics involved, and their followers, the theory of deterrence which was being formulated seemed to be both universal and timeless. However, US nuclear theory, where it was comprehensible, was seen to be far less than universal in relevance to an advocate of independent nuclear power (France) or to an aspiring nuclear giant (China) or to an adversary superpower (the Soviet Union). Robert S. McNamara, when Secretary of Defense, typified US insensitivity to different national outlooks, and also personified the conceit of the military-intellectual complex when he described the independent nuclear powers as 'dangerous', 'expensive', 'prone to obsolescence', and 'lacking in credibility'.[18] As these comments testify, when the doctrines of other countries were judged against the doctrines of the whiz-kids, they were seen to be the products of inferior minds. This was evident in speeches, discussions, and in the tone of much American writing (including the echoes bounced off British disciples).

The ethnocentric bias of Anglo-American deterrence theorists contributed to a massive conceit. If this caused difficulties with ostensible allies such as the French, it was only to be expected that it would cause difficulties with an adversary such as the Soviet Union. It was generally taken for granted by Anglo-American theorists (and still largely is) that Soviet strategists did not properly understand the nature of deterrence (note the assumption of *one* revelation of its nature).[19] Not only has the Soviet approach been dismissed as primitive, but their programmes have been seen to be so misconceived that the type, level and character of their weapon deployment has threatened to undermine the stability of the balance of terror. Against such an adversary, it has been argued, over-insurance is the only rational policy. The conceit of the Anglo-American theorists has been evident in the tone of their comments and also in their general ignoring of what little writing has been done on Soviet military doctrine either in the Soviet Union itself or by the small but worthy group of Western specialists on Soviet military affairs. Where it was not ignored, this existing material tended to be treated in a perfunctory manner. Given the importance of Soviet doctrine this neglect would appear amazing, were it not for the fact that incuriousness has been such a frequent companion of strategic thinking.

Ethnocentric outlooks have affected the assessment of a wide range of other strategic doctrines. The active and passive attempts by the US Navy to track Soviet ballistic-missile-firing submarines (SSBNs) has been regarded as properly prudent and not undermining deterrence. Soviet efforts to track US SSBNs on the other hand have been criticised as destabilising and providing evidence that Soviet strategists do not understand deterrence. Informed by similar reasoning, the US programme for developing multiple independently targetable re-entry vehicles (MIRVs) was justified as strengthening deterrence by increasing the costs of war, and by decreasing what some choose to call the 'attractions' of a first-strike posture. In contrast, the less advanced Soviet programme for putting multiple warheads on missiles (MRVs) was interpreted by some as a step towards a first-strike posture. In the same way the size of Soviet ICBMs is a matter of great concern to US planners, because it gives the adversary an unfair advantage and a significant counter-force threat: on the other hand these same commentators see nothing unto-ward in a US lead in nuclear warheads of 8,500-3,300. For their part Soviet planners evidently remain oblivious of the extent to which their own counter-force capabilities worry US planners, although they them-selves take full cognisance of the potential counter-force threat repre-sented by the greater accuracy and numbers of US warheads. Such mirror-imaging is common through the whole defence posture. Critics of the SALT talks have complained that the Soviet Union is seeking strategic 'superiority' or 'parity-plus'. However, this definition is entirely one-sided, depending upon what one chooses to count. By doing a different set of sums the United States can be seen as not only striving for 'superiority', but of having achieved it. It has a roughly 3:1 advantage in warheads. As the students of bureaucratic politics say, where you stand depends upon where you sit. US representatives in SALT have so far adopted a firm attitude on the question of Forward Based Systems, much to the satisfaction of their European allies. Soviet forward bases, however, have always been seen as highly provocative. Soviet missiles had to be removed from Cuba in 1962, apparently at any cost to the United States, not to mention the world. Again, the US ABM programme in the late 1960s was justified as 'defensive', and part of a prudent strategic posture: the Soviet ABM programme on the other hand was seen as 'offensive', threatening to undermine deterrence by making war 'thinkable', and perhaps being an element in a first-strike posture. With strategic doctrines, legitimacy is evidently a geographical appraisal.

A recent example of this same phenomenon occurred in the debate about the Soviet civil defence programme. The ethnocentric tendency to overestimate one's influence as a target has resulted in some com-mentators attempting to persuade their readers that the Soviet Union has been making impressive efforts in this field. It is then implied that this growing capability is evidence of a more threatening military posture to come, and of a readiness to consider nuclear blackmail. Others have questioned the scale, seriousness and purpose of the Soviet efforts. They have challenged both the evidence and its implications. The truth is not yet apparent, but it does appear that those commenta-tors who believe Soviet civil defence policy to be a threatening develop-ment all share common assumptions about Soviet ambitions. From this viewpoint whatever the Soviet Union does is seen as being motivated by bad faith. Such commentators would find it difficult to concede the possibility that an attempt to provide some measure of protection for the vital elements of society in the event of war might be a logical and reasonable precaution *in itself*. Some Americans once thought so: they would today if they could persuade themselves that such a precaution was feasible and affordable. Civil defence precautions bear no necessary relationship with an intention to engage in militant behaviour, although the possession of what seems an effective civil defence network would theoretically add an extra degree of self-confidence in any crisis which might arise. Soviet civil defence efforts have been perceived almost entirely in terms of US interests: the role which the growing threat from China might have on Soviet perceptions and policies, or the value of civil defence as a 'socialising' instrument, is ignored. Western civil defence measures would be justified on the basis of saving people in the event of a war which nobody wants. The same measures taken by the Soviet Union tend to be interpreted as readying that country for war.

The 'new strategy' announced by Dr James Schlesinger in January 1974 further illustrates a number of the ethnocentric perceptions already mentioned. The ostensible changes in US doctrine promised to give more flexibility (inherently a good thing), and in particular they promised the option of attacking Soviet targets more successfully and selectively. Some saw it as a morally preferable strategy, giving the United States the option of destroying specific military targets, whereas the earlier doctrine of Mutual Assured Destruction had meant that retaliation was synonymous with punishment, which in effect meant genocide. Interestingly, in adopting this change of emphasis US planners showed some convergence with existing Soviet doctrine, hitherto dismissed as unsophisticated. Strategists in both countries suddenly switched clothes. The Schlesinger Pentagon moved towards Soviet ways of thinking, while the Soviet leaders now expressed fears, real or imaginary, about the greater war-fighting emphasis in US doctrine. This switching of attitudes could have been a useful learning experience for both sets of planners, but whether they did in fact learn anything is a different matter.

American interpretations of Soviet doctrine have sometimes contained a tactical element, as occurs in the declaratory policy of all states, and have sometimes been affected by bureaucratic politics, where an organisation has found utility in defining or exaggerating a particular threat. But even after such political distortions have been stripped away, there still remain the cultural ones. There has been conceit, the view that one's own way is best. There has been a strong tendency to overestimate one's position as a target, and to interpret all adversary actions in terms of one's own vulnerability. There has been a widespread incuriousness about looking to see how the adversary's strategic doctrine might fit into his overall interests and policy posture. There has been the imposition of one's own strategic outlooks on the adversary. There has been little attempt to imagine how the adversary interpreted, and then felt about US strategic developments. In short, the commitment to know the enemy stopped well short of trying to recreate the world through the other nation's images. There is no evidence that Soviet planners have been any wiser.

The Superpower Arms Race

The preceding discussion reveals an important paradox. It suggests that those who espouse logic and rationality in strategy appear to be short-circuiting their own approach. Ostensibly rational men are failing to take steps to minimise avoidable distortions of adversary behaviour. This less than sensible approach is the more noteworthy because it takes place at a conscious level, or at least not far beneath. This is suggested by the general unwillingness of most strategists to invest much time and effort in studying other countries, including the Soviet Union. Stereotypes satisfy, bureaucratically and psychologically. They also save having to think too much. Whatever the motives, the willingness to live with ethnocentric distortion is inimical to the desire for rational strategic planning. While strategic incuriosity exists, strategic rationality will remain on vacation.

The US–Soviet arms race is a case study of such problems.[20] It should go without saying that Soviet perceptions of strategic questions are deeply affected by the

> unique culture, traditions, and institutions of the Soviet Union; and that what the Soviet Union decides to do in the field of military policy flows from the peculiar political processes of that country and, hence, is likely to differ from what an American analyst might do if the decision were his to make.[21]

However, as Matthew Gallagher and Karl Spielmann proceeded to point out: 'These propositions, perhaps accepted by all analysts as statements of fact, have been far from consistently applied in the actual conduct of American policy over the past decade or more.' This statement is as historically valid as the preceding one was commonsensical. Yet, as the authors argue, many of the misjudgements about Soviet policy that have affected the arms race 'have been rooted precisely in the belief that the obverse of these propositions holds true'.

Gallagher and Spielmann have adduced an impressive list of cases to support their contentions.[22] The best example is the 'missile gap'. They argue that it was the belief of the Eisenhower Administration that the Soviet Union would try to act in much the same way as the United States was then preparing to act that led to this scare in the late 1950s, which in turn resulted in the massive US strategic programmes of the Kennedy Administration in the early 1960s. This drive for superiority evidently took place with little consideration within the Kennedy Administration of its likely effects on Soviet attitudes. This was a major failure for an administration which in October 1962 won deserved fame for its ability to step into the other man's shoes.

In addition to the missile gap, one could add the earlier and similar example of the 'bomber gap'. More recently one could add the belief in some quarters that the Soviet Union would be satisfied with strategic 'parity'. US policy-makers, having become satisfied with 'sufficiency', thought that the Soviet leadership in turn would be satisfied with the replacement of gross inferiority by the gift of 'parity'. These US policy-makers were both annoyed and disappointed when the Soviet Union in the 1970s appeared to be expanding its strategic force levels to at least 'parity-plus', although such an effort was consistent both with Soviet definitions of peaceful coexistence and with the importance assigned to military power in assessing the correlation of forces.[23] The earlier estimate had been based on a mixture of hope and strategic theory devoid of Soviet political content. The SALT talks have been a fruitful source of illustration for such problems, and such recent manifestations of ethnocentrism have been all the more noteworthy because of the sophistication which the politico-strategic community in the West considers it has acquired. Early in 1977, for example, there was cause for serious concern that the new Carter Administration had presented its new SALT proposals without looking at them from the Soviet viewpoint.[24] If they had, they would have asked themselves why the Soviet leaders should have been willing to accept a package which seemed to the advantage of the United States, which included ideas objected to for a year, and which was now tied up with a human rights campaign. When the Soviet negotiators predictably rejected the proposals, gloom descended on Washington, and commentators talked about a further drift away from detente. The unanimous view of Soviet-watchers when the proposals became public was that the Soviet leaders' response had been quite predictable. One can only assume that this was a case of the administration not looking at the situation from the Soviet viewpoint and/or of failing to consult with its Soviet specialists. Why should the Soviet leaders have been expected to accept the formalisation of a balance which could be improved from their viewpoint? In the decade between their exposure in October 1962 and their achievement of formal parity in May 1972, the Soviet leaders had learned what was achievable by military exertion. They would not easily, with the stroke of a pen, write off the possibility of a more favourable bargain.

Ethnocentric bias is generally thought to be a peculiar proclivity of so-called hawks. However, many so-called doves have an equal but opposite bias. Characteristically, Western doves project their liberal values onto Soviet society: not only do they assume the existence of a similar hawk/dove divide in Moscow, but they also assume that these are birds of the same feather, whatever their habitat. This is not so: bad ornithology can also make bad strategy. While the Soviet hierarchy is certainly made up of groups with different interests, with some advocating less emphasis on defence spending than others, a simple translation of political sympathies is not appropriate. The apparent 'doves' in the Politburo and the Central Committee are not directly comparable with the 'doves' in the US Cabinet or Congress. There are no 'liberals' at the top of the Communist Party of the Soviet Union. Mutual interests can occasionally be identified between different policy-making groups in the two capitals, but this does not mean that their attitudes are based on common political outlooks. This fallacy of transferring national points of political reference was frequent in much British thinking about Japan in the 1930s. Some groups put their faith in Japanese 'moderates' and 'liberals' without appreciating that in the context of Imperial Japan these labels made no sense unless they were realigned very far to the political right of groups with similar labels in British society. The habit of transferring national assumptions is presently evident in discussions of the political influence of the Soviet military. It is common for the Soviet armed forces to be seen either as a mirror-image of a Western-type military-industrial complex, or as a faithful and non-political instrument of the Soviet political leadership. William Odom is one of several specialists on the subject who has argued that this is not satisfactory.[25] For one thing, the military/civilian distinction in policy-making in the Soviet Union is not so meaningful: in Moscow 'martial preferences are [not] limited to marshals'.

It is salutary to be reminded that ethnocentric perceptions in the arms race have not been confined to military establishments and their dovish critics. Some area specialists are by no means free of ethnocentric bias and, because of their greater knowledge and air of authority, may well be correspondingly more dangerous. In this respect it has been noted that the ethnocentrism which informed US thinking about Soviet military policy in the mid-1960s was 'community-wide.[26] Greater knowledge of a country is not synonymous with cultural relativism: it does not guarantee immunity from methodological infirmity.

By the mid-1960s the West was not short of knowledge about the Soviet Union. Whether one was talking about hawks or doves, area specialists or strategists, civilians or military professionals, it was not an absence of information which was primarily responsible for mistaken interpretations of Soviet behaviour. Rather, it was 'the false belief that the Soviet decision-makers were operating on much the same principles, and with much the same view of the strategic situation' as their American counterparts.[27] The source of many errors in the arms race has not been the absence of factual knowledge, but rather the absence of imaginative thinking.

Detente: or Peace and Ill-Will

'Detente' is the over-used and insufficiently understood label attached to the superpower relationship so far in the 1970s. It happens to be a particularly revealing illustration of the way in which the ethnocentric understanding of a concept can affect interstate relations.

The dictionary definition of 'detente' is simply 'a relaxation of tension'. In the euphoric days of 1972 many Westerners were predisposed to think that it meant more: to live and let live; more security with less defence expenditure; 'positive' peace; in short, peace and goodwill. Soviet actions in the intervening years have resulted in a growth of disillusionment among important sections of Western opinion. The Soviet arms build-up, dubious behaviour in SALT, 'meddling' in the Middle East, internal repression, 'adventurism' in Africa, rejection of the spirit of Helsinki — all these actions have been considered to fall short, sometimes well short, of what Western opinion has considered to be the proper standards of a detente relationship. The hopes of 1972 have dissipated: instead, Soviet policy is now seen in terms of betrayal, bad faith and untrustworthiness. To some observers this has merely confirmed their worst expectations about the Soviet Union: to others is has merely added another layer of confusion and uncertainty to their already complex picture of international relations. As a result, in the last few years we have witnessed an abrupt change in much Western thinking about detente, from the belief that it was a wholly desirable process to the present situation where some observers regard it as one of the most dangerous illusions on the international scene.

Moods matter. The 'atmosphere of relations' can be more important than 'objective reality'. The sense of disillusionment felt by both superpowers is a more important political fact than any new weapons system they have developed over recent years. One might expect that the hardening of opinion resulting from a sense of disillusionment will play into the hands of those leaders in the West who can promise to deal with the Soviet Union in the tough way it apparently deserves. Such a hardening attitude, in turn, would seem destined to provoke a similar trend in the Soviet Union. Such possibilites have very practical relevance during a period when leadership power struggles are taking place, as with the run-up to a US presidential election, or when a president is under siege and looking for success, or during the prolonged jockeying for position in Moscow which inevitably takes place as the years sit increasingly heavily on the incumbent's shoulders.

The questions are simple: is detente an illusion? has the Soviet Union been acting in 'bad faith'? has it been engaged in 'deception'? The answers are difficult, for the evidence is ambiguous, and much depends on the meaning one attaches to terms. However, it can be argued with some confidence that whatever else they have been doing, the Soviet leaders have not been engaged in an exercise in deception. To the extent there has been deception in the recent superpower relationship it has not been by the Soviet Union; rather, it has been self-deception on the part of Western observers.

The current disappointment with detente is more a consequence of earlier US ethnocentric perceptions rather than later Soviet 'bad faith'. The false and inflated Western expectations about detente in the early 1970s were based on the always dubious assumption that detente meant the same thing to Soviet spokesmen as it did to themselves. This was never the case, and Soviet spokesmen have never said it was. The Soviet view of the superpower relationship has been a consistent one, and they have acted within the norms of that relationship as they have understood them. Those norms are those established by the concept of 'peaceful coexistence'. Mr. Brezhnev has explained on a number of occasions since the Helsinki Summit of July 1975 that peaceful coexistence still means what Soviet spokesmen said it meant twenty years ago, namely that it was an 'economic, political, and ideological struggle, but not a military one'.[28] Those who were lulled into thinking that detente meant an end to the conflict and then were surprised by Soviet behaviour in Angola, for example, were primarily victims of their own wishful thinking. Mr. Brezhnev has been consistent: he has never questioned the principle of Soviet support for national liberation struggles as being in any way contrary to the spirit of peaceful coexistence.

Soviet spokesmen have hardly missed an opportunity to explain the concept of peaceful coexistence.[29] Essentially, it is defined as a form of regulated competition, which will be to the immediate tactical advantage of the Soviet Union while at the same time hastening the eventual victory of communism. Despite the Soviet exegisis, they largely failed to get Western opinion to understand their concept of detente/'peaceful coexistence'. Interestingly, Western strategists were at the same time failing to get their Soviet counterparts to accept and understand American nuclear theology in their 'SALT seminar'. If Western opinion fails to understand the Soviet exposition of peaceful coexistence – or chooses not to – then Soviet observers must conclude that their opponents are either stupid or mischievous. Faced with this choice, the heirs of the Bolsheviks will invariably project a conspiratorial motive on their opponents. They will assume that they are trying to sabotage detente.

Whatever else one might say about recent Soviet foreign policy, one cannot criticise it as a 'betrayal', at least of its own principles. Clearly, the present state of disillusionment would not have been severe if Western observers, from the start, had understood what the Soviet leaders meant by peaceful coexistence. Such understanding is not easily achieved, for Soviet conceptions of such a term as 'peace' include ideas which Western thinking cannot stomach.[30] 'Peace' in the Soviet conception does not mean 'peace and goodwill': instead, it is 'a continuation of the politics of war by other means', a 'temporary, unstable armistice between two wars'. To Lenin, a peace treaty was 'a means of gaining strength', and a peace policy was one 'designed to further a communist takeover'. In sum, peace and goodwill towards the bourgeois world is a belief which is impossible for a communist to hold. It should go without saying that such unfamiliar and uncongenial connotations to the word 'peace' must be thoroughly assimilated when considering any Soviet statement about peaceful coexistence or detente.

There is now a generally better understanding of the nature of the detente relationship than was the case in the early 1970s. More observers are now more willing to accept Soviet declarations and to recognise that peaceful coexistence is an instrument in a strategy of conflict. One manifestation of this changed outlook, spurred on by the US presidential elections, was an attempt to change the terminology. At the start of 1976 President Ford disavowed the term detente and stated his belief that the United States must 'seek to relax tensions so that we can continue a policy of peace through strength'. But 'peace through strength' never caught on. It turned out to be easier to relearn the meaning of detente rather than change the terminology. In this task Dr

Kissinger contributed to the public debate by carefully using a more limited formulation of the meaning of the term.[31]

It is one thing to know that detente is not synonymous with peace and goodwill, but this leaves many questions unresolved: in particular, it does not clarify the 'rules of the game' in practice, or the degree of risk the Soviet leaders consider to fall within their understanding of the detente relationship. While this is so it is inevitable that much ambiguity will surround such Soviet—American issues as aid to national liberation struggles, the degree of co-operation in arms control verification, and the meaning of non-interference. We would be foolish if we assumed that the Soviet representatives would not try to define terms to their satisfaction, or not try to manipulate treaties to their advantage, or not try to have their cake and eat it. These are universal political aspirations.

If Soviet leaders carry out policies of which we disapprove, we should hesitate before criticising them for 'betrayal' and 'bad faith'. From the Soviet viewpoint there is nothing inconsistent or hypocritical in intensifying the ideological struggle or in supporting national liberation struggles in a period of so-called detente. But they can properly be criticised, however, where they have clearly failed to live up to specific agreements solemnly undertaken, as with the human rights provisions at Helsinki in 1975, reaffirmed at Belgrade in 1978, and agreed to be 'essential' for detente. The Soviet treatment of Yuri Orlov and other members of 'monitoring groups' greatly casts doubt on Soviet good faith on such matters, but it does not mean that they always 'cheat' or that their policy of detente is one of massive deception. Our confusion about their posture will be reduced if we remember that their basic commitment is to peaceful coexistence, which is seen by the Soviet leaders as an opportunity to improve their position and to manipulate the atmosphere of relations – to work on the 'gullibles' and 'lullables', as Charles Manning once put it.[32] Peace and goodwill may have been the earlier Western conception of detente, but Soviet spokesmen have never hidden the fact that their own conception of the superpower relationship is one of 'peace and ill-will'.[33] In this sense, Henry Kissinger's definition of detente as a *process* is most helpful. It recognises that we have not reached a satisfactory 'peace', but rather are in the important business of trying to come to some sort of agreement about the means of the contest. Detente is about the rules of the game; it is not an outcome. A sophisticated understanding of detente recognises that peaceful coexistence does not imply that coexistence will foreseeably be peaceful.

Arabs, Jews and Outsiders

The illustrations so far have been taken from the superpower relationship. Lest it be imagined that the mighty have a monopoly of strategically relevant ethnocentrism, the Arab–Israeli conflict is instructive. This relationship shows the effect of ethnocentrism in a prolonged crisis which has military implications far outside the Middle East. It is the most dangerous cockpit of our time.

Both Arab and Israeli planners have suffered from the dangerous effects of ethnocentrism. Egyptian ethnocentrism, and especially the combination of the Arab sense of superiority and the alien nature of Israel, contributed to Egypt's failure to make a thorough study of the enemy they would have to fight in 1967.[34] Mohamed Heikal, a close observer, has written: 'Because Israel was a country we felt ought not to exist we behaved as though it did not exist.' An apparently ludicrous example of this was the fact that before 1967 a lecturer at the Egyptian Staff College was discouraged in his efforts to analyse the Israeli war machine. With President Nasser's backing, and a jolt from history, the Egyptian approach changed significantly after June 1967. With hindsight, Heikal recorded that the earlier attitude was 'almost incredible'. In terms of rational strategic thinking he was correct: but as many episodes in this book make clear, strategy is not a treasure-house of rational activity.

The Egyptian success of October 1973 was one of the results of improved Egyptian planning, including a more conscious attempt to know their enemy. On the other side, the failure to predict this attack was a costly example of Israeli ethnocentrism. General Chaim Herzog's study of the war has made clear that the fundamental error in Israeli intelligence before 1973 was their inability to penetrate the Arab mind. As with all the other well-known intelligence failures, a variety of factors was at work in this case, but the cultural factor certainly played a part. Israeli feelings of superiority, the culture-bound character of Israeli thinking and the Israelis' habit of projecting their own assumptions on the Arabs – each of these factors seriously affected the weighing of odds and the sorting out of information. Responsible Israelis in 1973 could not think like Egyptians. The Israelis assumed that Arab values and reasoning were the same as their own. From this they assumed that the Arabs would be either unable or unwilling to attack with the balance of forces as they then seemed to be. Once this assumption had been made, 'Every new development in the intelligence evaluation was adapted to this concept, instead of being evaluated independently.'[35] This meant that they failed to see the combined significance of a wide variety of events in the days and weeks leading up to the Egyptian attack.[36] Such a misreading of events is very familiar in the long story of intelligence failure. As Herzog so exactly entitled his chapter on this problem of intelligence and its evaluation: 'Eyes Have They But They See Not.'[37]

Good intelligence gathering and interpretation is particularly important for a small, encircled and embattled nation such as Israel. Not surprisingly, the profound shock of 1973 resulted in a number of reforms. Of particular interest in the intelligence field was the creation of a special group of devil's advocates, formed to challenge existing views and to act as a more effective ear to discordant information.[38] This was an imaginative innovation, but whether it works in practice will depend on the quality of those involved and the receptivity of relevant participants in the policy process. The danger is that the innovation might degenerate into mere tokenism, one of the fashions of our time.

Another costly example of ethnocentric thinking on the part of the Israelis has been described by Edward Luttwak.[39] He records that after October 1967 there was nearly a year of relative quiet on the cease-fire line along the Suez Canal. The Israeli troops built no hard fortifications. Opposite them lived over 900,000 Egyptians in the Port Said, Ismailia and Suez governates; these were also the most modern and industrialised parts of Egypt. It seemed reasonable to the Israelis that no conceivable tactical advantages could possibly induce the Egyptians to sacrifice their cities and industries by making the canal the scene of large-scale fighting. Since Israeli command of the air seemed completely to rule out an offensive across the canal, the only option which seemed open to the Egyptians was a static artillery bombardment. Luttwak argues that the Israelis also ruled out this option, 'since according to *their own scale of values* its limited, almost symbolic gains would be outweighed by the destruction of the three governates' cities and industry'. The Egyptians thought otherwise. In October 1968 they laid down a series of artillery barrages. They sacrificed the canal-side cities in order to do so. After this episode the Israelis were forced to defend their positions and to undertake the large-scale construction of hard fortifications, and 'at a greater cost than would have been the case earlier'.

Generally after 1967 the Israelis failed to appreciate the importance to the Egyptians of a psychological as well as a military recovery. In the traditional literature of the Arabs the sense of racial superiority is intense. The defeats of 1948 and 1967 were felt very deeply. Indeed, a prime motive force of Arab political life in the twentieth century has been the desire to recover status and dignity after a long period of humiliation at the hands of superior powers.[40] In 1967 they had persuaded themselves that triumph was at hand.[41] When only abject defeat followed, doubt grew in the validity of the faith, and self-respect was eroded.[42] A costly war of attrition had to be endured, and eventually the canal had to be crossed not only for politics and strategy, but also for psychological reassurance. Those observers who could not understand and feel this sense of Arab humiliation could not begin to predict how those who did experience it might behave.

Clearly, the cultural differences between the societies involved in the Middle Eastern conflict have had an important impact on that region's recent military history. Unfortunately, the overcoming of ethnocentric distortion is particularly complicated in that region because, in Luttwak's words, 'two variants of one civilisation face an Arab–Islamic culture which is not only very different but which is also undergoing a process of disintegration under the pressure of economic change and nationalism.'[43] The difficulty both sides have had in penetrating the minds of their adversaries has proved costly in war-fighting and continues to prove equally obstructive in attempts at peace-making.

In addition to the culture-bound local countries, the problems of the region are not assisted by the ethnocentrism of the interested external powers. Traditional Russian ignorance of the outside world is legendary, and it continues to have strong echoes at the highest levels. It even affects regions which have been as significant for Soviet foreign policy as the Middle East. Evidently the opinions of area specialists have been dismissed in a cavalier fashion, as happened to a Soviet expert on Israel named Nikitin, whose analysis of the Middle East in mid-1967 concluded that the Arabs would be defeated if they began another war.[44] Furthermore, the expertise of important Soviet policy-makers hardly developed after that experience, if Boris Ponomarev was typical. Ponomarev was a member of the Politburo and the Central Committee, and was also a noted ideologue with a reputation for taking a keen interest in Third World affairs. Nevertheless, it is evident that he had an imperfect knowledge and a less than compelling interest in the Arab world.[45] Evidently, ideological universalism is no antidote for the powerful habit of strategic incuriousness.

Western shortcomings are more serious still, given our great interests and responsibilities in the area. Unfortunately, there has been a persistent failure to understand some of the major dynamics of the situation, and this has partly been the result of false liberal assumptions and their related mechanistic diplomacy: this approach misses an important point, namely that the problem of the Middle East is not so much about discrete concrete issues, such as the tactical siting of a cease-fire line, but about the outraged feelings of the Arabs. As Gil Carl AlRoy has put it, 'at the root of the problem stands the reluctance and perhaps sheer inability in the cultivated and liberal circles in the Western world to acknowledge the vehemence and violent bitterness of the Arab rejection of Jewish political assertiveness in the Middle East'.[46] Significantly, although the Western world created a state in the region, the liberal view finds it impossible to conceive the elimination of one. Similarly, 'reasonable' Western thinking finds it very difficult to accept that there are some conflicts which cannot be 'settled' other than by brute force. Such attitudes encourage the playing down of the violent language of the Arabs, while at the same time exaggerating their friendly actions in a determination to fix them in an understandable framework.[47] Our culture-bound thinking prevents us from recreating the world through Arab eyes. If we do not simply reject Arab ways of thinking as uncivilised, we tend to compress Arab attitudes into a mould we think reasonable and therefore manageable. This is distorting, but reassuring. For most of us, a comfortable distortion always beats a tormenting truth.

A characteristic liberal argument is that firmly held beliefs cannot be changed by force: strategic bombing against morale is therefore deemed to be counter-productive. On the other hand, the proponents of this liberal viewpoint would probably act on the assumption that such deeply held beliefs as those of the Arabs and Israelis might be manipulated and accommodated by persuasion or diplomacy. It is not clear why talk should be more effective than force in changing minds, though this is a prejudice that most of us feel should be given its chance.

Allies: Know Your Friends

Lest it be thought that adversaries have a monopoly of strategic problems caused by ethnocentrism, it is useful to be reminded of the difficulties sometimes caused between allies.

NATO in the 1960s was a case study of disintegrative tendencies. The allies demonstrated a generous propensity for misunderstanding, some of which was grounded in ethnocentric perception. This was so even between such countries as the United States and Britain, two nations with a long association and a more or less common language. Despite many common interests, relations were occasionally strained because both governments failed to understand the other's attitudes and intra-governmental bargaining processes.[48] Each government tended to project the ways of its own capital into the different milieu of that of its ally. With two such states false expectations arise as a result of the easy assumption that the partner will see a situation in a similar way. If such mistakes occur between states with a 'special relationship', it is hardly surprising that cultural distortions and therefore unreal expectations arise between countries which have much less in common.

France and the United States in the 1960s provided a continuing illustration of the difficulty which two allies can have in understanding each other's position. The different strategic conceptions were symbolised by the McNamara Strategy and the *force de frappe.* Underlying the dispute were different national aims and aspirations, but these normal problems were exacerbated by a mental blockage which seemed to prevent the respective leaders and commentators from admitting any reasonableness in the other's viewpoint; they could only see stubborn and selfish national interest. Strategic incomprehension and national pride were too powerful to be overcome by an 'agreement to disagree' formula: the outcome was a prolonged crisis in NATO which was broken only when France withdrew from its integrated military structure. This outcome was not surprising. Governments, like individuals, have great expectations of reasonable behaviour from those they think are like themselves. They will naturally expect them to see the world in the same way and to behave sensibly, which in political practice does not mean behaving with 'good sense', but rather means behaving 'like me' or 'in accordance with my wishes'.

Friends, by definition, are supposed to be friendly, so that when a close associate fails to act in a desired manner, the disappointment is all the greater. Just as most murders take place within families, historically speaking it is a fact that more emotional heat has been generated by the heretics within the gate than by the barbarians without. Theological metaphors are relevant when considering allies with ideological affinities. The Sino-Soviet relationship in the last twenty years is an instructive study. It shows the effects of several manifestations of ethnocentric perception, particularly the effects of racial antipathy, culture-bound thinking and the tendency to project one's own assumptions. Each set of leaders had expectations of what constituted proper revolutionary behaviour on the part of the other, and disenchantment resulted when those expectations were not fulfilled. In the mid-1950s the Soviet leadership did not find China as suppliant to Soviet authority as they would have expected in a relatively weak power under the protection of a great one, and one (as they saw it) which also happened to be the base of the communist revolution. The Chinese were equally disappointed about Soviet behaviour. Soviet missile developments in the late 1950s encouraged the Chinese to believe that a fundamental change had taken place in the world balance of power, with the east wind now prevailing. In contrast with the ostensible position of the Chinese leaders, the Soviet leaders saw fewer revolutionary opportunities opening up, and they were much less willing to engage in risky behaviour either in theory or in practice.[49] The resulting Chinese disappointment was characteristic of states which do not bear responsibility for acting.

Some of the problems of Soviet–Chinese relations were also evident in Soviet–Egyptian relations after 1967. Ethnocentric distortions are always likely to be magnified when there are big differences in size, outlook and level of development between the countries concerned. Mohamed Heikal's eyewitness account of this relationship has described the trouble caused by Soviet tactlessness which was largely a result of their lack of affinity with Egyptians. Heikal has also given evidence to show that the Egyptians themselves failed to appreciate Soviet policy as a whole, and that this resulted in expectations about arms deliveries and support which were far greater than the Soviet Union was willing to meet.[50] False expectations are a familiar problem in any arms supplier/receiver relationship: it is one of the reasons why military aid diplomacy has proved to be such a relatively undependable instrument of policy. In this case both Soviet and Egyptian leaders failed to imagine how their partners saw the situation. Had they done this their expectation would have been more realistic, and their diplomacy would have been adjusted accordingly. A specific illustration of the effect which the different viewpoints had took place at the end of 1967, when the Soviet Union attempted to support Egypt by deploying warships in ports which might have been vulnerable to Israeli attack. Luttwak has argued that this supportive action by the Soviet leaders may have been stripped of much of its significance because Egyptian opinion would not readily recognise the intent of the signal. In the face of an Israeli threat which [Egyptian] street opinion does comprehend, the Soviet deployment could be seen and criticised as 'inaction'[51] in the face of an active threat. One man's risky and potentially costly gesture of solidarity is often another man's idea of pussyfooting.

Across a wide range of alliances therefore – those between equals, those involving a 'special relationship', those grounded in ideology or those between superpowers and Third World countries – ethnocentric perceptions can have strategically significant effects. Perhaps surprisingly, the strain caused by enigmatic friends is probably more troubling to governments on a daily basis than the problems posed by evergreen enemies.

Crises: Signalling without Signal Books

Crises are moments of opportunity and fear. Major interests clash; dangers intensify; and time is compressed. Crises usually involve complicated psychological relationships between the opponents but less than perfect communication channels and a relatively crude ability to read each other's signals. In such circumstances a distorting mechanism such as ethnocentrism can have very serious implications.

The danger of thermonuclear war has increased whatever degree of native caution existed in the minds of the leaders of the superpowers. The nuclear nightmare encourages more than second thoughts when a leader contemplates actions which might involve a military confrontation with another superpower. This is fortunate because US analysts have shown a 'disturbing' inability to predict Soviet crisis moves,[52] while the Soviet record in forecasting US behaviour has probably been worse. Obviously there have been some successful forecasts by both sides, but it is the failures that are of greatest concern given the costs of a crisis which goes wrong in the nuclear age. US passivity over Czechoslovakia in 1968 and Soviet passivity over the mining of Haiphong harbour in 1972 were correctly estimated. In general, the prediction of inaction has proved more reliable than the prediction of positive adversary moves. This verdict is of some comfort for those who want to act, but not so comforting for those who may be the targets of military action.

The Cuban missile crisis is generally regarded as a success in strategic practice. This verdict is valid, however, only in so far as nuclear war is taken to be the measure of failure. In most other respects the episode gave plenty of cause for concern. It was a crisis which by common consent brought the world nearer to nuclear war than any other. It began with both sets of planners being confronted by a 'behavioural surprise' on the part of their adversary:[53] the US leadership had ruled out the likelihood of the Soviet Union emplacing 'offensive' missiles on Cuba, while Khrushchev had evidently not expected the speed and decisiveness of the US response. Fortunately, as the crisis progressed, both sets of leaders showed more astuteness. Khrushchev avoided the temptation to be stubborn, while President Kennedy frequently attempted to put himself in his adversary's shoes. On many occasions Kennedy's arguments with the ExCom began with the words 'If I were Khrushchev',[54] and it was Robert Kennedy's recollection that his brother 'spent more time trying to determine the effect of a particular course of action on Khrushchev . . . than on any other phase of what he was doing'.[55] This act of statesmanship has often been described, but perhaps insufficiently recognised. Naturally, Kennedy was primarily concerned to ensure his own political survival, but he was also anxious that Khrushchev was not dangerously humiliated. Feelings are one of the most important but least understood aspects of crises: to his lasting credit John Kennedy recognised that the outcome of a crisis will not simply be a matter of the interaction between two sets of sober cost-benefit analysts. Feelings are facts, but how are they to be weighed? 'How does my adversary feel about the situation?' is a simple question, but finding a good answer is inordinately difficult. The proverbs of the nations attest to the difficulties of getting under another's skin. Crises involve excited and frightened human beings: they involve people who are 'not their normal selves'. This makes prediction more difficult, and in the circumstances of a crisis a major error in estimating the adversary's feelings may be far more significant than a comparable error in counting his missiles.

Estimative failures in the past are disturbing because they undermine our confidence about the future. We understand so little. Robert Bathurst has argued that the understanding of such a basic question as 'who will shoot first and when?' is primitive indeed, even granting that such questions will not be amenable to any precise answers. Political behaviour is such a contingent activity that prediction can never be a science, but there is even a shortage of educated guesses. Significantly, Bathurst has argued that dependence on the analysis of enemy intentions devoid of any feeling for cultural relativity seems to promote an arrogance which has lead to disastrously wrong answers. His recommendation that the estimative process needs examining and improving is valid but always easier said than done. But one thing is clear: effective crisis management demands more than an ability to think logically. The point at which the other side will decide to shoot will be 'intuitive, culturally determined, and made to the roll of a different drum'.[56]

Historians often suffer from the vice of their virtues. Paradoxically, one of the reasons why we do not better understand crisis behaviour is the result of academics trying to do their job properly, by sticking to what they consider to be reliable sources. As far as the study of post-war crises is concerned, this means that we are largely restricted to American material. Soviet archives are not open and there are serious doubts about the memoirs available. In general, little attempt is made to complete the picture from the Soviet side, and what work has been done by Kremlinologists rarely finds its way into the reading and writing of mainstream strategists. This information imbalance again overemphasises American concepts and assumptions about crisis management.

The narrow compass of Western thinking about crisis management is further increased by the almost exclusive preoccupation of Western strategists with Soviet—American crises. The important experience of the Chinese has been largely ignored. An examination of Chinese crisis behaviour, however, gives at least two important lessons to ethnocentric Western students.[57] Firstly, it shows how sophisticated a non-Western state can be both in declaratory policy and military display. Secondly, it is an important reminder that even sophisticated crisis managers can be misunderstood and can fail. In October 1962 there were two major international crises, both of which involved quite sophisticated sets of crisis managers. We would do well to remember that only one of these crises did not result in war.

The strategy of crisis management needs more than megalogic. Even that favourite device of crisis theorists, the chicken analogy, has been criticised on the grounds of its rationality. For example, if resolve in a game of chicken can best be demonstrated by the throwing away of the steering wheel, what happens if both players 'rationally' decide to throw away the steering wheel, *but at the same time?*[58] This over-attended analogy can also be criticised from a cultural perspective. It may happen that the two adversaries decide to tug at their steering wheels in order to avert disaster. But what if their habits, training and cultural conditioning are diametrically opposed? Both players may decide that they do not want to collide, but if one has been conditioned to drive on the left hand side of the road, and the other has been conditioned to drive on the right, then the 'natural' avoiding action of each will result in them swinging onto another collision course. In such an episode it is clear that the players know the rules of the game and the risks involved; what they insufficiently understand is the different cultural conditioning of the adversary. If war were to result from analogous behaviour, it would surely represent the ultimate irony in strategic thinking. Civilisation would rush towards Armageddon not because of a clash of ideologies or of grandiose ambitions, but because the participants were desperately attempting to engage in rational war-avoiding strategic behaviour.

Notes

1. See the Report by Captain G. Vivian (British Naval Attache in Tokyo) to the Director of Naval Intelligence, 18 Feb. 1935. This report was widely circulated within the British Government, and few challenged it. Public Record Office, Adm. 116/3862, quoted by Stephen W. Roskill, *Naval Policy Between the Wars,* vol. II (London: Collins, 1976), p. 188.

2. Richard D. Challener, *Admirals, Generals, and American Foreign Policy 1898-1914* (Princeton, N.J.: Princeton University Press, 1973), pp. 404-5.

3. For example, J. Bowyer Bell, 'National Character and Military Strategy: The Egyptian Experience', *Parameters,* vol.V(I) October 1973.

4. Ralph K. White, *Nobody Wanted War: Misperception in Vietnam and Other Wars* (Garden City, N.Y.: Doubleday, 1968), pp. 27-30, 122-30, 222-8.

5. Robert Jervis, *Perception and Misperception in International Politics* (Princeton, N.J.: Princeton University Press, 1976), p. 369.

6. Bernard Brodie, *Strategy in the Missile Age* (Princeton, N.J.: Princeton University Press, 1959), p. 52.

7. Jervis, *Perception and Misperception,* p. 36.

8. See Bernard Brodie, *War and Politics* (London: Cassell, 1973), p. 261.

9. Jervis, *Perception and Misperception,* Ch. 9.

10. Carl von Clausewitz, *On War,* trans. J. J. Graham (London: Routledge and Kegan Paul, 1966). The book was first published in 1832. The Graham translation first appeared in 1908. The latest translation, with extensive commentary, is Carl von Clausewitz, *On War,* trans. by Michael Howard and Peter Paret (Princeton, N.J.: Princeton University Press, 1976).

11. B.H. Liddell Hart, *The British Way in Warfare* (London: Faber and Faber, 1932).

12. B. H. Liddell Hart, *History of the Second World War* (London: Cassell, 1970).

13. Guillio Douhet, *The Command of the Air,* trans. D. Ferrari (London: Faber and Faber, 1942).

14. His main work was *The Influence of Sea Power Upon History 1660-1783* (Boston: Little, Brown and Co., 1890).

15. The Soviet conception of 'command of the sea' is explained by Michael MccGwire, 'Command Of The Sea In Soviet Naval Strategy' and Peter Vigor, 'Soviet Understanding of "Command of the Sea" ', Chs. 32 and 33 of Michael MccGwire, Ken Booth and John McDonnell, *Soviet Naval Policy: Objectives and Constraints* (New York: Praeger Publishers, 1975).

16. In addition to the numerous histories of the Cold War, see also U. Bronfenbrenner, 'The Mirror Image in Soviet–American Relations', *Journal of Social Issues,* vol. XVII (1961), pp. 45-56; William A. Gamson and Andrew Modigliani, *Untangling the Cold War: A Strategy for Testing Rival Theories* (Boston: Little, Brown and Co., 1971).

17. See the comments of Sir William Hayter, a former British Ambassador in Moscow, in his *Russia and the World: A Study of Soviet Foreign Policy* (London: Secker and Warburg, 1970), p. 23.

18. Quoted in Henry A. Kissinger, *Problems of Nuclear Strategy* (New York: Praeger Publishers, 1965), p. 12.

19. This is discussed below, pp. 82-5.

20. Matthew P. Gallagher and Karl F. Spielmann, *Soviet Decision-Making for Defense. A Critique of U.S. Perspectives on the Arms Race* (New York: Praeger Publishers, 1972).

21. Ibid., p. 80.

22. Ibid., pp. 76-82.

23. See Stephen P. Gilbert, *Soviet Images of America* (New York: Crane, Russak and Co., 1977), p. 126.

24. See the comments of Arthur M. Schlesinger, Jr., *The Times,* 25 Apr. 1977.

25. William E. Odom, 'The Soviet Military and Foreign Policy', *Foreign Policy,* vol. 19 (Summer 1975), reprinted in *Survival,* vol. XVII(6) (Nov.–Dec. 1975), pp. 276-81.

26. For example, see Colin S. Gray, 'Nuclear Strategy: The Debate Moves On', *RUSI Journal,* vol. 121(1) (Mar. 1976), pp. 48-9.

27. Gallagher and Spielmann, *Soviet Decision-Making,* p. 80.

28. Quoted in M. P. Gehlen, *The Politics of Coexistence–Soviet Methods and Motives* (Bloomington, Ind.: Indiana University Press, 1967), p. 67.

29. For example, see the article by Dr E. M. Chossudovsky, *The Times,* 3 July 1974.

30. Peter Vigor, *The Soviet View of War, Peace, and Neutrality* (London: Routledge and Kegan Paul, 1975), Ch. 3, 'The Soviet Concept of Peace'.

31. As quoted in *Time,* for example, 17 Nov. 1975.

32. C. A. W. Manning, *The Nature of International Society* (London: Macmillan, 1975), pp. 191-3.

33. Vigor, *Soviet View.*

34. Mohamed Heikal, *The Road to Ramadan* (London: Collins, 1975), p. 241.

35. Chaim Herzog, *The War of Atonement* (London: Weidenfeld and Nicolson, 1975), p. 279.

36. Ibid. See also Richard Deacon, *The Israeli Secret Service* (London: Hamish Hamilton, 1977), pp. 257-70.

37. Herzog, *War of Atonement,* Ch. 4.

38. BBC News, 31 Aug. 1977.

39. Edward N. Luttwak, *The Political Uses of Sea Power* (Baltimore: Johns Hopkins Press, 1974), pp. 20-1.

40. This is one of the themes of Peter Mansfield's *The Arabs* (London: Allen Lane, 1976), esp. p. 503.

41. Ibid., pp. 537-8.

42. Edward N. Luttwak, *American Naval Power in the Mediterranean Part II* (Newport, R.I.: Center for Advanced Research, Naval War College, 1975), pp. 78-9.

43. Ibid.

44. Robert Kaiser, *Russia: The People and the Power* (Harmondsworth, Middx: Penguin Books, 1977), p. 354.

45. Heikal, *Road to Ramadan,* p. 144.

46. Gil Carl AlRoy, *Behind The Middle East Conflict: The Real Impasse Between Arab and Jew* (New York: Capricorn Books, 1975), p. 22.

47. Ibid., p. 23.

48. See Richard E. Neustadt, *Alliance Politics* (New York: Columbia University Press, 1970); and 'White House and Whitehall', reprinted in Morton H. Halperin and Arnold Kanter, *Readings in American Foreign Policy. A Bureaucratic Perspective* (Boston: Little, Brown & Co., 1973), pp. 387-401.

49. See Raymond L. Garthoff (ed.), *Sino-Soviet Military Relations* (London: Praeger, 1966) and the essay by Malcolm Mackintosh, 'The Soviet Attitude' in M. H. Halperin, *Sino-Soviet Relations and Arms Control* (Cambridge, Mass.: MIT Press, 1967), pp. 193-226.

50. Heikal, *Road to Ramadan,* pp. 46-8, 165-84.

51. Luttwak, *Political Uses of Sea Power,* p. 66.

52. Captain Robert B. Bathurst USN, 'Crisis Mentality: A Problem in Cultural Relativity', *Naval War College Review,* Jan.–Feb. 1974, pp. 55-62.

53. See Klaus Knorr, 'Failures In The National Intelligence Estimates: The Case of the Cuban Missiles', *World Politics,* vol. XVI (Apr. 1964), pp. 445-67.

54. Edward Weintal and Charles Bartlett, *Facing the Brink: An Intimate Study of Crisis Diplomacy* (New York: Scribner, 1967), p. 67.

55. Robert F. Kennedy, *Thirteen Days: A Memoir of the Cuban Missile Crisis* (New York: W. W. Norton, 1969), p. 124.

56. Bathurst, 'Crisis Mentality', p. 62.

57. See Allen S. Whiting, *The Chinese Calculus of Deterrence* (Ann Arbor, Mich.: University of Michigan Press, 1975).

58. Herman Kahn, *On Escalation, Metaphors and Scenarios* (New York: Praeger Publishers, 1965), p. 11.

4 PROBLEMS IN STRATEGIC THEORISING

Let nothing be called natural/lest all things/Be held unalterable.
Berthold Brecht

... the world cannot be prised away from our manner of conceiving it: and our conception of the world is something that philosophy can help to change. *A.J. Ayer*

Alongside the replacement of the strategy of military victory by the 'diplomacy of violence',[1] there has been a corresponding replacement of the fog of war by the mists of strategic theory. In this chapter the focus moves from failures in strategic practice resulting from varieties of incompetence by commanders and planners to some problems involved in theorising about strategy, a domain which is largely that of so-called defence intellectuals. Of particular relevance in the present discussion are those gaps between fact and theory opened up by cultural factors. It is a major problem, for it is largely in terms of cultural influences playing upon them that individuals and groups react to situations as they do; political perceptions are signally affected by their cultural milieu.

Ethnocentrism is a factor which must therefore be entered into the account, whether one's interest is in theorising for its own sake or in the hope that better practice will be a by-product or out of a belief that there is nothing so practical as a good theory. The greater the ethnocentrism, the wider will be the gap between strategic theories and behavioural facts.

Rationality: Know His Culture

The idea of rationality is at the centre of Western strategic thinking. We cannot engage in strategic analysis unless we assume that decision-makers attempt to think rationally (though accepting that they will be prone to do the opposite). In strategy, rationality is usually conceived in an instrumental sense. It is concerned with means, not ends. Rationality is 'choosing to act in the manner which gives best promise of maximising one's value position on the basis of a sober calculation of potential gains and losses, and probabilities of enemy actions'.[2] This definition implies several decision-making characteristics,[3] namely that all possible alternatives must be considered, that the alternatives must be considered on their merits and in terms which provide the best 'value-mix', that calculations will be made consciously and correctly, that they will be based on accurate information, and that decisions will be made coolly, with a clear head. Ethnocentrism may add distortion to any or all stages of an attempt at such rational calculation, from the gathering and screening of information to the discussion of what is likely to constitute the best course of action.

When decision-makers calculate what is likely to give 'best promise' of achieving a particular end their reckoning is culture-dependent. 'Best promise' only makes sense in terms of a particular set of values, which in turn have their roots in a particular culture. The concept of rationality itself may well be acultural: an omniscient being could presumably determine which course between several options gave best promise of achieving certain goals, but at a human level one man's god is another man's heresy, and manifestations of rationality, like those of religion, are a matter of geographical accidents and cultural heredity.

The calculation of rational behaviour is culture-dependent in two main ways. Firstly, one's cultural heredity can prevent an individual or group from seeing (or seeing as acceptable) certain options which might nevertheless be rational in an objective sense. The *kamikaze* pilot is a good example. Amongst a group of Western military planners it is very unlikely that such a ploy would have been considered an acceptable method for stopping enemy warships, although in the circumstances of a hard-pressed Japan the tactics met the criteria of rationality. We must not mistake rational for reasonable behaviour. Not all rational behaviour might be thought to be reasonable: more often than not, 'reasonable' behaviour is that which we ourselves (whoever we are) are used to. Secondly, culture is important because it shapes the ends which create the problem to which rational thinking has to be addressed. If an outsider cannot understand or sympathise with the reasonableness of particular ends, he may not appreciate the rationality of the means. This can be seen in the familiar reaction of the Western military to the Soviet institution of military commissars. This institution is not infrequently derided as 'not making sense', especially for those periods when such commissars had equivalent or greater power than the actual military commanders with whom they worked. But the 'sense' to which the critics appeal is that of Western military logic, not Soviet political priorities. Military efficiency might argue for the abolition of the *zampolit*, but it should go without saying that the Communist Party of the Soviet Union does not exist simply to maximise military efficiency. The military commissar is a rational idea, even if not a militarily efficient one.

When thinking about the rational behaviour of others, strategists tend to project their own cultural values. The habitual assumption is: 'If my opponent is rational, he will do what any other rational man would do in his situation. I am rational. Therefore he will do what I would do in his shoes. If I were in his shoes I would . . .' This is how most strategic thinking proceeds, but it should be apparent that one can only predict the behaviour of 'a rational man' if both observer and observed share the same values, have the same set of priorities, and have similar logical powers. Ethnocentric perceptions interfere with this process: they mean that one's own values and sense of priorities are projected onto the other. By this process ethnocentrism undermines the central act in strategy, that of estimating how others will see the world and then will think and act.

The problem of projecting one's own assumptions about rational behaviour is compounded by the prevalence of what Graham Allison called the 'rational-actor' type of analysis.[4] The rational-actor approach simplifies thinking. From this perspective governments are seen as monolithic entities (black boxes) which rationally decide between the options they perceive in order to maximise the values they support. However, as Allison and others have explained, foreign policy and strategy are not the rational products of black boxes. The policy process is essentially a bureaucratic one: policy is not 'made' by one rational unified entity, but by a conglomerate of large organisations and political actors. We would commit a double mistake if we were to assume that another country's past behaviour represented the rational outcome of strategic reasoning, and then went on to predict its future behaviour on the basis of what we project any rational entity (i.e. ourselves) would do. Needless to say we would add a third mistake if we did adopt a bureaucratic perspective, only to project our own bureaucratic behaviour onto others. Bureaucracies have their own cultural idiosyncracies. Together, ethnocentrism and the bureaucratic politics approach seriously undermine ideas about strategic rationality.

When we move from the general to the particular, we can see that the implications of the relationship between culture and rationality has affected some of the most important strategic appreciations of recent years. Estimating the Soviet military threat is one such example. In the late 1960s General Goodpaster, then Supreme Allied Commander Europe, argued that Soviet force levels were well above what were necessary for what he called the Soviet Union's 'legitimate' self-defensive needs. This view has been frequently repeated, and is now a constant refrain. But nobody seems to have asked how we should define a 'legitimate' level of self-defence. Can a universal definition be agreed? Who decides what is 'legitimate'? To the last question there is at least a clear practical answer. It is for the Soviet leadership to decide its own legitimate level. This calculation, in turn, will be affected by the values, interests, priorities, problems, requirements and capabilities of the state leaders. In this respect the terrifying history of the country is particularly relevant. Little imagination is needed to understand this, and it is hardly surprising that Soviet leaders have always been hyper-sensitive to threats and matters of security. The Russian people have a deep fear of war. For its part the Soviet military establishment has good reason to remember with horror the failure of 1941, and the need to prevent its reoccurance. To all Soviet people, whenever they were born, World War II remains 'only yesterday'.[5] We learn feelings from history, as well as facts, and these learned responses help to determine a group's reaction to certain stimuli and its commitment to certain ideas and interests. Security is the first interest of all groups, and the Russians have more reason than most to be over-sensitive about it. As well as being sensitive, they have a wide range of military needs which inflate their requirement for armed forces. Add to this the ready availability of military manpower and a society which has been willing to put guns before butter, and one will certainly have a level of military power which will appear worrying from a Western perspective. But what appears to be over-insurance and threatening from a Western viewpoint *might not yet meet* what appears from a Soviet perspective to be the 'legitimate' self-defensive needs of that country.

The point is that the word 'legitimate' has some misleading connotations when used in a military context. There are no laws or universal standards in this area. Instead we should think of the way great powers act on issues affecting their security, and then add the sorts of perceptions, values and responsibilities shared by Soviet leaders. From this perspective Soviet military capabilities in Europe should not be a cause of surprise. That does not mean that we should be complacent about them, but it should temper alarmism. To the extent the concept of legitimacy has any meaning in this context, it is only a national meaning, pertaining to the traditional thoughtways of the culture concerned.[6] By its own standards Soviet defence efforts are obviously not illegitimate. Indeed, it can even be questioned whether the Soviet Union makes more 'effort' for its defence than do Western states. Certainly, quantitive indicators show Soviet defence effort to be higher than in the West, but this does not necessarily mean that their *effort* in a wider sense involves more strain or sacrifice. Tolerance of strain and willingness to sacrifice vary between nations as they do between individuals. Effort can be measured, but it also has to be felt. One can question whether individual Russians feel the 'burden' of defence more than their richer and more secure Western counterparts. Although the individual Westerner gives up less in standard of life for defence needs (in terms of both direct and opportunity costs), he is probably more *aware* of the pinch of the defence effort and feels that he is *sacrificing* more for his country's defence (especially as he may not think there is a 'real' threat) than his poorer and more heavily burdened Soviet counterpart (who does believe there is a threat, and who wants to help avert it). Because by Western standards the Soviet people seem to be sacrificing themselves for their arms build-up, this does not mean that they are: indeed the perception of the average Russian is that his life is getting better, while Westerners feel a decline in their expectations. A nation's effort can be measured by physical and economic indicators, but it should also include an estimation of what the members feel about their commitment. Furthermore, what seems an excessive Soviet exertion cannot be read to mean that their intentions are necessarily militarily aggressive. Under the Czars the Russians engaged in continental diffusion characteristic of the time; under the Soviet regime they remained in the forward positions made possible by a defensive war. They have occasionally engaged in the 'competitive meddling' characteristic of all great powers, but they have no history of military aggression in the Hitlerian style. Soviet military behaviour has been typically prudent and defensive.

From the standpoint of a planner in Moscow Soviet defence efforts fall short of an ideal posture. They face several major threats and manifold military problems in attempting to deal with them. They also have important deficiencies. Soviet planners have to fear the worst about NATO and/or China, and they have to consider their own vulnerabilities. If they are attacked, Soviet planners have to attempt to ensure that they have enough to further their purposes in war. Possibly their forces would discharge their missions successfully, and so emerge with enough intact to call themselves victors. But at what cost would this be to Soviet society? Until the Soviet leaders can have some confidence that victory can be a meaningful concept, even in a nuclear environment, can it ever be said that they have achieved a 'legitimate' level of defence?

From a Soviet viewpoint it can be argued that US force levels are well above what is required for their 'legitimate' defensive needs. Throughout the post-war period the Soviet experience has been one of trying to catch up with a technologically superior society; outside Eastern Europe this experience has not been that of exploiting its military strength in the extensive manner of the United States. 'Legitimacy' really belongs to the wrong category of words to be used in this context. If instead we concentrate on the way great powers behave, and remember that all states like to insure to the fullest extent they can afford, we will have a sounder basis for thinking. Both superpowers have over-insured since 1945. This may have been undesirable from many viewpoints, social as well as strategic, but the costs of mistakes are greater still, and this thought stimulates the appetite of the prudent. The fact is, as President Coolidge put it on one of those occasions when words rather than moths issued from his mouth, 'No nation ever had an army large enough to guarantee it against attack in time of peace or insure it victory in time of war.'

Although high force levels can be justified from a Soviet viewpoint on the grounds that they are only attempts to meet defensive needs, it is hardly surprising if these levels appear threatening from a Western perspective. However 'defensive' the reasons for the accumulation of Soviet armaments, they inevitably provide its leadership with impressive capabilities, a wide range of options and a powerful image of looming military might. These advantages could all be brought into play if Soviet intentions changed significantly or if external constraints lifted. Furthermore, there is also the possibility that the instrument might shape the will to use it. Capabilities accumulated for one set of reasons can be used for another. Indeed, the mere possession of an instrument can change expectations and intentions. Therefore, even if one argues that the Soviet Union is defensively oriented, there is still plenty of reason for concern. We are faced with the oldest strategic problem of all. What is seen as a rational posture of defensive insurance from one perspective may well appear as a threatening or offensive posture from another. In strategy, one man's prudence is another man's overkill.

Cultural heredity and national perspective, therefore, affect levels of military effort: they also affect levels of tolerable suffering. The idea of 'unacceptable damage' is a basic consideration in deterrence theory. It is a concept, however, like 'legitimacy', which is both subjective and contextual. The difficulty of determining what is likely to constitute unacceptable damage was demonstrated by the British experience with strategic bombing over Germany and the US experience over North Vietnam. Ethnocentrism affected estimates of the likely effectiveness of strategic bombing in several ways. There was an assumption that rational behaviour by the enemy would result in a speedy surrender.

In both cases this was generally assumed without an understanding of the other nation's commitment to the cause for which it was fighting. Furthermore, 'bad anthropology' frequently resulted in an assumption that the enemy's backbone was more brittle than one's own and would snap under a hail of bombs. Events proved both these ethnocentric assumptions to be false: to date experience has generally ridiculed the hopes of airpower theorists about 'rational' adversary behaviour under the impact of strategic bombing.

The costs which societies are willing to bear varies considerably. A good example of this has been the human steam-roller employed by Czarist and then Soviet Russia. In both eras there was a greater willingness to accept heavy casualties than was the case in the West. In World War II this was demonstrated to some Western commanders, to their horror and surprise, by the way that Soviet commanders cleared minefields simply by sending troops across them, rather than by slower and less costly technical means.[7] Western commanders could not be so lavish with their own men's lives if there appeared to be an alternative. National attitudes to costs vary greatly, therefore, and outsiders often fail to appreciate the depth of feeling which others have about particular objectives. In the late 1960s the Israelis could not appreciate the depth of Egyptian humiliation, while many Americans underestimated the level of punishment which the North Vietnamese were willing to suffer. Maxwell Taylor, the US Ambassador in Saigon, frankly admitted that he could not understand how his opponents maintained their morale.[8] Ethnocentric perceptions distort our understanding of the value preference of other societies and, therefore, the price they are willing to pay and the burdens they are willing to bear. Definitions of unacceptable damage are as peculiar to societies and to a specific context as are tolerances of pain with individuals. It is well to remember that Stalin in the 1930s was willing to allow millions of deaths in order to change his agricultural policy.

The limitations of projecting Western assumptions can be seen in the general failure of strategists to contemplate what Yehezkel Dror has called 'the crazy state'.[9] The importance of this thesis is in its attempt to disturb the cosy world of American deterrence theory, applicable as it is to adversaries exhibiting 'normal' rational behaviour for 'normal' (if sometimes unacceptable) ends. In Dror's conception, a crazy state may behave rationally in an instrumental sense, but its goals may be 'crazy'. Conventional approaches to deterrence may not therefore suffice,[10] although some theorists have attempted to deal with the problem by stressing the need for building in what Kahn called a 'safety factor', that is an overkill capability large enough to impress even the irrational and irresponsible. What degree of overkill will impress the irrational and irresponsible is, however, an open question. How much is more than enough?

In analysing the US—Soviet arms race ethnocentrism often manifests itself in the sense of faulty methodology. In the case of US—Chinese relations, on the other hand, bad anthropology has often been the dominant force. Crude stereotyping led Western opinion to believe that Chinese motivations were outside the bounds of normal understanding. Indeed, China is the one major country in the last generation which has sometimes been given the status of a 'crazy' state, either implicitly or explicitly. A TV film of the mid-1960s was entitled 'China: The Roots of Madness', and the widespread belief of that decade was that the Chinese leaders not only believed that nuclear war was inevitable, but also that their country would emerge victorious. Not surprisingly, many Western observers were led to believe that the possession of nuclear weapons by China would be more dangerous than their possession by the Soviet Union. Soviet propaganda and China's own declaratory policy added to this impression. However, China's action policy gave off different signals, and those observers who paid attention to the latter were always more moderate in their judgements about Chinese rationality than those who believed Soviet pronouncements or who took on face value such widely quoted Chinese statements as the declaration that if the United States started a nuclear war, the victorious Chinese 'would create very swiftly a civilisation thousands of times higher than the capitalist system and a truly beautiful future for themselves'.[11]

Knowledge about China has accumulated since the mid-1960s. Much remains ambiguous, and Chinese policies are not easily predicted, but the same is true of most countries. Western Sinologists, as opposed to superficial commentators, have never thought of China as a 'crazy' state. Rather, they have seen Chinese strategic behaviour in terms of its emergence from a unique political culture and geopolitical situation, and have concluded that what has emerged has, on the whole, been both sophisticated and rationally responsive.[12]

The Arab world is another area which many Western observers have found difficult to comprehend, for 'normal' behaviour is often overturned. In a revealing and candid discussion about Arab politics between King Feisal and President Nasser just before the latter's death, the King suggested that everybody concerned was mad. President Nasser was more guarded: he suggested a doctor be appointed 'to examine us regularly and find out which ones are crazy'.[13] This was an intriguing exchange. Feisal's comment shows that from some perspectives we are all at least a little mad: but Nasser's comment, on the other hand, underlines the almost universal assumption that it is always the next person who is crazy. When strategists understand the implications of both these outlooks, and account for them in their analysis, some of the problems of strategy will become a little clearer, though the answers will remain as elusive as ever.

'Craziness' is an ethnocentric as well as a medical conception. The movements and states which Dror has described as 'crazy' are so judged in terms of contemporary Western culture: craziness is a culturally given and time-bound value judgement.[14]

Strategic Criteria: Comparison Is Obligatory

Maps can be illuminating cartographic reflections of ethnocentric souls. In the best world maps of the late Middle Ages, European cartographers tried to fit America into their own preconceived world map. They wasted much ingenuity in trying to make the Americas a part of their own land mass. The Americas had to be joined on, for medieval Europeans could not conceive a 'New World'.[15] Early Chinese map-makers, conceiving their kingdom as *Thienhia* or 'everything under the heavens', drew their maps in accordance with a similar outlook. When they later came to conceive the earth as a globe, with China as only a part of it, their 'total confusion' about the outside world resulted in their putting the kingdom of China right at the centre, with the great empires of Europe as distant and obscure satellites rotating around it.[16] The inspiration behind Chinese cartography has not significantly changed: it has only been given a Marxist–Leninist–Maoist twist. In 1968 the *People's Daily* twice presented annotated maps of the 'Excellent World Situation'. The only city marked was Peking, and both showed China roughly in the middle, but a little left of centre.[17]

Such manifestations of national outlooks are not uncommon in great powers, and they hint at an important but largely unexplored methodological problem in strategic theory, namely that of articulating the critera by which different countries should be judged. More often than not, the criteria used are implicit rather than explicit, and unsystematic rather than carefully formulated. More often than not, they are also ethnocentric. The roughness and inappropriateness of the criteria inhibit the development in strategy of a 'scientific approach' (in a loose sense) in which comparison and categorisation are obligatory.

International politics and strategic history are full of examples of societies attempting to fit the behaviour of others into their own preconceived outlook. This increases the temptation to project one's own assumptions. Such faulty methodology is particularly significant when an established society has to account for a new phenomenon, such as a revolutionary state or the rise of a new great power. Hypersensitivity is the usual response, involving a rush to demonic stereotypes and playing safe militarily. *Nations in Darkness*[18] was the title John Stoessinger appropriately gave to his essay on the perceptual mishaps in Chinese—American and Soviet—American relations. Equally appropriate was his use of the phrase 'through a glass, darkly' to describe the relationship between societies which are geographically and culturally remote, such as the United States and China. Attempts to fit Chinese strategic thinking into Western strategic frameworks have proved to be mistaken, as the small number of Sinologists with a military interest have tried to show. Indeed, some have argued that not only has China's military tradition been 'refreshingly different' from that of the West, but that at times it has also been more fertile.[19]

It is not only states which are culturally different which have problems: those which are culturally close can also have trouble understanding each other. Like European cartography of the late Middle Ages, Eurocentric strategic outlooks have continued to find it hard to admit a New World. This has resulted in a widespread misconception of American strategic behaviour. More often than not, American strategists are seen as Europeans gone wrong, but with more muscle. Significantly, the Eurocentric perspective has been successfully projected into much American thinking itself. This is largely the result of the prevalence of the European immigrant perspective: those with relatively recent European backgrounds seem to have had a disproportionate influence on the development of international relations in the United States.

American strategic history has been the victim of inappropriate and unarticulated strategic criteria.[20] Commentators on US strategy have invariably used continental European criteria (perhaps even Prussian criteria) rather than judging the United States on its own terms. These continental European frameworks for judgement are not appropriate for a continental-sized country whose circumstances have been unique amongst the great military powers in terms of relative size, power, remoteness, traditional degree of security, industrial capacity and more recently its global responsibilities and multiplicity of relationships. Writers have implicitly, and sometimes explicitly, tried to interpret American strategy, conceived as a strategy of *choice,* in terms of the criteria and preoccupations of countries whose outlooks have been dominated by strategies of *necessity.*[21] Those used only to thinking in terms of strategies of necessity have largely ignored important features of American strategic history which stand in favourable comparison with all other great military powers, namely the vitality and plurality of its arms debate, the record of civilian control, the avoidance (with the exception of Vietnam) of tragic errors, the attempt to bring systematic planning into policy, and the historic consciousness of the desirability of preventing the military instrument from shaping the political will. The problem of appropriate criteria is of more than academic interest. It has policy overtones. It is only one step from Americans thinking that Prussian criteria are the appropriate ones by which to be judged, to their attempting to follow that style of behaviour in practice. Does anybody, including America, really want Gulliver to behave like a Prussian?

War Is a Continuation of . . . What?

The study of philosophies of war is of great significance for strategy because, as Anatol Rapoport has put it, 'the nature of war is itself to a large extent determined by how man conceives of it', and the general character of a nation's strategy is, in turn, determined by its philosophy of war.[22] Strategic theories have their roots in philosophies of war which are invariably ethnocentric, though naturally philosophies of war are not as constrained by national boundaries as are strategic theories. National strategies are the immediate descendants of philosophies of war.[23] If war is seen to be nature's way of insuring the survival of the fittest (as with some nineteenth-century German romantics), then the militarist ethos and strategic affairs will be elevated to dominating concerns in national life. If war is conceived as an absurdity (as among the Eskimos), then one will live one's life untroubled by strategic theorising and planning. If one were to view war as a gentlemanly pastime (as was the case in the age of chivalry), adventure and the satisfaction of honour are its justifications: war is not concerned with imposing new political systems on foreign communities. If one possesses an eschatological philosophy of war (such as the Nazi doctrine of Master Race), then one's destiny would be to carry out a preordained mission, like a sleep-walker. On the other hand, if one's philosophy is 'ethnocentric/cataclysmic' (like Lenin's just after the Bolshevik Revolution), then war is seen as a disaster that threatens to befall one's nation, and so demands 'herculean efforts' including draconian discipline to meet it. If one views war as a crime (like pacifists), then one does not participate in military activity. At the least one takes no personal part in fighting; at the most one seeks to win over others to one's own viewpoint, and so strengthen the laws of war and the promotion of disarmament. Finally, if one conceives the nature of war in a Clausewitzian sense (as being rational, national and instrumental in Rapoport's formulation[24]), then one engages in strategy along the lines adopted by the major European powers in recent centuries.

The Clausewitzian 'political philosophy of war' still prevails today though its scope is more inhibited than in earlier periods. Nevertheless Western strategists with evident pride frequently proclaim that 'we are all Clausewitzians now'. But we are not. We are not Clausewitzians in at least two important ways. Firstly, the Clausewitzian political approach is not the only philosophy of war; there are many philosophies of war. However, when Western strategists talk or write about 'the concept of war' (note the ethnocentric assumption of *one* concept) they always mean, implicitly or explicitly, the Clausewitzian concept of war which emerged from early nineteenth-century Europe. To imply that the Clausewitzian paradigm is synonymous with the meaning of war is to exhibit an extreme of ethnocentrism. Secondly, we are not all Clausewitzians in the sense that even where Clausewitz is thought relevant, Clausewitzian ideals may not be attained. Warfare is not always rational and instrumental. It may sometimes be everything but a continuation of political intelligence. The reasons why men and groups engage in war are complex. A particular war may be a continuation of politics, but for many participants, including those responsible for policy, this aspect may be a side-effect, a bonus or even irrelevant.[25] As 'aggressive instinct' or 'human nature' theories have become discredited, analysts have come to stress the social and cultural roots of war. Conflicts arise everywhere, but as Otto Klineberg has explained, 'there is nothing inevitable about the way in which they are expressed, or in the reactions they elicit'.[26] War, in short, is an extension of culture, as well as of politics.

Cultural conditioning, together with psychological considerations, affect the character of a group's decision to fight. Three illustrations suggest the inadequacy of an exclusive Clausewitzian paradigm: (i) The guerrilla movements of Latin America cannot be understood apart from their social and cultural setting. Indeed, in explaining why men become guerrillas culture may well be more important than politics. In 'sheer lyricism for Che', the students of the 1960s went into the jungle 'with no more than ham sandwiches'. For these groups, war was a continuation of what Anthony Burton nicely termed a 'self-consciously hairy-chested' view of masculinity.[27] Catholicism and machismo were more significant than the Clausewitzian philosophy of war. (ii) The importance of individual psychological factors abound in military history. The character of particular campaigns has often been affected by commanders who have allowed their desire for personal glory to influence their planning.[28] General Montgomery in north-western Europe and General MacArthur in the South Pacific are two recent examples. Ego-satisfaction certainly does not rank in any list of the principles of war, but it is of considerable explanatory value in military history. In campaigns where this factor has been important the prosecution of war has had political effects, but they have been a by-product of personal ambition as much as a continuation of political intelligence. Clausewitz has been no more than a vehicle and a rationalisation for the massaging of superegos. (iii) Self-image is largely the product of cultural conditioning. The effects of this have been evident in the Arab world, and were significant in the declaration of at least one war. On the eve of war in 1948 Golda Meir tried to dissuade King Abdulla of Jordan from taking part. The King bore her a grudge from that point on. According to the King, Mrs Meir had placed him in an 'impossible position', for she had given him the alternative of 'submitting to an ultimatum through the lips of a woman or going to war'. This was no choice for an Arab King. He was obliged 'of course' to go to war. Jordan joined the other Arab states in their invasion of Israel.[29] On this occasion war was not a continuation of politics as much as an expression of Arab male chauvinism.

For better or worse, we are not all Clausewitzians, even if we wear ostensibly Clausewitzian hats. Western strategic thinking has to accommodate to this realisation if fact and theory are to become closer, and if much relevant activity is not to be overlooked. A narrow conception of war means that important matters pertaining to inter-group violence are not included within our purview. In particular it means that the many varieties of internal violence tend to be ignored. This in turn means that a picture of peaceability is created which does not exist. Ethnocentric perspectives allied to a preoccupation with East–West concerns also means that the alternative outlooks, problems, interests and philosophies of Africa, the Middle East, Asia and Latin America are ignored. If one allows one's conceptual framework to be dominated by Clausewitz, one will miss important areas of reality. Clausewitz is necessary for the modern strategist but he is not sufficient.

Philosophies of war, like strategic theories, are products of time and place. This might be regarded as a cause for optimism. It might suggest that there is not simply one immutable philosophy of war, the Clausewitzian–Prussian one, which the world community is destined to endure evermore. If men's ideas about the nature of war are mutable, efforts must be made to change them in the 'right' direction. Changes do occur.

The traditional doctrines of Islam were ameliorated, from essentially a world domination theory to one which accepted integration into a Western-originated world order.[30] More recently, Khrushchev amended the Leninist doctrine about the 'fatalistic inevitability' of war. These are encouraging illustrations, and lead us to consider whether different societies can be persuaded that war is merely an outmoded custom or an absurdity, and so help to relax the grip of the war system. Such logic is beguiling, but the problems are apparent: how can national societies be created in the modern world free of power drives?[31] The record is not encouraging. It shows that just as bad money drives out good, war-like philosophies tend to drive out the more pacifistically inclined. Nations must ask themselves where there is any sense (or demand) in having an Eskimo philosophy of war if one is surrounded by Prussians? History, so far, has given only one answer.

Conceptions of the Utility of Force

Estimating the utility of military force is important in strategic analysis. Forecasts of how allies, adversaries and third parties may calculate the costs and benefits of military behaviour will affect one's views of the risks of pursuing particular policies and the feasibility of particular goals. Such important forecasts are very vulnerable to ethnocentric misconception, for the utility of military power can only be assessed within a national framework: it is the balance between aggregate values and aggregate costs as felt by a particular national group. It is also a calculation which may change, and is therefore both a subjective and contextual phenomenon.[32]

Historically, military force was a 'normal' aspect of international relations. However, questioning traditional assumptions about its utility has been one of the characteristic features of Western strategic discourse since the mid-1960s. In the light of a lost war in Vietnam, nuclear overkill, an endless struggle in Northern Ireland and a perceived Western failure to translate military power into diplomatic effectiveness, it has often been claimed that armed forces are not as useful as formerly. At best they are dismissed as 'intellectual time-lags'; at worst they are criticised as being counter-productive and dangerous. Certainly military force is a dangerous and savage method by which to carry out international relations, but those who sweep aside its utility underestimate the continuity of attitudes and behaviour both in relation to those Western societies at which the comments are primarily directed, and even more so in relation to most other societies.[33] Such beliefs can contribute to policies based on shaky foundations. The ethnocentric tendency (in this case largely amongst non-strategists) is to argue that since our own forces do not seem as useful as formerly this must be how other nations see their own: this is how 'any rational Man' must react. But other nations do not have the same attitudes. Furthermore, states which do not understand our style are apt to accept at face value the self-denigrating habits of Western democracies. A double error is thereby committed.

Western liberal ideas about the utility of military force cannot be safely projected onto other societies. Ideas about the usability of force are always likely to decline most amongst those with nuclear overkill, settled frontiers, a horror of violence, vivid memories of total wars and a reduced need to project force beyond their own frontiers. But these conditions do not pertain outside the Western world: more traditional outlooks persist. Western observers project their own attitudes in another way. There is a familiar Western penchant for adopting patronising attitudes towards less developed societies, and some writers seem to believe that it is 'only a matter of time' before they catch up in their attitudes.[34] This viewpoint contains the ethnocentric assumption that Western ways are better, right and will inevitably be followed by reasonable people. Whether or not such hopes are justified, they do suggest that some ethnocentric attitudes can be very attractive.

Force remains the *ultima ratio* on a broad range of international issues. During the late 1960s and early 1970s it was commonplace in the West to hear about the declining utility of military force. However, at the very same time extensive military efforts were taking place throughout the Third World (between 1965 and 1974 defence spending increased by 100 per cent, 39 per cent more men were placed under arms, and arms imports more than doubled[35]); the Soviet Army was efficiently imposing socialist unity on Czechoslovakia; a massive procurement of strategic weaponry was establishing for the Soviet Union a recognised position of superpower parity with the United States; Iran was spending vast amounts of money on modern military equipment to make itself policeman of the Gulf; Israeli commanders were conquering and holding territory to improve their state's security; Indian forces were detaching East Pakistan and assisting in the creation of the new state of Bangladesh; and the North Vietnamese and Vietcong were rounding off a prolonged struggle and imposing their own kind of unity on their part of Indo-China. These were only the most dramatic developments. While the leaders of these countries might fully attach themselves to the rhetoric of peace and disarmament at the United Nations and elsewhere, one need hardly waste any time discussing whether they think the maintenance and use of military power represents an intellectual time-lag. Their armed forces are usable and have been used.

Assertions that the utility of the armed forces of Western nations is in rapid decline are often exaggerated. In general Western forces have actually had more utility than some recent episodes might have suggested, be that utility in the form of negotiating from strength, specific threats, maintaining order at sea, internal security, peace-keeping or utility in non-use. The latter is of particular importance. An instrument does not have to be actively used to be useful: indeed, it is often argued that the use of brute military force represents a bankruptcy of military power. When a government has actually to use military violence, this is usually evidence that its forces lack credibility — either to deter attack, successfully impose a threat or achieve an objective by the clever manipulation of military signals.

It is also important to remember the changeability of the concept of utility, and hence to be wary of projecting impressions gained from the 1960s into the different world of the late 1970s and 1980s. In a world in which the level of violence is not reducing, and in which there are numerous sources of conflict, the extreme anti-military attitudes engendered by Vietnam may well prove to be the exception rather than the rule. Indeed, attitudes may have already changed in many sectors of Western society. The late 1970s are not yet bellicose, but they have become more hard-nosed. As time passes, criticism directed against the Vietnam War may well focus on matters of political purpose and direction rather than on the military instrumentality itself. The American armed forces will be seen as victims as much as culprits. Furthermore, if Soviet leaders in the late 1960s believed that their own arms build-up would provide them with leverage over a post-Vietnam United States, they were predictably mistaken. The United States has not turned into a superpower ostrich. Furthermore, the better-than-the-military-Joneses attitude of the Soviet High Command has done more than anything to remind the American public that military power still has an important role in world affairs.

Opinions about the utility of military power vary between countries, but they also vary within countries. This difference is more complicated than the simple divide between hawks and doves. In the United States some differences in one esoteric aspect of this debate were personified by Dr Kissinger and Dr Schlesinger. The latter argued in 1974 about the advantages of strategic strength and of the psychological impact of *numbers* of strategic weapons on third party perceptions. Dr Kissinger's view, as stated in the Soviet Union, was that strategic superiority loses any political meaning at the levels of weaponry currently possessed by the superpowers. In a now famous piece of rhetoric he asked: 'What is the significance of it [strategic superiority] politically, militarily, operationally at these levels of numbers? What do you do with it?' That a Secretary of State expressed such doubts is significant in itself: what is equally significant is the likely answer which the Soviet High Command might have given to Kissinger's question. According to one specialist their answer would have been: 'Use it'.[36] Apparent support for this guess was given by Admiral Gorshkov, Commander-in-Chief of the Soviet Navy. One of his underlying themes in a series of articles which he had published in 1972-3 was the argument that naval power was an effective political instrument.[37] Evidently the Soviet High Command took a far more traditional view of the utility of high levels of military power than the Harvard professor-cum-statesman with extraordinary intellectual subtlety.

Many 'liberal' thinkers in the West tend to underestimate the utility which groups in other countries attach to their own armed forces. Neither do they readily appreciate, with their own preference for what we call 'peace' (that is the present status quo), the demands and preference of other societies for *justice* rather than *peace*. This is partly a result of the widespread horror of violence in the West arising out of the experience of two total wars. It is difficult for Western liberals to accept that in some societies military violence has none of these connotations. In black Africa, for example, organised violence has sometimes been more a matter of theatre than of strategy. War and martial activities have had more to do with the meaning of manhood and the universe than with politics in a Western sense.[38] In many parts of the world, attitudes towards death and the use of violence differ from those in the West, where the trend has been towards humanitarianism. Other societies or groups within them often show a much greater willingness to take risks. It will always be particularly difficult for the successful, advantaged, secure and problem-free to appreciate the difficulties and unpleasantness of the world for those who are none of these. Contrary to appearances, movement and revolution are more characteristic of the modern world than stability and legitimacy, and ideological conflicts are stronger than moral accords: 'peace is scarcely a shared value in this century'.[39] If ethnocentric misconceptions result in a failure to appreciate the risks which the disadvantaged will take in order to change the fat cat's peace, then a very important input into forecasting will be lost.

These misperceptions are not all one-sided, however. If some Western commentators tend to project their own attitudes towards violence on Third World countries, the latter tend to accept what is said about Western attitudes towards force at face value. This is a particular problem for the United States, given its world-wide interests. Third World countries, but also allies and adversaries of the United States, often do not understand the US political process well enough. They tend to accept the self-depreciation of the 'goldfish-bowl democracy' without question. This self-denigration and apparent lack of confidence in turn feeds the confidence of those who would exploit US weaknesses. The faulty methodology of US commentators and the culture-bound habits of their listeners mean that both sides are likely to be surprised by the behaviour of the other. In both cases, the commentators are led to suppose that the other nation or nations are less willing to use force than in fact they are. The fact is that nowhere is the profession of arms about to go out of business.

Word Problems Can Be World Problems

For strategists, whose business concerns life and death, words as vehicles of both thought and communication have a peculiar importance. Unfortunately the language of strategy has received relatively little attention, [40] and even the analysis of relevant concepts used by different societies is comparatively rare. [41] What is more familiar are grumblings about the use of language in the American-dominated social sciences, especially the plethora of euphemisms and jargon, and the mixture of academic equivocation and natural humility in the face of complex issues which has led strategists into developing forms of expression which allow them to escape the sharpest intellectual hooks. [42]

Strategy suffers from many word problems. Sometimes the problems are the result of our own confusion: we are not sure of what we mean by some concepts. But some of the problems arise from ethnocentrism. We sometimes do not know what strategists and politicians in other countries mean by the concepts they use. And we sometimes assume that they mean the same as we mean, especially when the same word is used. All this places a premium on the most careful use of language.

In order to analyse and compare different strategic concepts, it is necessary that we understand them in relation to the social and political environment from which they emerged. This is a difficult but by no means impossible task; the convergence of thinking on the iron facts of strategy is sufficiently strong that one does not have to become a practising Sinologist or Sovietologist before one can engage in comparative strategic analysis,[43] though of course it helps.

Some of the problems involved in the projection of one set of concepts onto a different national experience were discussed earlier in relation to naval strategy.[44] Robert Bathurst has developed this theme in terms of the problems caused by the words we use.[45] He has argued that when Admiral Gorshkov, the Commander-in-Chief of the Soviet Navy mentions 'control of the seas', it is assumed in the West that Gorshkov means what US naval planners mean by 'sea control'. It is assumed that when Gorshkov writes of 'internal struggles', he is engaging in Washington-style inter-service battles and is trying to build a 'blue-water navy' free from army domination. The last phrase is interesting: because the Soviet Navy operates in all oceans, it is now argued that it has become a 'blue-water navy', a phrase which carries very specific connotations and historical memories for British and American navalists. Because Gorshkov has called for a 'balanced fleet' it is assumed that he means 'balanced' in the Anglo-American sense, and that this would mean that the Soviet Navy could be expected to behave offensively. When considering the budgetary and doctrinal problems facing Gorshkov, Americans have tended simply to project US institutional behaviour on the Soviet Union. In short, Western observers assume that Gorshkov is influenced by what influences us, that the Soviet leaders have no imagination or experience of their own, and that they have an institutional and geographical environment almost like ours. In Bathurst's view, without a far deeper understanding of Gorshkov's personality and his cultural and geographical environment, reconstructions of his decisions are 'simply interesting games which should not be taken very seriously'. Unfortunately, many naval commentators, with no sense of Russia in their minds, do regularly engage in these games and do take them seriously.

No less important differences also arise within the field of nuclear strategy. Differences in political culture are very important. For one thing US thinking about nuclear strategy has become dominated by civilians, whereas that of the Soviet Union has remained firmly dominated by the military (though final decisions are made by civilians in the Politburo). The differences between the resulting strategic concepts are consequently magnified by both national and professional perspectives. Between a Soviet military journal and a Western academic journal the differences of focus and approach are considerable. On the other hand, between Soviet and American military journals one would at least notice some similarities in focus and approach. Some military subjects, whose bones are formed more by logistic constraints than by esoteric theory, do sometimes have common thought-patterns. But even a general comparison of two sets of military journals would reveal big differences, because one military establishment is a product of a pluralistic society, whereas the other belongs to a closed society.

In the Soviet Union there has never grown up, as in Western countries (and especially the United States), a habit of public defence debating. In the Soviet Union there are no academic strategists as we understand the term, no civilian specialists in ostensibly independent research institutes, and no independent newspaper defence correspondents. There are defence debates, but the milieu in Moscow is such that their character is very different from the free-for-all Washington model. The debates are more cautious, they are technically rather than politically inclined, and outsiders have no role. Strategic debate is dominated by a smaller, more inbred and more professionally involved group. Similarly, Soviet military writings tend to be narrower, more professionally relevant (more technical), less political and more traditionalist. As was discussed earlier, the products of this system have been seen by US theorists as simpler, more partisan and less sophisticated.

Many of these considerations can be seen in the different Soviet and US conceptions of deterrence and defence.[46] The most striking contrast between the two conceptions is the fact that Soviet strategic thinking has not made the same doctrinal distinction between 'deterrence' and 'defence' which has been made by Western strategists. In Western nuclear strategy the distinction is crucial, but in Soviet thinking the concepts are interrelated, or even synonymous. Thus the Soviet conception conforms with the traditional military view (in all countries) which comprehends deterrence in terms of a threat by an impressive war-fighting capability. The Anglo-American conception, on the other hand, has crystallised into the idea of *mutual* deterrence. This theory includes the idea of being solicitous about mutual vulnerability and about the survivability of the adversary's retaliatory forces. It has also involved the development of doctrines and weapons for the creation of an impressive war-avoiding rather than war-fighting military machine. In comparison, the traditional military outlook which characterises Soviet thinking has in most respects been more logical, and this has given Soviet approaches a coherence which has been lacking in Western thinking. There is no mental blockage in Soviet thinking, for example, caused by the thought of deterrence 'failing'. If war breaks out, the Soviet attitude is then to move onto the next stage. In preparation for this possibility Soviet military planners have given much more explicit attention to fighting and winning a nuclear war than Western (especially civilian) strategists. Another traditional aspect of Soviet thinking arises from the belief that what is good for defence is good for deterrence.

The military postures which have resulted from this distinctive Soviet attitude have often been disturbing to Western thinkers. A dominating theme in US strategic doctrine has been the priority of deterrence over defence. This has produced complications because deterrence and defence have sometimes pulled in different directions as far as planning and weaponry are concerned. What is theoretically good for defence ('damage limitation' capabilities such as ABMs) has been argued to be bad ('destabilising') for deterrence. Alternatively, what might be thought good for deterrence (massive counter-population weapons) might be considered to be bad for defence (they provide no disarming capability or flexibility if war breaks out). Such contradictions are resolved for Soviet planners by their traditional belief that what is best for defence is best for deterrence. However, the military postures which emerge from such thinking, logical as they are, create severe complications and misunderstandings when they are seen by an adversary which does not consider deterrence and defence in the nuclear context to be synonymous, but rather sees them as distinct, in terms both of doctrine and resultant strategic posture.

The reasons for Soviet dissatisfaction with the doctrine of mutual vulnerability should be apparent from the preceding discussion. From the Soviet perspective what matters is not the deterrent doctrine of the mutual survivability of retaliatory forces: what matters is increasing the chances for the actual survivability of the Soviet system if the worst happens. From the Soviet viewpoint the doctrine of Mutual Assured Destruction (MAD) was inconsistent with effective war-fighting and survival strategies. The Soviet position was neither unsophisticated nor mischievous. It was built on Russian sense. MAD, on the other hand, had a certain American strategic logic, but as it was applied by some minds there was ground for suspecting that it was also sheer prejudice passing itself off as strategic theory.

The emphasis in Soviet doctrine on fighting a nuclear war has been difficult for many Western observers to accept. It has been particularly difficult to grasp for those without a grounding in strategic history. To those with such a grounding the 'sense' of traditional doctrines is usually readily apparent, but to those for whom 'deterrence' simply and entirely means the doctrines developed in the United States in the 1950s and 1960s, the Soviet approach appears at least awkward. It should not. From a traditional (and Soviet) viewpoint there is nothing inconsistent between preparing to fight and win a war should it break out, and hoping that this eventuality will never occur. Because they have developed doctrines and capabilities for fighting a nuclear war, it does not necessarily follow that the Soviet leadership is bent on making that eventuality come to pass, or that 'victory' in nuclear war has any meaning for them except in the worst of all possible worlds. Nuclear war is a finite possibility: we all recognise that. But the Soviet Union has done something about facing up to the possibility. And every little bit might help. That surviving let alone prevailing might not be possible in nuclear war does not necessarily mean that it is an objective which should not be pursued. The search for the desirable, even if unattainable, has rarely inhibited the efforts of great powers.

Soviet attitudes towards nuclear strategy have a steady consistency. To maximise their own security, the Soviet position is that more is better. What could be simpler or more traditional? However, they appear to fail to appreciate why this should appear 'destabilising' through the eyes of adversaries, just as many of their opponents fail to appreciate the Soviet perception of multiple enemies and of their own economic and technological inferiority to the United States. Both the United States and the Soviet Union have frequently failed to appreciate the impact of their own logical efforts and doctrines on the threat perceptions of the other. Both sides have failed to be sensitive to the insecurity which has been provoked in the other by their own military efforts. This is a cause for regret amongst strategists in the United States, in the light of their ideas about 'stability'. In the Soviet case it is just the opposite, for as Arnold Horelick has put it, 'the USSR's security tends to be viewed as synonymous with the insecurity of the potential enemy; indeed, the latter is expected to behave more "reasonably" only when the correlation of forces shifts in his disfavour'.[47] These different perspectives present a formidable barrier to hopes of finding mechanisms by which to stabilise and manage the US–Soviet strategic relationship; the more so because 'the gap separating the two outlooks is less likely the consequence of a temporary "lag" in Soviet strategic sophistication than of profound differences between the political cultures of the two societies'. It is a familiar feature of international politics. Governments fail to appreciate the impact of their own actions on others. In the past such problems have sometimes resulted in arms races, crises and war. In the past even 'total war' could be afforded. But this is no longer the case. In the past, strategic theories have come and gone, and more has often been learned from defeat than victory. But a nuclear nightmare would be a wholly different category of horror. At the highest levels of military power there is nothing worthwhile beyond deterrence:

however conceived, it is the last hopeful strategic theory.

The discussion of word problems has pointed to an interesting irony. Not only is there a tendency to assume that our own strategic conceptualisations are superior to those of other countries, but at the same time we are by no means always confident about what some of our own conceptualisations mean. 'Detente', 'command of the sea', 'flexible response', 'strategic superiority', 'parity', 'peace', 'seapower' — these are just some of the familiar concepts whose meaning is not even clear to those who share the same cultural background. There are honest differences of opinion about definition and also about the way the concepts should be operationalised. What are the norms of a detente relationship? What is the meaning of peace? In the case of the latter, a good definition would amount to a comprehensive political theory. One of the most persistent examples of the way in which we are unsure of our central concepts is the idea of the 'balance of power', an idea which explicitly or implicitly underlies much strategic thinking and practice. While Western writers have filled thousands of pages in trying to clarify the concept, however, it is instructive to note that thinking in some other countries is more systematic. The Russian language, for example, breaks the conceptual knot by simply using different phrases to describe the various nuances which the single phrase has in the English language.[48] In contrast with this logical approach, Western writers over the centuries have engaged in time-consuming academic gyrations, in order to save their multipurpose concept for posterity. Their industry might be described as eight [49] realities in search of a theory.

If we are not sure in our own minds about the meanings of various familiar and important strategic concepts, then we are doubly compounding the problem of ethnocentrism. Not only are we visiting our own concepts on foreign societies, but we are not even sure about the meaning of the concepts we are projecting. This puts a premium on focusing inwards, just as much as outwards. As in other aspects of the study of human behaviour, we help to know ourselves better by knowing others, but we also help to know others by better knowing ourselves.

International Negotiation: Words as Action

Strategy can be conceived as a form of bargaining. Sometimes it involves words; sometimes it does not. Since bargaining is more than anything a psychological relationship, it is inevitably prone to the problems of ethnocentric perception. This is a matter of growing significance, for in an interdependent and shrinking world, strategic seminars between the militarily mighty will cease to be a novelty, as was the case at the start of the SALT negotiations, and instead will become more a way of life.

Students of international negotiation ('negotiation' is bargaining made verbally explicit) have discussed a number of problems which have cultural dimensions.[50] Most obviously, these arise out of the difficulties associated with translation, the misunderstandings which might arise from different national styles, and the misperceptions which can result from a lack of knowledge about the unique domestic settings in which the foreign policies of different countries are made. For a long time, and one suspects still today, many Western diplomats have not been sufficiently sensitive to the problems of diplomacy in a multi-cultural world. For several centuries Western diplomats were trained in the classical diplomatic tradition, which instructed them to adhere to trivial homilies and fine generalities such as 'compromise is a good thing', 'be honest' and 'negotiate in good faith'. This genteel bourgeois approach was satisfactory as long as one's opponents shared the same outlook, but it was no preparation for Anglo-Saxon diplomats when they came face-to-face after World War I with negotiators from Soviet Russia and Nazi Germany. The good chaps from the foreign offices of the democracies were bewildered by the new game. They were not prepared for the strategies, tactics and styles of those with totally different aims and a totally different background. How could a good chap cope, let alone negotiate successfully, with bounders from Central Europe and beyond who did not think that compromise was a good thing (but who saw it, like the Bolsheviks, as a sign of weakness)? who did not think that honesty was one of life's more important virtues (note Hitler's appreciation of the instrumentality of the 'great lie' over the small one)? and who thought that negotiating in good faith was a rather silly principle, because the important thing was to win (Lenin said that promises were like piecrusts — 'made to be broken')? In the inter-war years the good chaps — the Chamberlains, Baldwins and Halifaxes — lost out in negotiations with their totalitarian counterparts. Their failure nearly resulted in the end of liberty for all the nations of Europe. In the event half of them were subjugated. For the others the rescue came in the form of military force, and the leadership of bulldogs like Winston Churchill.

Democracies do not have a monopoly of blindspots in this activity. Indeed, the problem of culture-bound thinking is always likely to be greater in closed societies. The Bolsheviks and their heirs have often found it difficult to understand the liberal democracies. They have been regularly surprised by the ideological and idealistic character of US foreign policy. This has occurred despite some deliberate attempts on the part of US representatives to hide it. US representatives have often been conscious of the need to couch their decisions in terms which they hoped that Soviet decision-makers would understand, even though it meant in World War II justifying decisions in ways the Americans themselves would not have used to each other.[51] When American representatives failed in this approach, or ignored it, they met obstruction from the Soviet side. A small illustration occurred at the end of the war, when Soviet negotiators apparently failed to appreciate that the US Government might want American prisoners-of-war returned from Germany as quickly as possible simply out of humanitarian feelings. Giving attention to such emotions was not the strong point of the Stalinist regime. Evidently American urgency would have been understood if the US negotiators had simply stressed that the POWs were needed to help prosecute the continuing war against Japan.

Contrasting national styles in diplomacy have been a regular cause of uncertainty and misunderstanding. The significance of rhetoric (and its role in domestic politics) is always difficult to handle. Arab rhetoric, with its overemphasis and apparent 'extremism', has always been a problem for Western negotiators. When British tact and understatement meets Arab over-assertion and exaggeration, the resulting mixture can be a perfect recipe for misunderstanding.[52] The nuances of translation can magnify the problems. *Jihad,* for example, is invariably translated as 'holy war', though Peter Mansfield has explained that it means 'striving' or 'exerting' oneself in the Way of God, and that such striving does not necessarily involve the instrument of the sword.[53] To Western minds, however, 'holy war' inevitably connotes a ferocious crusade.

Cultural factors affect bargaining and negotiation in various other ways. Western fallacies with respect to the Middle East have already been mentioned, as have the problems of the 'spirit' of agreements in relation to detente.[54] One directly military manifestation of the latter is the question of 'good faith' in arms control agreements. This issue was of lively interest in 1975 because of allegations that the Soviet Union was violating the SALT agreements. The arguments on both sides were finely balanced. Granting that there will always be ambiguities and suspicions surrounding an arms control treaty, the basic problem resolved itself into the question: can one clearly distinguish between the gathering of intelligence for the purpose of expanding one's knowledge of the other side's military system (old-fashioned spying) and the gathering of intelligence to further arms control verification (and hence achieve greater confidence in the other side's intentions)?[55] This problem is further compounded by the fact that the qualities which make a weapon difficult to verify are usually the qualities which make it survivable and hence militarily useful. If one concedes the peculiarities of the Soviet approach to arms control one can certainly defend their position as not 'cheating', though this conclusion will probably not make some of their behaviour any the more comfortable. In such circumstances, it must be remembered that 'good faith' is a culturally defined quality, and one must consider this before assuming the worst. One man's 'cheating' is another man's 'different standards'.

Churchill's aphorism that 'jaw-jaw' is better than 'war-war' is one of the cliches of diplomacy, but jaw-jaw is not the same as friendship, nor is it certain that negotiations even improve strategic understanding, though the latter has been a familiar assumption. This has been one of the hopes expressed for the SALT exercise. However, after nearly a decade of talking about strategic arms we have not achieved the con-structive US–Soviet 'strategic seminar' which it was hoped would signally improve strategic understanding and international stability. But, more pertinently: is what we have an improvement on what went before?

The evidence is presently ambiguous. Soviet negotiators have not been overly co-operative in their approach, and have not negotiated in 'good faith' by Western standards.[56] They have exploited ambiguities; they have been sea-lawyers in their reading of the small print; they have not given detailed information about the country's strategic posture; and they have not even disclosed numbers. Colin Gray has argued that this merely confirms that they are still strongly committed to a distinc-tively Soviet approach to strategic questions, and hence the delivering of 'pedagogical homilies' by the US negotiators is a futile activity. Gray's conclusion was that Soviet strategic behaviour could only be moderated by actions ('a coercive arms race' and 'detente-linkage management') and not by an exercise in strategic persuasion kept alive by the hope of every generation of Western negotiators that it will be different 'this time'. Gray's approach to SALT, wet-blanket though it appears, is a healthy corrective to the artless assumptions of some arms control supporters. However, there is another side to the picture. Supporters of SALT can take some comfort from the fact that Gerard C. Smith, who has had experience as chief US delegate to SALT, changed his mind after his disappointment at the first round, and has since argued that negotiation has improved strategic communication.[57] Problems remain: he emphasised that different negotiating styles inhibited communication, and stressed the relative unpreparedness of the Soviet delegation. Nevertheless, despite these difficulties and the very complexity of strategic arms control, Smith was confident that progress was possible.

An important point to note from both these optimistic and pessimistic attitudes to SALT is that some analysts at least have recognised that cultural relativity is a factor of great significance; the understanding it gives can be exploited either by words or deeds or both, for purposes of arms control, arms racing or a combination of both.

There is certainly room for disappointment in SALT, but before the exercise is dismissed out of hand, two points need to be kept in mind. Firstly, there is the time factor. SALT may not be a lively learning experience, but one should not have expected rapid progress between the enemies of several generations. Secondly, there were too many inflated hopes at the outset. A strategic 'seminar', like other seminars, should be conceived as an *exchange* of ideas, not necessarily a *meeting* of minds. Those who expected the latter expected too much. As an exchange of viewpoints SALT has had impact. If the Soviet negotiators are not clearer about the US position than they were in 1969, then one can only conclude that they are professionally incompetent. As far as the US negotiators and defence community are concerned, there is no doubt that there is a much better understanding of Soviet strategic concepts in the second half of the 1970s than there was ten years before. SALT has not been the only factor causing this development, but it has precipitated much interest in and discussion of the problems involved. Out of this study has come a more sophisticated understanding of Soviet strategy. This does not mean that there is not yet a good way to go, nor is this better communication synonymous with 'convergence'. There has been no conceptual breakthough in SALT in the sense that both sides have come to speak the same strategic language and use the same strategic concepts. It would be fanciful even to think in terms of such an outcome. However, there has been a mutual clarification of their different standpoints, and this alone is not an insignificant development. Whether this advantage is worth the diplomatic and strategic risks of engaging in the highly publicised SALT exercise is open to debate, but it would seem that the time-scale is still too short to urge 'quit'.

The multicultural context of strategic negotiations is essential background to the development of theory. Bargaining and negotiating styles are peculiar to national cultures, and the understanding of them is vulnerable to ethnocentric distortion. It is important for both participants and observers to avoid transferring their own outlooks onto others. Furthermore, we should also give credit to the limited knowledge which other societies have of our own. Closed societies do not find it at all easy to understand Western liberal-democratic countries.

At the start of 1977 the Soviet leadership was confused by the Carter Administration's emphasis on human rights. How could this 'interference' be compatible with a declared commitment to detente and SALT? A few years earlier the Soviet leaders had been more perplexed still by the Watergate affair. Because wire-tapping, bugging and dirty tricks against the opposition are standard practices in closed societies, the Soviet leaders found it particularly difficult to appreciate why their adversary partner, President Nixon, was getting into so much trouble. It was especially puzzling for Mr Brezhnev himself, because, as one newspaper put it, he must surely have been one of the biggest buggers in the world. For American democrats on the other hand the President's behaviour was far from normal. When techniques of information gathering which are common in some countries, and in the competitive world of foreign policy, were transplanted into the competitive world of US domestic elections, the world's oldest republic was shaken. Americans can stand a second-hand car-dealer to handle foreigners – indeed Nixon maintained much support in this area – but they cannot stand a Tricky Dicky who directs his special skills at themselves.

Notes

1. Thomas C. Schelling, *Arms and Influence* (New Haven, Conn.: Yale University Press, 1966), Ch. 1.

2. G. H. Snyder, *Deterrence and Defense* (Princeton, N.J.: Princeton University Press, 1961), p. 25.

3. See Sidney Verba, 'Assumptions of Rationality and Non-Rationality in Models of the International System' in Klaus Knorr and Sidney Verba (eds.), *The International System, Theoretical Essays* (Princeton, NJ: Princeton University Press, 1961), p. 107.

4. Graham T. Allison, *Essence of Decision: Explaining the Cuban Missile Crisis* (Boston: Little, Brown and Co., 1971).

5. Hedrick Smith, *The Russians* (New York: Quadrangle/New York Times Book Co., 1976), Ch. 12.

6. The point has been made in relation to another important area of international studies by Adda B. Bozeman, *The Future of Law in a Multicultural World* (Princeton, NJ: Princeton University Press, 1971).

7. Raymond L. Garthoff, *Soviet Military Doctrine* (Glencoe, Ill.: Free Press, 1953), pp. 236-7.

8. Neil Sheehan *et al.*, *The Pentagon Papers* (New York: Bantam Books, 1971), p. 372.

9. Yehezkel Dror, *Crazy States. A Counter Conventional Strategic Problem* (Lexington, Mass.: Heath-Lexington Books, 1971).

10. Ibid., p. 34.

11. Quoted in Allen S. Whiting, *The Chinese Calculus of Deterrence* (Ann Arbor, Mich.: University of Michigan Press, 1975), p. 227.

12. See, inter alia, Harry Gelber, 'Nuclear Weapons and Chinese Policy', *Adelphi Papers*, no. 99 (London: IISS, 1973); Harold C. Hinton, *Communist China in World Politics* (New York: Macmillan Co., 1966); Arthur Huck, *The Security of China* (London: Chatto and Windus, 1970); Whiting, *Chinese Calculus*.

13. Mohamed Heikal, *The Road to Ramadan* (London: Collins, 1975), p. 100.

14. Dror, *Crazy States,* pp. 23-4.

15. Daniel J. Boorstin, 'The Birth of Exploration', *The Listener,* 13 Nov. 1975, p. 633.

16. John Stoessinger, *Nations in Darkness − China, Russia, and America* (New York: Random House, 1975), pp. 10-11.

17. Huck, *Security of China,* pp. 22-4.

18. Stoessinger, *Nations in Darkness.*

19. Frank A. Kierman and John K. Fairbank, *Chinese Ways in Warfare* (Cambridge, Mass.: Harvard University Press, 1974), p. 2. See also Scott A. Boorman, *The Protracted Game. A Wei-ch'i Interpretation of Maoist Revolutionary Strategy* (New York: Oxford University Press, 1969), p. 3.

20. This is elaborated in Ken Booth, 'American Strategy: The Myths Revisited', Ch. 1 in Ken Booth and Moorhead Wright (eds.), *American Thinking about Peace and War* (Brighton, Sussex: Harvester Press, 1978).

21. The philosophical background of strategies of *choice* and *necessity* are discussed by Arnold Wolfers, *Discord and Collaboration* (Baltimore: Johns Hopkins Press, 1962), Ch. 15, 'Political Theory and International Relations'.

22. Anatol Rapoport, *Clausewitz: On War* (Harmondsworth, Middx: Penguin Books, 1968), pp. 13-17, 38-40.

23. The examples in this paragraph are taken from ibid.

24. Ibid., p. 13.

25. As Rapoport has explained, the findings on the Correlates of War Project revealed that there were no outstanding correlates: if we do not conclude that the causes of war are random, we must therefore assume that they are exceedingly complex. Anatol Rapoport, *Conflict in a Man-Made Environment* (Harmondsworth, Middx: Penguin Books, 1974), p. 229.

26. Otto Klineberg, *The Human Dimension in International Relations* (New York: Holt, Rinehart and Winston, 1964), pp. 10-11.

27. Quoted by Anthony M. Burton, *Urban Terrorism: Theory, Practice, and Response* (New York: Free Press, 1976), p. 78; lecture at the University College of Wales, Aberystwyth, Feb. 1977.

28. Norman Dixon, *On the Psychology of Military Incompetence* (New York, Basic Books Inc., 1976).

29. Moshe Dyan, *Story of My Life* (London: Weidenfeld and Nicolson, 1976), p. 108.

30. See Majid Khadduri, *War and Peace in the Law of Islam* (Baltimore: Johns Hopkins Press, 1955).

31. Note Morgenthau's relevant remarks in *Politics among Nations: The Struggle for Power and Peace* (New York: Knopf, 1964), p. 30.

32. The best discussion of the concept of utility is by Klaus Knorr, *On The Uses of Military Power in the Nuclear Age* (Princeton, NJ: Princeton University Press, 1966). He reviewed his propositions in the light of twelve years further experience in 'On the International Uses of Military Force in the Contemporary World', *Orbis,* vol. 21(1) (Spring 1977), pp. 5-27.

33. For representative views on the utility of military force by academic strategists see *Adelphi Papers,* no. 102 (London: IISS, 1973); John Garnett, 'The Role of Military Power', Ch. 3 in John Baylis *et al., Contemporary Strategy: Theories and Policies* (London: Croom Helm, 1975); Knorr, *Uses of Military Power;* Robert E. Osgood and Robert W. Tucker, *Force, Order, and Justice* (Baltimore: Johns Hopkins Press, 1967).

34. Knorr, 'International Uses of Military Force', p. 27.

35. Ibid., pp. 12-13.

36. This was the view of John Erickson, 'Soviet Military Policy. Priorities

and Perspectives', *Round Table,* no. 256 (Oct. 1974), p. 370.

37. Detailed analyses of the Gorshkov series can be found in *Admiral Gorshkov On 'Navies in War and Peace',* Center for Naval Analyses, Institute of Naval Studies, Sept. 1974 (CRC 257).

38. Although the book exaggerates the extent to which 'Violence . . . carries no approbrium,' see Adda B. Bozeman, *Conflict in Africa: Concepts and Realities* (Princeton, NJ: Princeton University Press, 1976).

39. Bozeman, *Future of Law,* p. 182.

40. Although it is not narrowly concerned with meaning in strategy, Thomas M. Francis and Edward Weisband, *Word Politics, Verbal Strategy among the Superpowers* (New York: Oxford University Press, 1971) is important because it recognises the peculiar importance of words as instruments.

41. Peter Vigor, *The Soviet View of War, Peace, and Neutrality* (London: Routledge and Kegan Paul, 1975) is an exception. For an attempt to analyse what Soviet spokesmen say about themselves, see Stephen P. Gilbert, *Soviet Images of America* (New York: Crane, Russack and co., 1977), esp. pp. 21ff.

42. For some relevant comments see Bernard Brodie, *War and Politics* (London: Cassell, 1973), pp. 197-209.

43. See Whiting's relevant comments, *Chinese Calculus,* pp. xix-xx.

44. Above, p. 38.

45. Captain Robert B. Bathurst, 'The Patterns of Naval Analysis', *Naval War College Review,* Nov. 1974, pp. 16-27. The points below are taken from this interesting essay. Textual and strategic analysis of the Soviet concept of 'command of the sea' is provided by Michael MccGwire, 'Command of the Sea in Soviet Naval Strategy' and Peter Vigor, 'The Soviet Understanding of the Concept of "Command of the Sea" [*Gospodstvo na More*]', Chs. 33 and 32 in Michael MccGwire, Ken Booth and John McDonnell, *Soviet Naval Policy: Objectives and Constraints* (New York: Praeger Publishers, 1975).

46. For two excellent analyses of these concepts see Peter Vigor, 'The Semantics of Deterrence and Defence' and Geoffrey Jukes, 'The Military Approach to Deterrence and Defence', Chs. 25 and 26 respectively in MccGwire, Booth and McDonnell, *Soviet Naval Policy.*

47. Arnold Horelick, 'The Strategic Mind-Set of the Soviet Military', *Problems of Communism,* vol. XXVI (Mar.-Apr. 1977), p. 85.

48. This is discussed by Raymond L. Garthoff, *Soviet Military Policy. A Historical Analysis* (London: Faber and Faber, 1966), Ch. 4 and William Zimmerman, *Soviet Perspectives on International Relations 1956-1967* (Princeton, NJ: Princeton University Press, 1969), Ch. 7.

49. As far as the number of 'realities' is concerned, you pay your money and take your pick. Eight is the number discussed by Ernst B. Haas in his well-known 'The Balance of Power: Prescription, Concept, or Propaganda?', *World Politics,* vol. V (July 1953), pp. 442-77.

50. The standard text is Fred Charles Ikle, *How Nations Negotiate* (New York: Harper and Row, 1964); more specifically on strategy, see Jeremy J. Stone, *Strategic Persuasion. Arms Limitation through Dialogue* (New York: Columbia University Press, 1967).

51. Discussed in Robert Jervis, *Perception and Misperception in International Politics* (Princeton, N.J.: Princeton University Press, 1976), p. 48.

52. See E. Shonby, 'The Influence of the Arab Language on the Psychology of the Arabs', *Middle East Journal,* vol. 5 (1951), pp. 284-302.

53. Peter Mansfield, *The Arabs,* (London: Allen Lane, 1976) pp. 32-3, 63, 189.

54. Above, pp. 48-51, 54-5.

55. A sensible discussion of this can be found in *Strategic Survey 1975* (London: IISS, 1976), pp. 111-16.

56. See Colin S. Gray, 'SALT: Time to Quit', *Strategic Review*, Fall 1976, pp. 14-22.

57. See Gerard C. Smith, Negotiating at SALT, *Survival,* vol. XX (3) (May–June 1977), pp. 117-20.

5 MILITARY EFFICIENCY VERSUS POLITICAL PURPOSE

> Know your enemy and know yourself: in a hundred battles you will never be in peril. *Sun Tzu*

> Few people can be happy unless they hate some other person, nation or creed. *Bertrand Russell (attributed)*

> You cannot organise civilisation around the core of militarism and at the same time expect reason to control. *Franklin D. Roosevelt*

By concentrating upon strategic failure and doubtful theory, the preceding two chapters will have created the impression that ethnocentrism is completely dysfunctional in the world of military affairs. This is not so. On the contrary, the first part of the present chapter argues that ethnocentric attitudes can contribute significantly to the prosecution of a variety of military tasks. However, this does not lead to the overall conclusion that ethnocentric attitudes are desirable for society as a whole. What is good for military efficiency is by no means necessarily good for political purpose.

Force and the Utility of Ethnocentrism

Paul C. Rosenblatt has aggregated a useful compendium of propositions about ethnocentrism and nationalism.[1] These will be applied to the main areas of military life in order to suggest where ethnocentrism may be functional.

Group Identity

It goes without saying that group identity is of paramount importance if a military machine is to work efficiently. Prejudice and a sense of identity are often closely related,[2] and ethnocentrism straddles both. Ethnocentrism therefore aids military efficiency by unifying groups.

Military organisations inculcate group identity by a variety of means. Some of these play upon the ethnocentric predispositions of their members. 'Hate' may be specifically cultivated in the so-called educational programmes of armed forces in order to intensify in-group feelings. All armed forces engage in this activity, though some do it much more blatantly than others. Those societies which are least self-confident, and whose armed forces have a socialising as well as a military role, are less subtle in promoting hate education than are those well-established

94

societies where the military profession is regarded as a necessary evil. The Soviet Union belongs to the former group; in it there has developed 'an enormous military-educational complex' in civilian as well as military life[3] cultivating the ethnocentric predispositions of the population. A major theme in the indoctrination of Soviet troops is 'Hate the Enemy: Love the Motherland'. Such a theme is thought crucial in building up the 'perseverance and heroism' of Soviet troops. It is not insignificant that there is more emphasis on whipping up hatred against enemies than in emphasising love for the motherland.[4] A happier and more self-confident regime, with a deeper sense of commitment, would surely feel freer to call for greater sacrifice from its citizen-soldiers. Significantly, its indoctrination programmes do not have the confidence to lay any emphasis on dying for the cause.

Military organisations can also be unified by the satisfaction which ethnocentrism helps provide by fulfilling psychological needs concerned with 'belonging' and 'supra-individual goals'. The latter is especially important for soldiers, because they above all others have to give themselves to the national cause. Unto death, they allow their bodies to become the property of the state. It therefore helps if the individual believes in what he is doing, believes that his own nation is superior and right, and believes that the enemy is inferior, evil and in the wrong. A soldier can go through the motions of fighting without any of these feelings, but it can help if they are present.

Ethnocentrism not only intensifies in-group feelings within military organisations but also within society as a whole. It helps make the group concerned sensitive about what it regards as its rights and interests, and helps identify enemies and threats. Propaganda is important for this purpose, and it is interesting that such strange bedfellows as Adolf Hitler and Bertrand Russell both well understood that propaganda was most effective when stirring up hatred and being directed against a single enemy.[5] Identifying enemies helps define who we are *not*, which is a necessary part of defining who we *are*. In this sense all political communities find it useful to have somebody to hate. The insecure ruling autocracy in the Soviet Union fears the spread of communism (at least that version called 'eurocommunism') in Western Europe. On the other hand, they depend upon their enemies (or 'adversary partners') to help give them legitimacy at home. Clearly the Soviet leaders fear their potential friends but need their potential enemies. This partly explains why the Soviet Union has found it more necessary to invade 'friends' rather than 'enemies'. An insecure ruling autocracy finds it safer to live with a responsible enemy rather than an heretical friend.

Nations live by their enemies. We need enemies, like we need culture, to realise who we are. Consequently, whether one is talking about the motivating of troops or the sense of identity of a national group, ethnocentrism is a magical compound which helps oil the military machine while solidifying the home front.

Intensity of Commitment

By polarising in-group/out-group feelings, ethnocentrism makes it easier for society to accept the institution of compulsory military service, for individuals to accept a life-long commitment to the military profession, or for the man-in-the-street to support the payment of taxes for the upkeep of his country's armed forces. At the least, ethnocentrism helps persuade us that armed forces are a necessary evil. As President Eisenhower put it, in a moment of obligatory rhetoric in his first inaugural: 'In the final choice a soldier's pack is not so heavy a burden as a prisoner's chains.'

Ethnocentrism increases commitment to the national military cause and it also tends to make the experience of military life more satisfying. It encourages a sense of purpose lacking in many ordinary lives. Patriotism can bring out the best in people (at least a narrowly conceived 'best'), and the greater the degree of ethnocentrism, the more intense will be the sense of purpose and belonging: the group will feel all the more that it is fighting for an important cause. Soldiers need causes as well as capabilities. They might march on their stomachs, and kill with weapons, but in a nationalistic and ideological century they also fight with their hearts and souls. Ethnocentrism is nothing if not a producer of noble causes.

For those individuals who have a strong need to feel associated with things which are ideal, ethnocentrism is a fertile source of ideas about virtue, strength, glory and independence from outside influence. Military history within the military profession often serves nationalistic ends, by attempting to increase an individual's sense of affiliation. However remotely, the individual can participate in a tradition of victory, of righting wrongs and of heroic deeds against the enemies of the community.

All armed forces face problems of motivation, especially in periods of peace. If there is no immediate enemy, one's professional rationale may well appear to be undermined. In practice, to be described as an 'insurance against future contingencies' is a pale morale-booster alongside 'defending the Republic' or 'fighting the Queen's enemies'. The cultivation of ethnocentric predispositions, which increases suspicion of outsiders, helps to fill in the motivational gaps in peacetime. This is one reason why detente is not matched by ideological and propaganda disengagement on either side.

Unity under Threat

Ethnocentrism helps groups to pull together in times of threat. This unifying process should assist national policy-makers. A military threat imposes a critical common interest on people who were hitherto a collection of individuals. It imposes the most important common interest of all, namely physical security. And when threats do materialise, ethnocentric perceptions help to simplify the issues and give the sense of self-righteousness immortalised in Stephen Decatur's infamous maxim, 'our country, right or wrong'. However extreme, such ideas help to keep a community together. The resulting sense of unity should be beneficial to the group either in the maximising of deterrence or in the prosecution of war.

Efficiency

Ethnocentrism can make for administrative efficiency by facilitating communication and co-operation within a group. In its turn the development of behaviour patterns which increase identity and the mutual recognition of roles further increases ethnocentrism. Ethnocentrism probably speeds decision-making by defining friends and enemies, by simplifying situations and by clarifying priorities. Stereotypes help one to avoid having to think about problems from first principles. Furthermore, if it can be argued that one has 'no choice' in the face of hostile outsiders, then making decisions becomes easier. To see 'no choice' eases the strain on one's conscience and intellectual resources. Whether the ethnocentrism which can produce this activity can at the same time produce well-directed activity is another matter, for most international situations are not amenable to simplification.

Deterrence

Ethnocentrism tends to isolate groups and to minimise mutual understanding. Mutual wariness will be increased. This can be militarily advantageous if it contributes to the deterrent strength of the groups concerned. On the other hand, greater understanding between groups can produce a decreased desire to act in a hostile manner, or alternatively, a better ability to exploit each other's weaknesses. In contrast, ignorance, as well as intensifying suspicion and conflict between groups, can enhance deterrence through 'the fear of the unknown'.

Nationalism and ethnocentrism intensify international conflicts. They distort perceptions and exacerbate suspicions and hatreds. But they can also be stabilising features in the international system. By contributing to a sense of unity and military purpose within a group, they can make clearer the group's determination to defend its patch of territory. This determination has always been a major factor in the maintenance of whatever degree of international order has existed.

Toughness

Nationalism excuses all, or almost all. Alix Strachey has pointed out that whereas only a madman would say 'I am always right', the same sentiment may be said, consciously and self-approvingly, on behalf of one's country. Strachey correctly argued that such an attitude involves a regression to a lower level of mentality, which interferes with the use of common sense and reason.[6] However, from a narrowly military viewpoint, especially at the tactical level, this way of thinking can have the advantages of its blindness. At the sharpest end of military execution, ethnocentric attitudes help to make the inevitable brutalities of war easier to accept and easier to justify both for those who have to carry them out and for those who are responsible for explaining them away.

However noble the cause, war is always a dirty business. Ethnocentric predispositions make it easier to bear. Ethnocentrism contributes to the 'vilification of the human', which makes killing easier. Soldiers do not need to hate — they need only obey — but it does help if they believe that their enemies are devils or thieves or barbarians who do not deserve to live.[7] If for some people army life or a 'splendid little war' takes one's mind off one's troubles, ethnocentric predispositions help to take one's mind off the unpleasant side of one's business, and help to reduce dissonance. Ethnocentric conditioning, cultivated by propaganda, helps to make it easier for those engaged in military activity — how much so depends upon the individual conscience — to do things which in the rest of their lives they are socialised to believe is wrong. It was Voltaire who told us that we do not think that killing is murder as long as it is done in large numbers, and to the sound of trumpets.

Ethnocentrism therefore helps to shape and toughen the cogs in the military machine. Like 'bull' and some other aspects of military life, it can be a substitute for thought. By exaggerating the alien character of the out-group, ethnocentrism helps an individual to reconcile his dirty job with those humanistic traits which he manifests in family life. Other factors obviously contribute to this: obedience, coercion, fright and fear of one's own commanders play important parts. Propaganda helps, and language is often used in such a way as to ease one's task: it is always easier to destroy things which have been deprived of their humanity by being classified as 'savages' or *Untermenschen.* When it comes to the sharpest end of military life, fighters and machines are required, not humanistic beings. At the tactical level, when soldiers face each other, it is no longer a question of Right and Wrong, but of winners and losers, the quick and the dead.

Authoritarianism and Ethnocentrism

From a narrowly military standpoint, therefore, ethnocentrism is by no means an unmitigated disaster. It can contribute to the efficient fulfilment of various military goals. However, this is to look at its impact from an overly narrow angle, and in isolation from other considerations and especially those characteristics which make up the 'authoritarian personality',[8] which one writer has recently argued has been a major factor in military incompetence.[9] Military organisations, by their nature, attract individuals predisposed towards authoritarianism.[10] Once there, they will tend to foster militarism. However, the authoritarian personality has weaknesses as well as strengths from the military viewpoint. Aggressiveness, the willingness to submit to authority, and the cultivation of toughness are desirable military qualities. Indeed, in moderation some authoritarian values may be desirable for society in general, for a well-run society requires a degree of discipline, conformity and orderliness. These characteristics have been called 'rational' authoritarianism and are socially useful. On the other hand 'irrational' authoritarianism, which is compulsive (like 'blind anarchy') and which derives from an underlying ego-pathology, has evident disadvantages for both society and military effectiveness.

Irrational authoritarianism is a psychological state which has been at the heart of much military incompetence. Amongst its manifestations have been the serious wastage of human resources, the clinging to outworn tradition, the tendency to reject or ignore information, obstinate persistence in a given task, the overriding belief in brute force, and undue readiness to find scapegoats. The authoritarian personality is also ethnocentrically prejudiced: authoritarianism and ethnocentrism correlate very closely. To have the military advantages which go with ethnocentrism, therefore, one must also accept that ethnocentric individuals will probably be equally prone to all the types of incompetence just described, and more.

It was argued earlier that ethnocentrism helps to produce ruthless fighters at all levels; however, the present discussion leads us to doubt whether it makes for good commanders in the broadest sense. Certainly it could be argued that senior commanders should 'hate' the enemy and not be squeamish about sacrificing lives for the sake of a greater good:[11] as Shelford Bidwell put it, 'No general ever won a war whose conscience troubled him or who did not want "to beat his enemy too much".'[12] But there is a counter-argument, which Norman Dixon has expressed: 'it could be maintained that it is not hatred so much as understanding of the enemy, and not a conscienceless squandering but a humane conserving of his own forces, which are the hallmarks of an efficient commander.[13] Dixon's discussion of the 'great captains' bears this out, and in his view the great captains have all been non-authoritarians. There may well have been non-authoritarian generals who were hopelessly incompetent, but Dixon found it difficult to identify any great general or admiral who had all the characteristics of an authoritarian personality, including ethnocentrism. Thus we have what Dixon described as a 'terrible paradox' right at the heart of military life, namely that those characteristics which are demanded by war — 'the ability to tolerate uncertainty; spontaneity of thought and action; having a mind open to the receipt of novel, and perhaps threatening, information' — are the antitheses of those characteristics possessed by those people attracted to the controls and orderliness of militarism. The conclusion reached by Dixon is very significant: 'Those very people who . . . are in theory the best suited to warring behaviour, may be the very ones *least* well equipped for other components of successful fighting.'[14] What is good for military efficiency is not even necessarily good for military effectiveness.

To be non-authoritarian and non-ethnocentric is certainly not a prerequisite for military success. Strategy is too complicated a business for such simple conclusions. Authoritarians have sometimes been victors while non-authoritarians have sometimes lost. But non-authoritarians are more likely to be effective in dealing with complicated tasks and problems, and they are more likely to be able to appreciate the effect they have on others.[15] They are also less prone to stereotyping. Stereotyping may be reassuring, but 'One cannot know one's enemy by stereotyping him.'[16]

Knowing the Enemy

Ethnocentrism is a stereotyping activity: it produces the most simplistic versions of national character. More generally it has a number of effects on one's images of the behaviour and intentions of other groups, what motivates them, and why they act as they do. In all cases its effect is a simplifying one. Ethnocentrism and its consequences should therefore be central concerns, because strategy is based upon analyses and forecasts of intentions and behaviour, threats and promises, words and actions, and communications and signals. A strategic relationship is at least as much psychological as physical: weapons may finally settle the account but their triggering is the result of the strategies and tactics, myths and logic, fears and hopes, mistakes and talent, commands and anxieties, and perceptions and misperceptions which exist in the minds of men. As one of the mechanisms which crucially affect some of the psychological processes involved, ethnocentrism must take its place as a significant variable in the theory and practice of strategy. The most basic difficulty caused by ethnocentrism in strategic affairs, therefore, revolves around the way in which it can interfere with 'knowing the enemy', the base-line of all practical strategic analysis.

History is full of enemies (not to mention friends) who have not been 'known' sufficiently well to provide the basis for reliable forecasting. Their capabilities have been underestimated or overestimated or their behaviour has been the cause of a variety of types of surprise. Ethnocentrism is an important analytical disadvantage in this context because it obstructs one's understanding of the opponent's 'software' — his intentions, style, prejudices, hopes and fears. Without such an understanding it will obviously be difficult to forecast an opponent's likely response to different developments, and the most likely mode of employment of his hardware. It is therefore apparent that whatever advantages might lie in the cultivation of ethnocentrism for military efficiency, they will be greatly outweighed if ethnocentric attitudes percolate upwards to the policy-making level. At the level of strategic policy-making, not to mention tactical employment, ethnocentrism can be a serious disadvantage when it interferes with the attempt to know the enemy in order to predict his behaviour.

It may be argued that the phrase 'knowing the enemy' is a contradiction in terms. All societies tend to close their minds to the validity of thoughtways and behaviour patterns which are 'foreign' or 'alien'. These very words are synonymous for people and things which are repugnant, irreconcilably different and belonging to another (unattractive) nature. Significantly, many cultures use the same word for 'human' and for members of their own group, and equate outsiders/foreigners with the lesser animals.[17] Such attitudes are further intensified if the label 'enemy' is attached. It can be argued that the first thing we should *not do* if we want to get into somebody else's mind is to label him 'enemy'. The 'screen of symbolic language' usually does not help. As Anatol Rapoport has written:

Our enemies are those who have been defined as our enemies, not those who have actually done us any harm. We fear what we have been taught to fear by use of language alone, not by actual experience. Man's cruelty to man based on labels that men attach to each other exceeds anything observed in the so-called world reddened by tooth and claw.[18]

At worst we define our enemies out of their humanity: at best we define them out of our range of sympathy, and even understanding.

Ethnocentric perceptions mean that a nation which is labelled as an enemy will be suspected, whatever actions it takes or does not take. When the other party is viewed within the framework of what Kissinger called an 'inherent bad faith' theory,[19] the image of the enemy becomes self-perpetuating, for the model itself denies the existence of data which could invalidate it.[20] The other nation is suspected, *whatever* the character of its actions. Almost by definition, because the analyst is dealing with an 'enemy' the attempt to understand him in a full sense will be difficult if not impossible. Inconsistent information will tend to be rejected. The minds of most people naturally refuse to comprehend and 'feel' the world in an enemy's terms. An analyst might be able, as a start, to make a list of the enemy's hopes and fears and his stated rights and interests. But he may find it impossible to go beyond this intellectual exercise. He may well find it impossible to feel himself into his enemy's attitude. This does make a difference. There are at present a number of commentators who show an intellectual recognition of the existence of some special factors in the Soviet outlook (such as historical suffering at the hands of invaders) but who nevertheless write as if these factors should not affect Soviet behaviour: this is a foreign-policy equivalent of the social behaviour of those individuals who accept intellectually that another person has a medical condition, but who do not have the imagination to feel it, and so tell the other person, 'Yes, of course you are depressed, but that doesn't mean that you should not behave normally.' It may well be that national insecurity is like pain: as Samuel Johnson said about the latter, 'those who do not feel [it] seldom think that it is felt'. In international life, forecasting will be badly based without a feeling for the other person's political 'instinct': it will be difficult to guess the determination with which he will stick to a given course. Knowing the enemy therefore involves feeling as well as factual knowledge. A strategic analyst must sit himself in the desk of his counterpart, and attempt to see and feel the problem as his counterpart might see and feel it. Inevitably this is an extraordinarily difficult habit, but this exercise is essentially what the attempt to know the enemy entails, and military history shows how infrequently it has been achieved in practice. That strategic analysts must have imagination as well as intellect is as obvious as it is rare, though clearly there are many difficulties involved in trying to grasp another's reality.[21] We tend to give a false attribution of motives to other nations, we fail to perceive the other's real hopes and fears, and we fail to appreciate what he considers his needs to be. With so much ignorance prevading the situation, both sides tend to overcome uncertainty and impose meaning on the relationship by projecting their own principles and ways of thinking.

Ultimately, what is required in an attempt to know another nation goes beyond an attempt to sympathise with its problems. What is required is best encapsulated in the concept of 'empathy'.[22] Empathy has been defined as the 'self-conscious effort to share and accurately comprehend the presumed consciousness of another person, including his thoughts, feelings, (and) perceptions. . .as well as their causes'. The empathiser tries to feel the other's hopes and fears by adopting his 'internal frame of reference'. To expect completely successful empathetic strategic analysts is to expect a great deal: but it is not too much to ask them to make more of an attempt than in the past, when they have been notably unsuccessful. The attempt to empathise should be an integral part of a national strategic exercise, because one cannot 'know' the enemy without having some feeling for his 'internal frame of reference'. Unfortunately, those given to authoritarianism and ethnocentrism — those for whom knowing the enemy is very professionally relevant — are likely to be those who are least well equipped to engage in the activity.

Ethnocentrism and enemy attribution will seriously interfere with an individual's ability to understand another nation. Ethnocentrism plays a part in the selecting of the information which an analyst uses and the techniques and attitudes which are applied to it. Ethnocentric perceptions filter out information and affect the way what remains is interpreted. 'Groupthink' will probably reinforce these tendencies even further.[23]

If an analyst approaches the problem of understanding another nation with the implicit assumption that the latter is an enemy, then his mental images and information-screening faculties will be informed and dominated by a particular set of biases. If strategic analysts perceive and organise their knowledge of allies, adversaries and third parties only in those terms and with those conceptual frameworks appropriate to their own limited plot of earth, then they are failing in the basic task of 'knowing the enemy' (or seeing 'the other side of the hill', as military commanders like to put it). Indeed, the central argument for dealing systematically with the phenomenon of ethnocentrism is that it does interfere so seriously with the task of knowing the enemy. In particular, it affects the problem of predicting motives and their associated behavioural patterns, an activity which is at the core of strategic analysis and practice. Trying to see the world as others see it, and thereby predict their behaviour, is the central creative act in the business of strategy: this may be seriously distorted by ethnocentrism, which involves seeing the other's world as we see it ourselves.

Diplomacy and the Disutility of Ethnocentrism

When ethnocentrism interferes with knowing the enemy, various unfortunate political and/or military consequences may follow unless good luck is present. These disadvantages must be set against the advantages of military efficiency discussed in the first part of this chapter.

Misplaced Confidence

When faced by an aggressive power, belief in racial superiority and intellectual conceit produces over-confidence — a belief that one understands or can cope with that power. If one's confidence is misplaced, this can result in dangerous appeasement, or defeat in war. History is full of cases of one state taking advantage of another, when the latter thought it knew its enemy but really did not. Who *knows* whom? is a preliminary step before determining who *dominates* whom? Knowledge is an element of power.

Misplaced Suspicion

An intense ethnocentric viewpoint produces extreme suspicion towards the behaviour of others. Stereotyping another nation as a dangerous adversary will affect one's own attitudes and precautions; these in turn will affect the attitudes and precautions of the other nation. The typical results of such a situation are the development of costly overkill capacities and intensified international tension. This is the disadvantageous corollary to the benefit of group identity, for as Rapoport has argued, strong and real as the substantive issues may be between groups, 'the need for identification with a group remains the strongest factor in instigating, perpetuating, and exacerbating social conflicts'.[24]

Surprise

A failure to understand the enemy's real hopes and fears may result in being caught out politically, strategically or tactically. Anglo–German and US–Japanese relations in the 1930s both illustrate the ways in which ethnocentric perceptions prevented an understanding of the challenger's objectives and determination. This failure added greatly to the eventual costs that had to be paid in lives, resources and money.

Inflexibility

Ethnocentrism can assist military efficiency by simplifying situations and unifying groups. The corollary to these advantages is the disadvantage of inflexibility. This phenomenon is particularly common in military planning because of 'groupthink', cognitive dissonance, bureaucratic inertia and the predisposition of authoritarian characters towards a rigidity of outlook. Ethnocentrism reinforces all these tendencies. Amongst the manifestations of this rigidity are the tendency to neglect unpalatable information and the adherence to existing plans longer than the circumstances justify. This puts a premium on having non-ethnocentric leaders. A particular leader can affect the character and atmosphere of the whole policy-making group, which in turn will affect the selection and slanting of information which helps structure policy and swing decisions. There is more to politics than impersonal forces: personalities can affect our destinies. It made a difference that it was President Johnson rather than John Kennedy who was responsible for US policy in Vietnam in the mid-1960s.[25] In predecisional phases, ethnocentrism seems likely to reduce a group's ability to change. Orthodoxy and dogmatism are intensified, at the cost of real learning. Together, ethnocentrism and nationalism tend to produce an inability 'to change when change is necessary for adaptation and high readiness for violent encounters with other groups'.[26] If an enemy is clearly and correctly perceived, however, such rigidity may well be glorified as national determination.

Rigidity in Crises

A particular instance of the problem of rigidity occurs in crises. In some if not all crises flexibility and understanding are at a premium at the decision-making level. The need to know the enemy is acute. However, the rise in ethnocentrism which invariably accompanies crises[27] might well obscure important parts of the decision-maker's picture and increase tendencies towards inflexibility. The danger therefore is that ethnocentrism will increase at political decision-making levels when the consequences of failure will be greatest.

Self-Fulfilling Prophecies

Ethnocentrism is characteristically associated with the phenomenon of the self-fulfilling prophecy, namely a 'false definition of a situation which makes the originally false conception come true'. As Kennan put it:

> It is an undeniable privilege of every man to prove himself in the right in the thesis that the world is his enemy; for if he reiterates it frequently enough and makes it the background of his conduct, he is bound eventually to be right.[28]

It can be argued that the more nationalistic and ethnocentric a group is, the greater will be its chances of survival in time of danger because of its sense of collective determination and identity. It would seem to be equally true however, that such groups may actually seriously decrease their overall security by increasing the number of dangerous situations in which they get involved, by decreasing the amount of constructive criticism by group members in the face of threats to survival, or by decreasing the likelihood of borrowing useful ideas from other groups.[29] Ethnocentrism and nationalism flourish on out-groups: the more an out-group is so labelled, the more will its behaviour tend to fit and be fitted to the label.

In a military context the danger of the self-fulfilling prophecy has been seen most often as providing fuel for an arms race, by stimulating the procurement of weaponry by one nation on the basis of the adversary's anticipated behaviour. By responding in this way, the adversary's anticipated behaviour is likely to become his actual behaviour. Between two suspicious nations, what one side sees as defensive, the other may well see as offensive preparations. In order to maintain the theoretical 'balance', further preparations have to take place which in turn stimulate more suspicion and still more precautions. This spiral is the classic arms race model. The militarised and ethnocentric outlook of the Cold War produced a reality which approached it.[30] During this period, US–Soviet relations were seen in narrowly military terms. The deteriorating relationship was compounded by the 'mirror-image' effect, whereby both adversaries developed similar but reverse attitudes towards each other. Pervasive military logic interacted in a hostile atmosphere to catapult the wartime partners into super-power rivals. The clash of national interests was real enough: what was even more dangerous was the interaction of myths.

Groupthink

'Groupthink' has been defined as 'a mode of thinking that people engage in when they are deeply involved in a cohesive in-group, when the members' striving for unanimity override their motivation to realistically appraise alternative courses of action...[it] refers to a deterioration of mental efficiency, reality testing, and moral judgement that results from in-group pressures'.[31] Groupthink is not necessarily a product of ethnocentrism, but there is an important relationship, for strategy in practice is 'made' by groups. Characteristic features of groupthink activity include the tendency to develop stereotyped and dehumanised images of the out-groups against whom the in-groups are engaged in competitive struggles, and the tendency for the collective judgements arising out of group discussions to shift towards riskier courses of action than the individual members would have otherwise been prepared to take.[32] Paradoxically, Irving Janis found that policymakers comprising an amiable group found it relatively easy to authorise 'dehumanising solutions' such as large-scale bombings: 'softheaded groups are likely to be extremely hardhearted toward out-groups and enemies'.[33] Furthermore, Janis showed that four of the worst disasters in recent American history were directly attributable to the psychological processes associated with group decision-making. Great misjudgements were made, eased along by such arguments as 'the plan cannot fail', 'it cannot happen here' and 'they will not do that'. In each case the mistakes were made easier because of the ethnocentrism of the participants in the policy-making process.

The problem of groupthink, however, is not basically one of intellectual shortcomings. Indeed, the decisions analysed by Janis were made by highly intelligent men, with specialised knowledge, who were both hard-working and dedicated. Group processes can subvert even the best and brightest. Amongst the main symptoms of groupthink are:[34] an illusion of invulnerability, which creates excessive optimism (the idea of superiority); the attempt to rationalise away discrepant information to protect existing assumptions (to maintain the integrity of the images of the group); an unquestioned belief in the group's inherent morality, enabling members to ignore the ethical dimensions of their acts; a stereotyped view of the enemy (based on culture-bound thinking); a rejection of non-conformist viewpoints (to reinforce in-group norms); a self-censorship of deviations from the apparent group consensus; a shared illusion of unanimity concerning judgements conforming to the majority view; and the emergence of self-appointed 'mindguards' to protect the group from adverse information that might shatter their complacency about the effectiveness and morality of their decisions. These symptoms are closely related to those involved in ethnocentrism. Enthnocentrism encourages groupthink, groupthink exacerbates ethnocentrism, and ethnocentrism reinforces groupthink. The interplay between them is subversive of rational strategic analysis and planning.

When the advantages and disadvantages of ethnocentrism are considered in relation to military efficiency and political purpose, the weight of argument lies strongly with the disadvantages. Ethnocentrism can help military efficiency in significant ways, but apparently only at the cost of bringing along in its wake a bundle of characteristics associated with authoritarian ways of doing things, which includes a propensity towards a variety of types of incompetence. Only at the lowest level of action, in producing the ruthless fighter, can ethnocentric predispositions be said to be really functional to the success of a system. The more it pervades upwards, however, the more dysfunctional it becomes. At the level of strategic planning, it results in the creation of false images of potential adversaries. The exaggeration of enemy images may be functional for budgetary purposes, but at what cost, if the imaginary enemy is subsequently engineered into being a real one?

Despite some ostensible advantages, therefore, ethnocentrism is a major disadvantage for the politico-strategic practitioner, because he wants to know the enemy *in order to beat him*, or at least to be able to deter him cost-effectively. For academic strategists, on the other hand, ethnocentrism can offer no compensation at any stage: it cannot be other than an impediment to those who want to know other nations simply because they want to know them.

Notes

1. Paul C. Rosenblatt, 'Origins and Effects of Group Ethnocentrism and Nationalism', *World Politics*, vol. XVI (June 1964), pp. 131-46.
2. G.W. Allport *The Nature of Prejudice* (Reading, Mass.: Addison-Wesley Publishing Co., 1954), esp. pp. 289-91.
3. William E. Odom, 'The Militarization of Soviet Society', *Problems of Communism*, vol. XXV (Sept.–Oct. 1976), pp. 34-51.
4. Herbert Goldhamer. *The Soviet Soldier – Soviet Military Management at the Troop Level* (New York, Crane, Russak and Co., 1975), esp. pp. 203-54.
5. Adolf Hitler, *Mein Kampf* (New York: Reynal and Hitchcock, 1941), pp. 227-42; Bertrand Russell, *The Conquest of Happiness* (London: Allen and Unwin), 1930), p. 6.
6. Alix Strachey, *The Unconscious Motives of War* (New York: International Universities Press, 1957), pp. 202-3.
7. This is so for most 'conventional' campaigns, but less so in those with an explicit 'hearts and minds' aspect, as in Northern Ireland.
8. See T. W. Adorno *et al., The Authoritarian Personality* (New York: Harper and Brothers, 1950). The idea of the authoritarian personality has subsequently come

under criticism. However, the essential concept remains valid, even if it is not as
rigorous or as easily testable as was originally thought.

9. Norman Dixon, *On the Psychology of Military Incompetence* (New York:
Basic Books Inc., 1976).

10. Ibid. This is one of the themes of Dixon's work. The distinctions below are
based on his argument, in *Psychology*, esp. pp. 152-3, 258-9, 263-6, 287-7.

11. Ibid, p. 275.

12. R. G. S. Bidwell, *Modern Warfare: A Study of Man, Weapons and Theories*
(London: Allen Lane, 1973), p. 18.

13. Dixon, *Psychology,* p. 275.

14. Ibid, p. 194.

15. Ibid., pp. 263-6.

16. Ibid., p. 266.

17. Jerome D. Frank, *Sanity and Survival: Psychological Aspects of War and
Peace* (New York: Random House, 1967), p. 104.

18. Anatol Rapoport, *Semantics* (New York: Thomas Y. Cromwell Co., 1975),
pp. 19, 77.

19. Henry A. Kissinger, *Necessity for Choice, Prospects for American Foreign
Policy* (London: Chatto and Windus, 1960), p. 194.

20. David Finlay, Ole Holsti and Richard Fagen, *Enemies in Politics* (Chicago:
Rand McNally, 1967), pp. 26-7.

21. See Joseph DeRivera, *The Psychological Dimensions of Foreign Policy*
(Columbus, Ohio: C. E. Merrill Publishing Co., 1969), p. 324 and *passim.*

22. Lauren G. Wispe, 'Sympathy and Empathy' in *International Encyclopedia
of the Social Sciences*, vol. 15 (New York: Macmillan Co. and Free Press, 1968),
pp. 441-6.

23. This is discussed below, pp. 164-5.

24. Anatol Rapoport, *Conflict in a Man-Made Environment* (Harmondsworth,
Middx: Penguin Books, 1974), p. 190.

25. Bernard Brodie, *War and Politics* (London: Cassell, 1973), pp. 126-44.

26. Rosenblatt, 'Origins and Effects', p. 143.

27. This is the conclusion of most studies. Ibid., p. 132.

28. George F. Kennan ['X'], 'The Sources of Soviet Conduct', *Foreign Affairs,*
1947, reprinted in *American Diplomacy 1900-1950* (London: Secker and
Warbug, 1953), p. 111.

29. Rosenblatt, 'Origins and Effects', p. 139.

30. See the relevant comments of Professor James E. King, quoted by Philip
Green, *Deadly Logic. The Theory of Nuclear Deterrence* (Columbus, Ohio: Ohio
State University Press, 1966), pp. 152-3.

31. Irving L. Janis, *Victims of Groupthink. A Psychological Study of Foreign
Policy Decisions and Fiascos* (Boston: Houghton Mifflin Co., 1972), p. 9.

32. Ibid., p. 6.

33. Ibid., p. 12.

34. Ibid., pp. 197-8. See also the relevant points in Ralph K. White, *Nobody
Wanted War: Misperception in Vietnam and Other Wars* (Garden City, N.Y.:
Doubleday, 1968), Ch. 9.

6 THREAT ASSESSMENT

Fear the man who fears you. *Jewish saying*

Nothing is so fatal to a nation as an extreme of self-partiality and the total want of consideration of what others will naturally hope or fear. *Edmund Burke*

Man cannot live by the Military Balance alone. As the last three chapters have shown, it behoves strategists to be as familiar with value systems as weapons systems. Strategy is a universal preoccupation, but its meaning is always contextual, set by the peculiar problems, perceptions, interests, traditions and ideologies of those with whom we are dealing. These cannot be understood without a feeling for cultural relativity.

In this chapter some of the implications of the earlier discussion will be applied to one of the central activities of strategy, threat assessment. Threat assessment is a basic function of the strategic planner, but correct threat assessment has proved to be exceptional in strategic history: there has been a 'curious failure' to recognise the difficulties of the task, and those professionally involved have done little to develop remedial measures.[1] And what improvement there has been has occurred in methods of information gathering rather than in analytical techniques. As a US Government report said in 1971, it is 'not at all clear that our hypotheses about foreign intentions, capabilities and activities have improved commensurately in scope and quality as more data comes in from modern methods'.[2]

It is not the aim of this chapter to deal with all the formidable problems of intelligence gathering, assessment, and prediction in so far as they impinge on the problem of threats in international politics. Rather, it will suggest the importance of cultural implications in threat assessment, and especially the role of ethnocentrism.

The Narrow Strategist's Syllogism

A 'syllogism' is a formal method of deductive reasoning; less commonly, it can also be used as a label for crafty argument. Normally, the 'strategist's syllogism' could usefully and ambiguously refer to either or both these meanings. In the present discussion, however, the concern is only with the latter: good strategic reasoning can take care of itself.

As it relates to threat assessment, strategic reasoning proceeds from conscious and unconscious assumptions as follows. *Stage one:* (a) Strategy abhors a vacuum. (b) Strategists need enemies. (c) Therefore enemy images (and 'inherent bad faith' theories) are elaborated.

Subsequently, enemy images are adapted to one's strategic outlook as much as one's own postures are shifted to meet changes in the strategies of one's adversaries. *Stage two*: (a) The capabilities of other nations are readily definable as threats because of their intrinsic destructive potential. (b) There is always room for doubt about a nation's intentions. (c) *Therefore* it is argued that threat assessment should concentrate on capabilities rather than intentions. Subsequently the preoccupation with capabilities leads to the guideline that what the enemy *can* do it *will* do.

The result of these two stages of thinking, when injected with a strong dose of native prudence, is to lead the analyst into dwelling upon the *possible* (hostile) behaviour of another nation almost unrelated to its cultural or political context. We are therefore left with an image of a hostile Strategic Man with a given amount of military capabilites and economic resources. The intentions of this other nation tend to be neglected, because they are 'uncertain'. Into the resulting political vacuum are projected one's own assumptions of what 'any rational [but hostile] man' would do. In addition, it is often assumed that 'what hurts me must help him', and that creating such mischief will therefore be an important adversary objective. When threats are identified, the tendency will be to worry more about one's own vulnerabilities (where can I be hurt?) rather than concerning oneself with recreating the other nation's view of its own interests and priorities. Once the other nation is perceived as an 'enemy' it will be seen to behave in a hostile fashion, almost regardless of its actual behaviour. After all, strategists must label some or other nation as an enemy, for strategy abhors a vacuum. The circle of the argument is complete.

The rational impulse behind these assumptions and ways of thinking is provided by common prudence. But there are a number of irrational elements in the process, each of which is subversive of sensible strategic planning. Bureaucratic politics provide plenty of clues. Military establishments need enemies to maintain their professional self-image, and the manipulation of enemy images is a common way of acquiring clout in resource-allocation debates. But the situation is rarely as simple or cynical as that. Lawrence Freedman has provided three relevant additional arguments. Firstly, government agencies do not always overestimate their adversaries' military potential. It would surprise its critics to learn that the CIA had demonstrated a 'marked tendency' to underestimate the future strategic capabilites of the Soviet Union. Secondly, it would be erroneous to believe that estimates were always politicised by the interplay of bureaucratic pulling and hauling, though it does seem reasonable to argue that 'as evidence becomes more hazy and the area of ambiguity is reached, the chances of disagreement grow'. In short, ambiguity encourages the propounding of bureaucratic preferences. And thirdly, institutional detachment or independence is not the same as being objective or free from bias.[3] Objective truth would not be the consequence of the abolition of bureaucratic politics.

Bureaucratic factors have various implications for threat assessment, but they are not the concern of this chapter. Instead, the focus is on the role of ethnocentrism, and the way in which it can reinforce the *rational* element in the strategist's syllogism in the direction of *irrational* threat assessment. Ethnocentric predispositions have an insidious influence. They make the activity of threat assessment seem clearer, more realistic and simpler than in fact it is. They provide the analyst with confidence in his approach, but they invariably mean that he is pursuing it less satisfactorily than he imagines.

Capabilities Versus Intentions

One of the most important and contentious issues in defence policy discusssion in general and in threat assessment in particular is the proper weighting of enemy intentions as against enemy capabilities. What emphasis should be put on each when trying to determine the character of a 'threat'? Many observers have no doubt whatsoever. Especially if they are spokesmen for a military establishment, their unvarying answer these days is that emphasis should be placed on capabilities. Intentions, it is iterated with the strength of dogma, 'can change overnight'.

At the basis of this argument is a prudential recognition that the international system is in some respects a threat system, and that relationships are kaleidoscopic: the friends of yesterday may become the enemies of today and vice versa. However, the prudential recognition that international politics do have some of the characteristics of a state of nature does not justify an extreme view of the propensity of most nations for war, or the view that capabilities offer a more sensible basis for threat assessment than do intentions. Indeed, the thinking which informs such attitudes rests on a number of weak assumptions, some of them deriving from or being reinforced by ethnocentric perceptions. In contrast to the conventional wisdom on these matters it can be argued that (i) intentions are not as changeable as stereotypes or theory might suggest, (ii) that capabilities are not necessarily the result of rational planning and are therefore not a safe basis for deducing intentions, and (iii) that capabilities are not as unchanging as is commonly assumed. If these counter-arguments are valid we can therefore conclude that the concentration on capabilities to the exclusion of intentions is misconceived. A more realistic approach to threat assessment would integrate both capabilities and intentions, and would do so within a broad picture of a nation's foreign and domestic political objectives and constraints.

It is frequently argued that the intentions of governments are unpredictable and can change overnight. In one sense this is true. Governments can decide to change their minds overnight, and on matters of detail they often do not themselves know from minute-to-minute what they will do on some matters. Furthermore, accurate prediction is an extraordinarily difficult art: there is no capacity for 'highly pinpointed prediction' such as to justify enough confidence to take it seriously.[4] Why, if we cannot satisfactorily explain the past, about which so much is known, should we have any confidence that we can correctly picture an uncertain future? However, recognising this difficulty should not be taken as an excuse for despair. Although innumerable spokesmen over the last ten years have stressed the unpredictability of intentions, there is reason to be more confident in thinking about the future than this argument suggests. The justification for such confidence becomes clearer once we distinguish between 'conjecture' and prediction, between major and minor matters, and between 'behavioural' and 'technical' surprise.

The claim of 'conjecture' is more modest than that of prediction.[5] Conjecture is 'low order' prediction. It is distinguished by an awareness of the impossibility of high-confidence prediction on a vast range of matters, and it carefully distinguishes between phenomena in terms of their conjecturability. By stressing conjecture we are admitting that we cannot accurately predict intentions, but we are also saying that we cannot accurately predict any human behaviour. Nevertheless we can go a long way with 'reasoned inference from admittedly defective evidence' (conjecture), especially on the pinnacles of 'high' politics.

On major matters, and nothing is more important than going to war, basic intentions rarely change 'overnight', although final decisions can obviously be traced to one moment. On the fundamental aspects of a country's foreign policy, such as its proclivity for war, the objective constraints within which decision-makers work are powerful. While one cannot accurately predict how particular governments will respond to some situations, one can usually infer with some confidence the issues over which they will run risks and be prepared to fight.

A knowledge of relevant history should add to the strength of a strategist's conjecture. History gives some indication of intentions, patterns and national styles. In relation to a given country it is usually possible to identify types of behaviour which will be avoided because they will be too costly (assuming the other nation behaves rationally in terms of its own values). 'Negative' interests are usually identifiable, and they are also to some extent controllable by outsiders. This is the basis of theories of deterrence. By demonstrating the will and capability to inflict certain costs on Nation B in the event of the latter undertaking certain undesirable actions, Nation A helps to shape the negative interests of B. This fact is of special importance to a defensive alliance such as NATO; it puts a premium on identifying Soviet interests and on devising strategies to deter the Soviet leaders from contemplating dangerous initiatives. History is not a perfect guide to present and future intentions, of course, but it is the only provider of perspective for educated conjecture. While it may be true that major wars have low predictability, the basic orientation of most great powers has shown an impressive degree of continuity. The real problem is not that history is not a guide to styles of national behaviour, but that it does not spark our imagination sufficiently to identify the *contingent* factors that so bedevil prediction. If we could know the accidental factors — assassinations, falls of government, coincidental crises, economic collapses and so on — our conjecture about the future attitudes of different countries would greatly increase in reliability. But obviously we cannot predict events whose occurrence, let alone timing, is inherently uncertain.

As well as distinguishing between prediction and conjecture, it is important to distinguish between 'behavioural' and 'technical' surprise.[6] A behavioural surprise occurs when the opponent's behaviour is incompatible or seems to be incompatible with one's set of expectations; a technical surprise, on the other hand, is not incompatible with the prevalent set of expectations but occurs because the opponent is successful in concealing a particular capability or in keeping a particular course of action shrouded in secrecy. At least from hindsight, behavioural surprises have been few on the issue of war, though technical surprises have been many. It is hard to think of examples of countries whose basic policy on war has changed 'overnight', except in response to attack (and in any case one assumes that self-defence is a basic propensity of all). There are no grounds whatsoever for arguing that a nation's propensity for war is so unpredictable that it can be cast out of the equation. Only those who do not know a particular country, and have no serious interest in knowing it, would make such a claim. (One might not always be right, but that is in the nature of any human activity.) If we had possessed more knowledge, and if we had avoided projecting our own ideas of 'reasonable' behaviour, would we have been wrong if we had concentrated on the intentions of Nazi Germany in the late 1930s, or Communist China in 1950 or Israel in 1967 or Egypt in 1973? Capabilities were hardly a certain guide: Hitler's war economy was not fully geared, Communist China was seriously vulnerable to US attack from the air, Israel was surrounded by a bevy of more populous states, and Egypt had both tactical weaknesses and less sophistication in its weaponry and personnel. In these cases, and others, intentions were stronger than capabilities. Nevertheless, capabilities remain the grist of all intelligence communities, partly because, as Freedman has explained, intelligence analysts as a body tend to be 'dedicated empiricists', with a shared respect for certain types of so-called 'hard' evidence and a corresponding scepticism towards what they classify as 'soft'.[7]

Capabilities are not only an uncertain guide to intentions: they are also much more changeable than conventional wisdom allows. In large part this is the consequence of the problems involved in the basic intelligence-gathering exercise, and then the enormous expertise required in assessing the meaning of the collected data. Recent history suggests that there have been as many failures in the analysis of adversary capabilities[8] as there have been faulty estimates of basic intentions.

The proposition that capabilities can literally change 'overnight' might seem outrageous to the proponents of the capabilities argument, largely because of the length of the lead-times involved in military procurement. But the fact is that adversary capabilities do change rapidly because *estimates* change overnight. The best known examples were the changing estimates that turned the bomber and missile 'gaps' of the 1950s into US surpluses. There have been plenty of other illustrations. In the mid-1960s Henry Kissinger wrote about the drastic and confusing alterations in US estimates of Soviet military strength,[9] and recently Lawrence Freedman has analysed in detail the variability of US estimates of Soviet capabilites throughout the nuclear age and the subsequent impact this has had on threat assessment.[10] Stanley Hoffmann has indicated that the same phenomenon has sometimes operated in US–Chinese relations. He has pointed to the contrast between the placid reaction of the United States to China's first explosion of a nuclear device in 1964 and the Secretary of Defense's 'apocalyptic presentation' of the 'facts' to the NATO Council fourteen months later. China's power and policy had not changed, but the American position in Asia and the American attitude towards Europe's complacency about Asia had.[11] It would seem that, sometimes at least, enemy capabilities are made to fit allied strategies rather than the other way round.

The preceding paragraph suggests that whatever changes occur in threat assessment as a result of new intelligence or better strategic book-keeping, there might well be a tendency for adversary capabilities to be manipulated to serve one's own domestic or foreign policy interests, or at least satisfy one's psychological susceptibilities. Policy-making man is a rationalising animal, as well as sometimes being rational, and this can affect estimates of adversary capabilties. Dissonance theory helps to explain what happens. Once a decision has been made dissonance may significantly affect the way we think about enemy capabilities. When a commitment has been made to a particular posture, evidence pointing to different conclusions will be minimised, as policy-makers try to increase their comfort with the decisions already reached; by this means two generations of German leaders helped to persuade themselves that Britain would not fight in a continental war or, if it did, that it would not be a major factor. There is a tendency, therefore, once a strategy has been decided upon, to make the enemy 'fit'. This distortion is made easier by the widespread lack of knowledge about other nations which results from strategic incuriousness, ethnocentrism or other blinkering factors. There is therefore reason to support Henry Kissinger's doubt as to whether 'estimates guide or follow our strategic policy'.[12] Under 'the facade of objectivity' in threat assessment there is plenty of room for the deliberate or unconscious manipulation of 'facts'. As a result of such possibilities one may reach the apparently absurd conclusion that enemy capabilities may sometimes be determined more by one's own strategy and policy than by the intentions of the enemy itself.

Enemy capabilities continue to change rapidly. Once a year for ten years after 1963 US intelligence estimates underestimated Soviet force levels: on ten occasions in succession, perceived Soviet capabilities literally changed overnight. More recently Western assessments of Soviet naval capabilities have tended to become moderated in the face of the more sophisticated 'interested public' of the mid-1970s. The picture of the Soviet missile build-up altered even more rapidly when the 1976 estimate of total Soviet warheads and submarine missile production was significantly downgraded.[13] And if the actual Soviet capabilities did not change, but only the US estimates of them, it is important to remember that, diplomatically speaking, it is *perceived* rather than *actual* capabilities which are most significant.

Assessing capabilities is therefore an imperfect art, and may be affected by other than the simple desire to count. Bureaucratic manipulation and strategic accounting errors make it a fickle activity, something far removed from the precise base-line for planning which 'dedicated empiricists' would like. Indeed, there have been so many overestimations and underestimations, subsequently revised, that one is justified in concluding that enemy capabilities are too changeable and too subjective to provide the main focus for threat assessment. The problem is compounded even further when one considers the expertise needed to understand the meaning of whatever capabilities are identified, in terms of tactics and strategy and potential threat. Rarely will the meaning of a given set of capabilities be clear, and the greater the ambiguity, the greater will the scope be for bureaucratic and analytical mind-sets to affect the estimating process. Despite all these problems and qualifications, however, a widespread assumption persists that we can learn more about other nations from photo-reconnaissance analysts and contingency-planners than from foreign policy specialists.

Capabilities are not unchanging 'facts'. Equally important, numbers of weapons do not necessarily add up to anything rational in terms of political planning. The Anglo-American experience suggests that force levels are rarely rationally determined. Force levels are often arbitrary: they are therefore not premises from which one can reasonably infer precise strategic intentions. The sources of arbitrariness are various. When officials trying to make difficult choices are confronted with many uncertainties, there is a natural tendency to seize uncritically on any constant that is offered, and to base calculations upon it.[14] US policy-makers once fixed upon $15 billion to simplify defence budgeting, while British policy-makers fixed upon £200 million. A proposal that a 70-group Air Force was needed became a fixed reference for the Congress. Similarly, the Royal Navy insisted upon the magic figure of 70 cruisers in the inter-war years. The US Navy maintained a standard of 15 capital ships for many decades after 1921, despite all the changes in missions and contingencies that the intervening years had brought,[15] and the make-up of the Sixth Fleet has been static for thirty years, despite many changes in mission and operational environment. Britain and the United States are not exceptions: there is no reason to suppose that force planning anywhere is any freer of inertia, arbitrary standards or irrationality. Only those who make no attempt to find out about other nations would imagine that their strategic policies were guided by unitary and utterly rational minds. The 'pull' of certain numbers suggests that strategies are the rationalisation of numbers arrived at by wheeling and dealing and hunches, rather than numbers being the direct outcome of strategic reasoning.

Those who stress capabilities as the base-line for planning find much food for thought in the looming Soviet arms build-up over recent years; and the assumption is encouraged that it represents the working out of a blue-print created by a centralised rational actor. It is more complex than that, however. A plausible account of the causation for the Soviet arms build-up must take into consideration not only a multiplicity of causes, but must also see it in terms of the dynamics of its evolution. The latter would bring out the rational responsiveness of Soviet strategy and the extent to which it has been reacting (in an improvising and opportunistic fashion) to developments elsewhere. Soviet capabilities would also have to be assessed in relation to the tasks they are supposed to perform under worst-case conditions: from this position what appears to be a potential threat in terms of Western vulnerabilities may well become an actual shortfall in terms of Soviet requirements.

The factors affecting the character and size of Soviet force levels are multifarious. They include any and all of the following: internal policing needs; internal socialising and nation-building (a state like the Soviet Union would need a mass army even if there were no foreign threats); the habit of not throwing equipment away (it might come in useful); bureaucratic and industrial inertia; bureaucratic rivalries; inter-service competition; budgetary and military inertia; the clout of the military-industrial complex; the clout of different branches of the services (the powerful branches tend to over-insure while the less powerful face over-stretch); an economic system prone to over-production (favouring inertia over initiative, and quantity over quality); doctrinal inconsistencies and compromises; the tradition of over-insuring (resulting from a historic consciousness of great insecurity and therefore a belief in 'the more the better'); and the related pull of numbers for their own sake, in the sense that military power might be seen as an absolute good, something of which it is impossible to have too much (like money, there may be a tendency for means to become ends, for people to amass quantities of a resource in excess of what they can use or spend).[16]

One might look at the Soviet Union and conclude that all these factors might significantly affect the size and character of its force structure *before* even admitting any detailed rational strategic planning into the analysis. The whole political culture (leaving aside strategy) is predisposed towards military over-insurance. It is a political culture with an historically socialised response to military stimuli.[17] Obviously, one must not completely disallow the possibility that rational strategic

Threat Assessment

thinking plays some part in determining Soviet force structures. Rational strategic factors would include responsiveness to changes in the perceived threat from the United States in particular (which stimulated naval expansion against the growing nuclear strike power of the US Navy at the turn of the 1950s/1960s, and the increase in ICBM production at the start of the 1960s in response to the adverse missile gap opened up by the vigorous arms-racing of Kennedy and McNamara); it would also include the provision of forces to provide deterrent power against the technically superior capabilities of its adversaries, to provide foreign policy leverage, to enhance prestige, and to garrison Eastern Europe. The adoption of an offensive military doctrine in the event of war further inflates manpower requirements. In addition, the 'correlation of forces' is of primary concern in 'scientific' decision-making. And at the basis of everything is the permissive fact that the Soviet Union, unlike Western democracies, has a regime and system which allow its expensive military tastes to be largely indulged. Two important qualifications need to be added to this picture of military expansiveness, however. Firstly, an aggressive strategic doctrine is not necessarily incompatible with a basically deterrent and war-avoiding foreign policy. One could argue that the Warsaw Pact is a defensive alliance in all senses except military doctrine. Secondly, the fact that the Soviet Union makes some serious preparation for the possibility of general war does not mean that its leaders believe the risk is 'high', but only that the risk is finite, and it certainly does not mean that general war is an option which they are preparing to grasp.

In sizing up a country's armed forces, therefore, especially a country as large and complex as the Soviet Union, it is important not to be too logical. Rather, like the historian, one should look for multiple causes. If 'hard' evidence does not exist for a particular explanation, that is no excuse for dismissing the possibility out of hand, for even those who are responsible for a country's capabilities probably never quite know why some things are done, or why the force mix is exactly how it is. As a British government document once put it, with disarming frankness:

The size of the forces of the Crown maintained by Great Britain is governed by various conditions peculiar to each service, and is not arrived at by any calculations of the requirements of foreign policy, nor is it possible that they should ever be so calculated.[18]

Inertia, pragmatism, opportunism, muddling through — such ways of proceeding are almost certainly typical of the defence planning of more countries than inter-war Britain. As often as not capabilities are not so much the rational outcome of what is euphemistically called 'strategic thinking' as of the habit behind the Great War ditty, 'we are here because we're here because we're here'.[19] Of all the things which capabilities reflect, strategic thinking is but one. Usually strategy is more rationalising than rational.

Whatever their complex origins, however, military capabilities do provide their possessors with a capacity for violence which inevitably represents a standing danger to potential adversaries. This is one of the reasons why those responsible for a nation's security stress the prudence of concentrating on capabilities rather than intentions, at least in respect of those countries which they categorise as enemies. (Paradoxically, it is the intentions of friends superpowers tend to worry about, not their capabilities.) The history of the Cold War demonstrated a constant preference by Western military thinkers for concentrating on Soviet capabilities (or rather imagined future Soviet capabilities) rather than on supposed Soviet intentions. Capabilities were thought to be 'facts', whereas intentions were only speculation. To the prudent mind the logic of this suggested that more weight be given in planning to those who claimed to be able to say what the enemy could do rather than those who claimed to be able to say what it might do. Analysis of the possible — a relatively easy skill — was generally preferred to analysis of the probable. George Kennan was familiar with this situation in the late 1940s. What George Kennan was saying about Soviet intentions counted for little in the face of what Soviet capabilities seemed to be saying to the military contingency planners. Kennan's understanding of the Soviet Union and his insights into Soviet conduct were generally overlooked.[20] He was overruled in favour of worst-case analysis. With hindsight most observers now think he was probably right in his cautious estimates of Soviet conduct, but how could anybody at the time be sure? With the military take-over in Eastern Europe being capped by the coup in Czechoslovakia, military aggression seemed to be an integral feature of Soviet ambition. It seemed to be Nazi-type expansionism all over again, with military force being welded to an aggressive ideology. At the time few gave credit to the possibility that Soviet strategy was determined by the desire to complete the counter-offensive against Germany and establish a secure defensive perimeter across Central Europe. Instead there seemed to be good reasons for thinking that Soviet intentions knew no natural limits (interestingly, however, Soviet capabilities for carrying out such a great plan were greatly exaggerated in the West's determination to prevent a second Munich). In such circumstances, the prudent response was to believe the worst and to make sure, and in the late 1940s, unlike the late 1930s, the Western nations now had a resolute and militarily assertive nation as its leader. The risks of a strategy of confrontation seemed less than the risks of appeasement. But who could guarantee that pursuing a Cold War strategy would not lead to an even worse disaster than a Soviet-dominated Europe? As it happens, we survived the Cold War. But the important question is: could we have survived it at less risk and at less cost, and arrived at a safer level of accommodation with the Soviet Union? Nobody knows. But what can be said is that the prudence and ethnocentrism which deprives an adversary of intentions (other than hostility) also deprives one's own policy of the constructive possibilities on which to build a stabler relationship.

Because it has been shown that assessing capabilities is an imperfect art, and that capabilities are as changeable as intentions, a sensible approach is to replace narrow realism by a posture of sophisticated and constructive realism which will integrate both capabilities and intentions. This largely means investing the 'intentions' part of the equation with more seriousness than at present. In practice, however, *a sharp distinction is impossible,* for to a greater extent than military planners would allow, estimates of intentions and capabilities are interdependent.[21] Hardware forecasts do require some judgement about military objectives. It is certainly mistaken to argue that ICBMs and tanks and such somehow represent solid 'facts' (we would do well to remember that aggressor states are hardly ever rationally 'ready' for war), whereas such woolly and unquantifiable factors as interests, hopes and fears are not relevant. Capabilities do represent a 'standing threat', by providing options, but it is important to make as rigorous an examination of intentions as possible if an effective and efficient policy is to emerge, one which will not be profligate with resources or unduly complacent or likely to miss chances for responding positively to situations in order to bring about a relaxation of tensions.

The thrust of the argument so far has been that ethnocentrism helps weight the capabilities versus intentions argument in favour of the former. It helps in the stereotyping and dehumanising of the 'enemy' which is dysfunctional in itself, and at the same time distracts attention away from the weaknesses of focusing on capabilities. The argument points to the need to place more emphasis on intentions in threat assessment. But this means the *educated* assessment of intentions, and not merely the projection of the ideas of 'any rational [hostile] man'. To be done well, threat assessment should be informed by a feeling for

cultural relativity. If this were achieved to any extent, the strategic analyst would cease to argue the rationality of emphasising capabilities
over intentions, except perhaps for cynical budgetary reasons. If, as
has been argued, capabilities are not necessarily the rational products
of a nation's foreign-policy intentions, and estimates of capabilities can
alter dramatically, we should therefore revise our traditional formulation and argue that, since capabilities can change overnight, we should
put more trust in our judgement about intentions.

Worst-Case Forecasting

Closely associated with the debate about intentions and capabilities is
the debate about worst-case forecasting. It is not intended to discuss
the many aspects of this concept, but instead to indicate some of its
problems in terms of the preceding discussion.

Worst-case forecasting is to strategic analysis what the 'god of the
gaps' is to theology. It fills in for what we do not understand. Worst-case
forecasting is inspired by native prudence, but it is often justified by
the belief that it is very difficult if not impossible to determine adversary
intentions. Because it is seen as unsafe to base policy on intentions, it
is argued that it is wiser to base it on the worst the other nation can do.
But intentions are not *so* unknowable: there is one very important difference between worst-case forecasting and the god of the gaps. The
latter fills in for what we do not understand, and perhaps cannot ever
understand. In strategy, on the other hand, there is the opportunity for
the filling in of at least part of the gaps. Analysing the intentions of
other nations is difficult, but a good deal can be known: one of the
biggest barriers is our own familiar incuriousness. In his conversations
with soldiers in Vietnam Ralph White noted that one 'striking common
characteristic' was the 'inhibition of curiosity both about the viewpoint
of the enemy and about the background of the war'.[22] Soldiers have
not traditionally been interested in such matters, but in the highly
charged and highly politicised atmosphere of the late 1960s, this
apparent lack of interest on the part of citizens of the world's largest
democracy was of special note. It adds to the theme of incuriosity
which runs throughout strategic affairs. Incuriosity is the mind-guard
of ethnocentrism.

And prudence is the bedmate of ethnocentrism. However, the two
are not inseparable. One does not have to be ethnocentric to believe
that one must attend to one's defences. A reasonable prudence might
dictate such a course. Even without a dangerously looming threat one
might decide that there is sufficient uncertainty in the world that one

must place a heavy emphasis on defence. The tendency towards worst-case threat assessment might be fuelled by either prudence or ethnocentrism. Although it may be difficult to prise them apart, it is worthwhile to try to distinguish them. In practice there is likely to be some difference between the tone and recommendations of a perspicacious strategist who is merely exercising professional caution – 'we must keep a wary eye on things' – and the dogmatic strategist whose thinking is largely the playing out of ethnocentric bias in the shape of 'unrealistic, exaggerated diabolism'.[23] The perspicacious strategist and the dogmatic strategist might both decide upon similar-looking military postures and doctrines, but they are likely to recommend related foreign policies of a significantly different tune. In such circumstances the 'realistic' tendency will be to defer to the more hawkish. The professional ethos favours thinking the worst: over-insurance is not a sin, but taking an avoidable risk is. On the other hand, the unintended and undesirable consequences of over-insurance tend to go unconsidered or are rejected. Professional and organisational pressures, not least within intelligence 'shops', push in the direction of conformity.[24] Professional socialisation, organisational inertia and ethos, group and psychological mechanisms all tend to sustain an enemy image once it has come into play.

In commenting on the many errors which are made in attempting to read the future, one is apt to underestimate the baffling problems involved. Forecasting the limits of another government's ambitions is an extremely difficult task. For one thing, the government concerned may not know itself the limits of its ambitions, for these might well change with circumstances. It takes great insight (and luck) to be able to predict anything with accuracy, let alone the extent of a potential adversary's aggressiveness. It therefore takes all the more self-confidence on the part of an analyst to advise his superiors that all will be safe on the basis of his educated hunches. In such circumstances worst-case forecasting appears a more realistic basis on which to start thinking about policy. The worst case is more easily definable than the probable case, and so provides a firmer basis for policy prescription. Worst-case forecasting also frees individual analysts from blame if things go wrong. This is another reason why the tendency is always to think the worst. To base policy on a less than worst-case forecast will turn out costly if the prediction is wrong. To underplay what turns out to be a real threat may bring defeat; but to overestimate, and perhaps provoke a potential threat into an actual one, might only increase tension. In the past, when war was a less serious business, it nearly always made sense to defer to the alarmist. In the context of the nuclear age the balance of the argument should logically change. Risks should be taken for peace rather than war: as George Kennan once said, what the system requires is more gardening and less militancy. There has been some movement in this direction in Western behaviour in recent years, but it has resulted from the drift of politicians rather than the changing perspectives of strategists.

Ethnocentrism fuels worst-case forecasting. It tends to produce policies based on negative but not positive realism: it encourages the attempt to be ready for the worst, but it tends to ignore opportunities for encouraging the bringing about of the better. The 'inherent bad faith' outlook means that any actions by any other nation are seen with suspicion. They are not amenable to any constructive or positive or non-hostile interpretation. Those who look at relationships through 'bad faith' lenses risk losing chances for conceiving policies which may enhance security by tension-reducing rather than confrontational and deterrent postures. Strategists with narrow perspectives are of limited use as foreign-policy advisers. They are no more than military technicians. Alfred von Schlieffen stands as a symbol of and a warning against such men: his temperament and narrow conception of his role helped to bring about that very outcome which it was his hope and duty to prevent.

The outlook and recommendations of a prudent and sophisticated strategist would be based on the recognition that there may be many possible causes for an opponent's behaviour. It would be argued that one's guard must be maintained, but that unless the evidence was uncontroversial, there would be no justification for thinking the worst. Preparing for the worst would not be advocated, while there would be a careful recognition of the effect that one's own behaviour might have on the other nation. Too often in the past policy-makers appear not to have realised the extent to which they have provoked threats to their own nation because of the threat they themselves have directly or indirectly made to others. In contrast a sophisticated and positive policy would be conducted so as to encourage and be open to positive signals from the other side. It would attempt to manipulate the other government's internal debate in a beneficial way. The main difference between the ethnocentric and the reasonably prudent strategist may be, in the words of Robert Jervis, that the former will 'neglect the possibilities of favourably affecting the other's behaviour by moderating one's own actions'. In contrast, his behaviour will tend to increase 'illusory incompatibility'. Jervis continues:

If the other's hostility is seen as rooted in autonomous drives, there is no reason to examine one's own policies to see if they may be self-defeating. There is no need to make special efforts to demonstrate your willingness to reach reasonable settlements.[25]

Such an undiplomatic sense of inevitability was exemplified for a moment during the Cuban missile crisis: Robert Kennedy has reported,

> We all agreed in the end that if the Russians were ready to go to nuclear war over Cuba, they were ready to go to nuclear war and that was that. So we might as well have the showdown then as six months later.[26]

This is a fatalism which justifies pre-emptive and preventive wars. Fortunately, in October 1962, the balance of argument tipped in favour of those who were willing to accept the risks of the peaceful assumption, rather than those who were ready to face the risks of the warlike possibility. It was decided to try to moderate the other nation's behaviour.

On many less critical occasions in the Cold War, perspicacity gave way to ethnocentric militancy. Possibilities for favourably affecting the opponent's behaviour were neglected. The worst was expected and might well have happened, though not because either side wished it. With a mutual belief in a devil-like opponent, there were pushes for military superiority and technical sophistication with little regard for the likely effect on the other nation. As hostility was expected whatever was done, 'full speed ahead' was the normal red-blooded outlook. The Soviet Union of Stalin and Khruschchev might not have responded positively to a more differentiated approach, but it might have, and this would have helped change Soviet–American hostility into that of 'normal' competition between great powers, rather than what it turned out to be – and still is – that is potentially the most destructive confrontation ever in history. If Soviet leaders had not responded to a less confrontational and threatening military strategy, then little would have been lost: there was always enough overkill to ensure that deterrence was not 'delicate'. Politically speaking, the balance of terror was never delicate: the error in thinking it was was the result of an imbalance in the outlook of worst-case advocates. Deep differences of interest existed between the superpowers, but mutually advantageous compromises were conceivable, and certainly neither side wanted war. More positive coexistence could not be pursued because of the atmosphere of fear and distrust, and 'the total want of consideration of what others will naturally hope or fear'. This made it difficult for either side to

consider a more accommodating approach.[27] Had the more positive
and sophisticated attitudes of the early 1970s been given an opportunity
in the relatively simpler international context of the mid-1950s, one
could assume that more progress would have been made in arms control
and questions of European security. There would at least have been the
possibility of more security at lower levels of risk. Even had this happy
outcome failed to materialise, it is hard to imagine how events might
have taken a more dangerous course than the one they in fact did.

While strategic planning is dominated by negative rather than positive
thinking, the operating principle will continue to be: when in doubt,
think the worst. There will always be professional deference to those
who can count missiles or who can conceive theoretical contingencies
rather than those who claim to know something about the intentions
of the country under consideration. Worst-case forecasting (except on
the rare occasions when it *is* valid) is not based on an educated appreciation of how another nation conceives its own intentions. It is not
meant to be. Furthermore, ignorance and ethnocentric predispositions
together result in the strong tendency for those who spend their time
conceiving the worst in theory, to see only the worst in practice. As it
happens rather few national armed forces have been built up in the
twentieth century to overthrow the international status quo, though
the few that have naturally dominate our thoughts. But should they?
Large-scale military aggression has not paid in the twentieth century,
and as the costs of war increase it will not pay in future. One of the few
consolations of the forseeable future is that we have probably seen
the last attempt by any national leader to carve out a New Order on a
continental scale by naked territorial expansion. This thought should
temper the temptation to think the worst. But it is unlikely to. Pessi-
mism and prudence are deeply ingrained in strategists, whether they are
policy-makers or academics. Amongst academics this was manifest in
the 'standard Sovietology' of the deterrence theorists of the 1950s and
1960s:[28] they seemed to believe that there were 'no apparent limits
to *how much* power' the Soviet Union and China would try to attain.[29]
Amongst policy-makers the case was put most clearly by Robert
McNamara, the troubled intellectual giant of defence secretaries: he
noted that 'A strategic planner must be conservative in his calculations;
that is, he must prepare for the worst plausible case and not be content
to hope and prepare for the most probable.'[30]

One of the implicit problems running through several of the aspects
of worst-case thinking discussed above is the tendency for the *possible*
to become thought of as the *probable*. As Klaus Knorr has explained:

What is merely possible is important when the consequences of its actual occurrence would be grave. But such a strategic assumption, which is prudent insurance, must not be confused with the estimate of a threat. In practice, unfortunately, such confusion is not rare. From postulating that an event is hypothetically possible, it seems easy to slip into the assumption that it is probable; and if one's behaviour is based on the assumption of probability, it may act like a self-fulfilling prophecy.[31]

Under McNamara the Pentagon attempted to cope with some of these problems by developing the concept of the Greater-Than-Expected Threat (GTE).[32] The concept arose out of the sensible realisation by McNamara's office that planning to meet an overstated threat (especially a worst-case threat) might involve great dangers and certainly excessive costs. The idea was developed that deployment decisions would be made on the basis of 'the most probable estimates of Soviet capabilities, while prudently maintaining options in reserve for introduction if the maximum, though unlikely, Soviet capabilities looked like emerging' (that is, the GTE).

Like worst-case forecasting, the estimate of the GTE was unreal, was as much concerned with US vulnerabilities as Soviet intentions, and bore only a remote connection with actual Soviet activity. Essentially, it was worst-case forecasting by another name, though it had the inestimable advantage of self-awareness.

Recommendations which flow from worst-case forecasting, which are based on estimates of practically possible behaviour on the part of a putative enemy, drive out recommendations based on estimates of how the other nation might see its own intentions, interests and capabilities. Matters are made even worse when decision-makers are unaware that they hold an 'inherent bad faith model' of the other nation, when they see all the adversary's behaviour as confirming that image, whatever it does or does not do. Everywhere they see evidence of the other's bad intentions, and everywhere they see evidence of the other's failure to reveal a friendly aspect.[33] Worst-case images cease to be a guideline and instead become a subjective truth.

With worst-case forecasting, estimates of the possible tend to drive out estimates of the probable. This can be damaging for both national and international security. Such thinking can dangerously fuel the arms race through the 'action-reaction phenomenon',[34] resulting in less security for all at higher levels of destructive power; and it can do a disservice to the image of an individual nation's strength by the publicising of the worst-case estimates of an adversary.[35] It must not be assumed that worst-case forecasting *inevitably* results in more dangerous outcomes, however. The action-reaction phenomenon is at best only one explanation of arms-racing, while preparing for the worst case does not necessarily mean taking precipitate action (as McNamara tried to show).[36] However, worst-case forecasting does inevitably entail the *risk* of such outcomes: thinking and acting on the basis of worst-case estimates may well change the character of relations between two countries, such that the possible tends to *become* the probable. This is one of the invariable consequences of overly suspicious strategic behaviour. In the nation state system, the security dilemma tends to swallow up its own.

The Level of Analysis Problem

Threats can be conceived as a level-of-analysis problem. Once they are conceived in this way, a number of confusions subside. There are two fundamental levels to contemplate in threat assessment, and they relate to the distinction made in the last section between possibilities and probabilities.[37] The first level is that of the foreign policy analyst; the second is the level of the contingency planner. The former is concerned with strategic analysis of a more political type, and with probabilities about the other nation's behaviour. At the second, lower (theatre) level, concern is with military contingency-planning and strategic analysis of a more technical character: attention is directed at what the other nation can do. At the strategic level intentions are very important; they are of less importance at the theatre level. Because intentions become increasingly significant as one rises up the scale of military activity, from tactics to strategic policy, the scope for ethnocentric distortion increases. On a practical level, therefore, threat analysis becomes more susceptible to ethnocentrism the more important it becomes.

As the discussion in Chapter 2 indicated, the tendency for strategists is to impose order on reality by concentrating on the system level and on rational Strategic Man. However, the implication of Chapters 3-5 was that strategists should integrate more levels of analysis into their discussion if they are to understand more fully why different groups are willing to engage in organised violence. Furthermore, such knowledge is essential for deterrence, the manipulation of force short of war, and crisis management. Sufficient evidence has been accumulated to show that the cultural dimension should suffuse analysis at all levels if 'enemies' are to be 'known'. However, with limited time the question arises as to where attention should be concentrated. It is not contended that there be a complete switch in foreign-policy analysis away from the system level. The system should not be slighted: its role in bringing about conflict should never be underestimated.[38] But realistic analysis must take account of cultural variables: the system may determine that wars happen, but cultural factors help to settle in detail how and why they take place.

Wars do not occur between individuals in the human family, but in the non-human family of states. However, it is not the states themselves which have the bogies, nightmares, stereotypes and myths which contribute to specific wars: all these occur at the level of people.[39] Recognising this is all the more important because of the widespread and sensible recognition that nuclear war could never be a rational act, and therefore is only likely to occur because of madness, accident, miscalculation or misperception. At least some of these contingencies might in part be brought about by ethnocentric perceptions and the related mechanisms which serve to exacerbate hostility by diabolising adversary intentions. The type of approach which concentrates on the system, at the cost of these other levels, will do a major disservice to strategic analysis.

Two things have therefore to be added to strategic theory if it is more closely to explain and approximate reality. The first is a sensitivity to cultural relativities at all levels of analysis, and the second is the paying of more attention to individual and group analysis as well as the system level of analysis. The latter will not be easy, nor should we overestimate Sidney Verba and note that personality variables do affect attitudes and behaviour, but admit that it is very much more difficult to assess 'how strong the effects are likely to be, in what direction they will operate 'how strong the effects are likely to be, in what direction they will operate, and under what conditions the non-logical influences are likely to be significant'.[40] The limitations of the rationality model have to be recognised, and this recognition has to be acted upon if strategic analysis is to describe reality more exactly. Even recognising this difficulty is a step in the right direction, for as Bernard Brodie has argued, the greatest need in thinking about the future is the need to be honest about uncertainty and to develop better ways for trying to handle it.[41]

The Irreducible Dilemma

Historically speaking, threat assessment has been very badly done.[42] There is not much reason for confidence that it is being done much better today. Perhaps because everybody seems to assume that it is easy, it remains, as Knorr has put it, 'one of the most primitive areas of statecraft'.[43] Strangely, therefore, there has been an 'absence of procedural rules for minimizing error'. Why should this be so?

Klaus Knorr has identified a range of problems which bedevil accurate threat assessment. These include: the problem of information-gathering, especially in closed societies; bureaucratic structures and proclivities; the ambiguity of incoming information; intrinsic intellectual difficulties; and predetermined expectations and beliefs. The latter are particularly important: 'Man, it seems, not only tends to be a prisoner of his perceptions, his perceptions also are slaves to his predispositions.'[44] This has had some particularly deleterious effects in intelligence gathering.[45] Ethnocentrism affects both perceptions and predispositions. It must therefore be counted as one of the variables which has resulted in threat assessment, historically, being 'nearly always more or less defective, often grossly so'.

In the present discussion of threats, as in the illustrations in earlier chapters, it can be seen that there is in strategy a pentagonal and usually reinforcing relationship between: (i) ethnocentrism; (ii) some of the types of misperception written about by Robert Jervis; (iii) some of the dynamics and characteristics of group decision-making and bureaucratic politics revealed by Irving Janis and Graham Allison; (iv) individual psychological features such as cognitive dissonance, conceived by Leon Festinger, and the authoritarian personality described by the Adorno group; and (v) the apparently inescapable dynamics of the international 'security dilemma' (some would prefer to call it the 'war system') which has been elaborated upon by most international theorists. Through these interactions, ethnocentrism causes, encourages and reinforces many of the characteristic features of the strategist's response to his complex operational environment.

From the viewpoint of an individual nation-state, as was argued in Chapter 5, ethnocentrism often does a disservice to policy-making. It compounds the biases in the strategist's outlook. Individual predispositions are consolidated by group dynamics: the working assumptions of a decision-making body become consolidated into groupthink, and the conclusions are then protected, advertently and inadvertently, by information-gathering and group discipline. Conclusions then resist change. Cognitive dissonance and other pressures to conformity come into play. Sometimes unchangeability is for the most banal and human of motives: 'The easy and lazy thing is to predict today what you predicted yesterday.'[46]

Misperception exacerbates international problems, though there is much more to international conflict than that. There is also 'the absolute predicament and the irreducible dilemma',[47] from which the strategic paradigm takes its essential meaning. Perfect perception, if that were achievable, would rid nations of imaginary threats, but there would still be many *real* threats to worry about. Indeed, everybody has enough actual challengers without having to invent enemies. The international system is a threat system because of what Butterfield called 'the structure of the situation' and the desire for self-preservation. This environment is pervaded by suspicion and the clash of interests: some would call this a 'realistic' view of international life, but others would prefer to emphasise its tragic quality. However its nature is conceived, it is hardly surprising that enemy-imaging, the emphasis on capabilities rather than intentions, and worst-case forecasting flourish. And each of these tendencies is exacerbated by ethnocentrism. It intensifies the suspicions and apparent clashes of interest which exist in the international system. This means that the normal conflicts and clashes of interest which exist in a world of sovereign and independent nation-states will expand beyond the level which objective analysis might indicate they should. Ethnocentrism increases the troubles of an already troubled world. If it is true that the 'security dilemma cannot be abolished, [but] . . . can only be ameliorated',[48] then overcoming ethnocentrism can be one part of the solution.

We are fortunate that so far in the superpower confrontation increased economic burdens and international tension have been the worst consequences of ethnocentric predispositions. We can also take some satisfaction from the fact that the balance of terror has imposed a novel caution on decision-makers: the objective danger, which it is difficult for anyone to miss, encourages a form of nuclear pacifism. But the nuclear age is still young. The time span with which we are dealing has been too short for us to be greatly optimistic about the future. Radical surprises, unthinkable accidents, collective irrationality and massive intelligence failures exist as skeletons in the cupboards of all major nations. There are numerous war cemeteries as testimonies. Some of the scenarios envisaged for the future may seem bizarre, but if the study of history is anything, it is surely a reminder of the predictability of the unpredictable.

Caution must be exercised, therefore, in projecting the apparent prudence and rationality of superpower behaviour over the past thirty years into the indefinite future. Contemplating the dangers of the Middle East is one useful antidote. This region regularly demonstrates the extent to which most of the world is still dominated by immediate fears of war. War is more than thinkable, it is almost a way of life. While there may be some nuclear pacifists, there are no conventional pacifists in the chancelleries of the world. In this situation, where there is a real security dilemma but, one always hopes, some prospect of ameliorating at least specific problems, the desirability of avoiding those pitfalls that are caused by ethnocentrism should therefore be evident. How this might be done forms the basis of the next chapter.

Victory Is Not Success

Western strategists generally think of the past as having 'worked' rather than failed in a military sense. This is especially true of the Anglo-American outlook. There have always been some who could call themselves 'victors' in strategic history, and even losers have often recovered quickly. As a result, although there have been some well-known scapegoats, the extent of the failure of strategic thinking and practice is seriously underestimated. This is partly because we concentrate on results rather than costs. In particular, like journalists, strategic writers tend to be insensitive about costs in proportion to the time and distance they are from an event. The costs of successful strategies in the past are now largely ignored. We know of the elder Moltke as a great military thinker, but does anybody consider whether his ideas were the best possible, as opposed to being merely the best at hand? And who now worries about the possibility that Nelson or any other great military leader might have secured his victories with fifty less lives, or thousands. At this remove, it does not seem to matter.

Results count in strategy. Victory helps to hide or play down costs. Victory is so sweet that the sight of costs tends to be lost. A Pyrrhic victory is better than no victory at all, and even the reputation of Stalin survives surprisingly intact. Victory excuses a great deal. A familiar example of this is the way the British have made a virtue of incompetence by elevating to dogma the strategy of the 'long haul' and by parading as cunning their lamentable tradition of losing 'every battle but the last'. Both phrases are euphemisms for unpreparedness. Real success is not just a matter of winning, but of winning well. Historically, strategies can only be said to have worked when victory in war was synonymous with success in a wide sense. Today success does not mean victory, but survival, and not only existing, but existing well.

The extent to which victories have been failures in strategy has not been sufficiently recognised either by strategists (who are reluctant to look at the past) or historians (who are reluctant to examine both strategy and 'if only' questions). The result is that the extent to which strategy has been an exercise in failure has not been internalised by the strategic community, and it goes untaught. The apparent success of nuclear strategy — in the sense that we have not had a major war in the last thirty years — adds a spurious reservoir of credibility to these attitudes. In the past the cost of victory has often been excessive. This portends ill for a future in which one thing above all is certain: however measured, the cost of using military force will be greater than ever before, whether or not the enterprise is finally attended by victory. In a world in which increasingly destructive weaponry threatens all nations, the responsibility upon those involved in the management of that power is correspondingly more serious. In such circumstances, those strategists who do not attempt to be part of the solution will undoubtedly become an increasingly important part of the problem.

Notes

1. See Klaus Knorr, 'Threat Perception' in Klaus Knorr (ed.), *Historical Dimensions of National Security Problems* (Lawrence, Kansas: Allen Press, 1976), pp. 78-119.

2. Lawrence Freedman, *US Intelligence and the Soviet Strategic Threat* (London: Macmillan, 1977), p. 62.

3. Ibid., pp. 58, 61, 196-7.

4. These points are from Klaus Knorr and Oskar Morgenstern, *Political Conjecture In Military Planning*, Princeton University Center for International Studies, Policy Memorandum No. 35, Nov. 1968, pp. 10-15.

5. Ibid., pp. 14-21.

6. Klaus Knorr, 'Failures in National Intelligence Estimates: The Case of the Cuban Missiles', *World Politics*, vol. XVI, no. 3 (Apr. 1964), pp. 455-67.

7. Freedman, *US Intelligence*, p. 188.

8. Ibid., *passim*.

9. Henry A. Kissinger, *The Troubled Partnership* (New York: McGraw-Hill, 1965).

10. Freedman, *US Intelligence, passim*.

11. Stanley Hoffmann, *Gulliver's Troubles: Or, The Setting of American Foreign Policy* (New York: McGraw-Hill, 1968), p. 160.

12. Quoted in ibid.

13. See Herbert Scoville, Jr., 'The Soviet Threat: Is There a Present Danger?', *Defense Monitor*, vol. VI(2) (Feb. 1977), pp. 2-3.

14. Joseph DeRivera, *The Psychological Dimensions of Foreign Policy* (Columbus, Ohio: C. E. Merrill Publishing Co., 1969), p. 75.

15. Matthew P. Gallagher and Karl F. Spielmann, *Soviet Decision-Making for Defense. A Critique of US Perspectives on the Arms Race* (New York: Praeger Publishers, 1972), p. 13.

16. Anatol Rapoport, *Conflict in a Man-Made Environment* (Harmondsworth, Middx: Penguin Books, 1974), pp. 188-9.

17. C.f. Rapoport's argument that complex behaviour patterns may not be the result of reasoning, but of a conditioned response to stimuli, and that by attributing foresight analysts may well be imposing too much of a pattern on reality. Ibid., p. 35.

18. A paper on imperial defence, 22 June 1926, quoted by Dixon, *Psychology*, p. 111.

19. See ibid. and 'The Military Heresy', *The Times Literary Supplement*, 30 June 1972.

20. See George F. Kennan, *Memoirs 1925-1950* (Boston: Little; Brown and Co., 1967), pp. 310-11, 352-3, 395, 403, 497-8.

21. Freedman, *US Intelligence*, pp. 10-11.

22. Ralph K. White, *Nobody Wanted War: Misperception in Vietnam and Other Wars* (Garden City, NY: Doubleday, 1968), p. 255.

23. Ibid., p. 318.

24. Freedman, *US Intelligence*, p. 11.

25. Robert Jervis, *Perception and Misperception in International Politics* (Princeton, N.J.:Princeton University Press, 1976), p. 353.

26. Ibid.

27. See William A. Gamson and Andre Modigliani, *Untangling the Cold War* (Boston: Little, Brown and Co., 1971), p. 38.

28. See Philip Green, *Deadly Logic. The Theory of Nuclear Deterrence* (Columbus, Ohio: Ohio State University Press, 1966), pp. 244-5.

29. Anatol Rapoport, *Strategy and Conscience* (New York: Harper and Row, 1964), p. 184.

30. Quoted in Freedman, *US Intelligence*, p. 85.

31. Knorr, 'Threat Perception' in Knorr, p. 116.

32. The points below are based on Freedman, *US Intelligence*, pp. 84-6.

33. Jervis, *Perception and Misperception*, p. 144.

34. McNamara's well-known formulation of it was in September 1967: see Freedman, *US Intelligence*, pp. 1-2.

35. Note the comments of US Secretary of Defense Harold Brown: quoted, ibid., p. 198.

36. Ibid., p. 85.

37. See also Michael MccGwire, *Soviet Naval Developments: Capability and Context* (New York: Praeger Publishers, 1973), pp. 1-5, 31-3.

38. The standard text is Kenneth Waltz, *Man, the State, and War: A Theoretical Analysis* (New York: Columbia University Press, 1959).

39. See C. A. W. Manning, *The Nature of International Society* (London: Macmillan, 1975), pp. 75-6, 82.

40. Sidney Verba, 'Assumptions of Rationality and Non-Rationality in Models of the International System' in Klaus Knorr and Sidney Verba (eds.), *The International System, Theoretical Essays* (Princeton N.J.: Princeton University Press, 1961), p. 97.

41. Bernard Brodie, 'The Impact of Technological Change on the International System: Reflections on Prediction', *Journal of International Affairs*, no. 2 (1971), pp. 209-23, esp. p. 223.

42. Knorr, 'Threat Perception' in Knorr, *passim.*

43. Ibid., p. 97.

44. Ibid.

45. See, for example, George H. Poteat, 'The Intelligence Gap: Hypotheses on the Process of Surprise'. *International Studies Notes*, vol. 3, issue 3 (Fall 1976), pp. 14-18.

46. Knorr, 'Threat Perception' in Knorr, p. 113.

47. The 'security dilemma' is at the core of the international theorising of political scientists. It is one of many variants of the 'state of Nature' idea. The phrase quoted is Sir Herbert Butterfield's classic encapsulation of the international predicament. See 'The Tragic Element in Modern International Conflict', esp. pp. 19-20, in his *History and Human Relations* (New York: Macmillan Co., 1952).

48. Jervis, *Perception and Misperception*, p. 82.

7 STRATEGY WITH A HUMAN FACE

> How horrible, fantastic, incredible it is that we should be digging trenches and trying on gas-masks here because of a quarrel in a far-away country between people of whom we know nothing. *Prime Minister Neville Chamberlain*

> One day everything will be well, that is our hope:
> Everything's fine today, that is our illusion. *Voltaire*

> What's Chad? *Secretary of State Henry A. Kissinger*

> I keep confusing Nigeria with Algeria because both end in 'geria'. *President Lyndon B. Johnson*

The last four chapters have shown some of the ways in which ethnocentrism can affect the theory and practice of strategy. They have shown it can have effects at all levels, from small group dynamics to the very philosophies of war which give shape to the military conduct of nations. The proposition that ethnocentrism is a pervasive feature in strategic life needs no further validation. The problem now becomes: what is to be done?

The Inertia of an Ethnocentric Profession

If bad anthropology makes for bad strategy, it certainly makes for bad strategic studies. Nevertheless, ethnocentrism continues to exercise a grip on the study of the subject, as it does on its practice. Within universities or research institutes ethnocentrism rarely appears as the crude racism and xenophobia sometimes witnessed in armed forces or society at large. But for some individuals at least, it appears to be a difference of tone and degree rather than of kind. For some, strategic theory seems to be the way that reason attempts to cope with prejudice.

If strategic studies are to be improved the grip of bad anthropology has to be relaxed. It will become apparent that there are no simple remedies, nor will good anthropology guarantee wise strategic studies or effective strategies; but it would be a step forward. The general sense of direction should be towards 'strategy with a human face', by which is meant the peopling of strategic discourse with real nations rather than stereotypes, with real governments rather than monolithic 'actors', with groups with national styles and traditions rather than rational strategic black boxes, with nations with hopes and fears rather than implicit enemy images, and with individuals affected by a distinctive cultural heredity as opposed to individuals supposedly driven by a universal political and strategic logic. The strategic anthropologist must come to terms with the fact that his subject is played out across a multi-coloured map, and not a chessboard made up of standard black and white squares.

If Strategic Man is to be buried, and replaced by strategic studies with a human face, then it is necessary to attempt to create strategic anthropologists, people who have been trained to identify and explain the diversity of behaviour by the comparative study (in a loose sense) of strategic conduct amongst a variety of nations. As long as the politico-cultural dimension is neglected, analysts will continue to develop theories which do not fit the facts, use words which do not fit the behaviour they are supposed to describe, and propose policies which will make more sense in a seminar room than in the world outside. That this has been so prevalent was revealed in the last four chapters. One can only conclude that strategic studies have been conceived too narrowly and that its exponents are inbred.

Strategic studies are often ethnocentric, but it should not be forgotten that strategy is a relatively new university subject and that some longer-established disciplines do no better. As a university subject strategy only had its birth in the mid-1950s. The present 'community' is therefore only the first generation of academic strategists. However, because of university retrenchment, it is evident that the same relatively small group of individuals (and their books) is likely to dominate thinking for a long time to come. Strategic studies have become respectable; the immediate problem now is whether and how the subject can be improved. With little new blood entering it the key question is: can the makers themselves be remade?

Students are largely the products of their teachers and the books they read. The most-studied literature and most of the current teachers are products of the so-called golden age of contemporary strategic theorising, which was born of US predicaments in the mid-1950s and which lasted until the mid-1960s.[1] In this period strategic studies was American nuclear strategy of the *Polaris/Minuteman* generation writ large. It was cast in an ethnocentric mould, and born into an ethnocentric environment. The strategic thinking of this period was not timeless as some have asserted. Strategic conventional wisdom has proved to have a greater rate of obsolescence than most missile systems. The changeability of politics has caused strategic fashions to rust even more rapidly than time has made obsolete the machines of war, even in a throwaway era.

Strategic studies have changed and developed since the mid-1960s, but not much. There was the occurrence of what Colin Gray termed 'the third wave'.[2] This was an attempt by a number of individuals to reopen the old questions, fill the lacunae, discipline the excesses and challenge some of the existing assumptions about the old answers. Two factors in particular encouraged this trend: the Vietnam War and the spread of the study of bureaucratic politics. Together, these developments convinced some observers of the limits of theory, the danger of over-confidence and the necessity for detailed area study knowledge. At the start of the 1970s area specialists and strategists began to be brought together to some extent, and the results were usually rewarding. But inertia remains powerful, and the impact of the change remains limited.

The physical growth of strategic studies continues, with new students and new journals spilling out of universities and colleges; however, several factors have inhibited commensurate intellectual development in the subject. (1) Conscientious strategists find it difficult to keep pace with the burgeoning literature even in their main areas of interest, and this discourages them from attempting to expand their expertise more widely. Publishing has got out of hand when those who are paid to read about a certain field cannot keep pace. There is little to suggest that 'more' means 'better' in strategic studies. (2) The exigencies of the academic profession encourage regular publication. This pressure itself favours the ploughing of familiar fields rather than the opening up of new ones or the allowing of fallow years in which intellectual energies might be freshened. This is a pity because it is one of the themes of this book that a wider perspective on strategy should result in a better approach to one's job. (3) There is over-specialisation. Academic strategists are seen to be worrying about the warheads on the top of a missile, while major changes are taking place in the world around them. In the world at large this is matched by the stultifying intricacies of SALT and MFR, which encourage outsiders to think that the practitioners are fiddling while Rome burns. (4) Academic strategists often continue to frame courses in terms of 'national security policy' as opposed to 'strategic studies'. In this case ethnocentric teaching is calculated, if not deliberate. (5) There is a widespread intellectual conceit in the profession, involving the view that our way is best and right. Sometimes this reveals aspects of solipsism and narcissism, which involve a failure to appreciate that there is more to the external world than our own thoughts, and that the objects we consider are persons with their own wishes and needs. Groups which tend to be absorbed in their own transcendence are unlikely to be those willing to hack away at new ground. (6) Amongst individual strategists there is a frequent and understandable (and sometimes necessary) tendency to drift into current affairs analysis and commentary. This means, to use Hugh Nott's nicely cynical distinction, that we have too many strategic talkers but not enough strategic thinkers. Today, academic strategists have largely ceased to inhabit ivory towers: instead they bustle through airport lounges. It is often magnificent, but is it the study of war?

Paradoxically, one of the impediments to the development of the subject has been the very vigour of strategic theorising in the United States, the country which first gave the subject its 'sophisticated' tag. The theorists of the late 1950s and early 1960s were enormously creative, but in some ways they did too good a job. They were too plausible and too influential. The academic empire of American strategic theorising was inspired by the missionary zeal of social science optimism and, like the British Empire, established its authority in a fit of absent-mindedness. For all its creativity and plausibility, however, the American strategic community was also ethnocentric in outlook. Consequently, together with many insights, the faults and fallacies of American strategic theorising were also implanted in the outposts of strategic studies in the Western world.

American strategic studies involve problems of content, approach and assumptions and values. (1) *Content:* Courses in US universities have often been conceived in terms of 'national security policy'. This means that the student learns about strategy only within the framework of US defence policy and its problems. This is an inadequate basis on which to develop an understanding of the nature of strategy. (2) *Approach:* American strategic studies share some of the problems of American approaches to foreign policy in general. Most of these can be subsumed under what Stanley Hoffmann called 'skill thinking'.[3] This approach includes the habit of using 'strategy' as synonymous with 'foreign policy', and of trying to inject certainty and predictability into an environment where ambiguity is the characteristic feature. It results from a mixture of the 'engineering approach' of many American defence intellectuals and also their ethnocentrism: this encourages them to project into their foreign-policy thinking their assumptions and beliefs about their own nation's past, its principles and its pragmatism. (3) *Assumptions and values:* In many cases, the assumptions and values of American strategic thinking are based on what Yehezkel Dror called a 'general *Gestalt* of fallacies'.[4] These include such fallacies as the personification of the adversary, the separation of political goals from strategic analysis, the assumption of widespread (essentially American) values, and the validity of extrapolating the past.

Despite its weaknesses, the peculiar character and enormous quantity of American strategic writing has had a major impact on all our thinking. Strategic discourse in the non-communist world is generally carried out in American terms. The writers whom we consult and to whom we refer are nearly always American writers. Elsewhere there has largely been underthink. The paucity of theorising in other countries is indicative of the non-American's lack of effort, interest, resources, commitment to academic brainstorming, opportunity and perceived need. Whatever else one may say about it, American strategic thinking has been an enormously vital activity. Critics of American approaches have been vociferous, and often patronising, but so far one waits in vain to see substantial products coming from their pens. Compared with the apathy, official dominance or deference to experts which characterises strategic thinking elsewhere, the character of the US debate should gladden the hearts of democrats.[5]

Interestingly, American peace research shares many of the problems of American strategic studies. Its drift to empire has been almost as extensive. It is at least as shot through with implicit value assumptions. It is equally full of superpower concerns. It is even more lacking in historical perspective. It is even more quantitative, thereby avoiding those areas that are not amenable to quantification. It projects Western liberal values and assumes that others share (or should share) the same norms about violence and war. It often demonstrates naivity about world affairs (equal but opposite to that of the archetypal strategist), and this includes a particular myopia towards strategists, whom it caricatures. Finally, the jargon of peace research is at least as obfuscating as that of strategic studies. Peace research should be important, but is presently not impressive. And as far as individuals are concerned, one is tempted to conclude that the virtues of peace researchers seem riskier than the vices of strategists.

The Demise of Strategic Man

If strategic studies are to be improved, it is necessary to embrace more completely the idea of strategic relativism, the idea that truth in strategy is relative to the individual or group in question and to the time and place in which the individual or group acts. In talking about the demise of Strategic Man it should be stressed that we are not contemplating eliminating the assumption of rationality from strategic analysis. In this respect we should keep in mind the distinction between strategic analysts and strategic decision-makers. As John Garnett has carefully pointed out, strategic analysts do sometimes assume rationality, 'not because they believe decision-makers will always act rationally, but because, for the purposes of analysis it is very difficult to make any other assumption. In short, the value of the rationality assumption is in its *explanatory* rather than its *predictive* power. It demonstrates the logic in strategic postures, but it offers no guarantees that statesmen will abide by that logic.'[6]

Rationality has its place, but Strategic Man does not, except in the context of a particular nation, and then only with the utmost caution. 'Strategic Man' in the abstract is Western Strategic Man writ large, which is a perfect example of the methodological fallacy of ethnocentrism. Strategic relativity is the counter to this, and three interrelated changes would help increase our sensitivity to this idea. They are: (1) *Interdisciplinary strategic studies:* In order to encompass all relevant ideas, and better explain what happens, the net of strategic studies needs to be cast more widely than at present. (2) *Cultural relativism:* In order to move towards a posture of sophisticated realism, in which threats are neither exaggerated nor ignored, there needs to be a conscious effort to work towards overcoming ethnocentric distortion. (3) *Administrative and procedural innovation:* In order to move in these directions, and also minimise the misperceptions and failures caused by groupthink and other distorting and irrational effects, we might introduce reforms to create a more favourable setting for independent, realistic and broad thinking.

The obstacles to change are considerable. Strategic Man is more alive and kicking in most of our heads than we would care to admit. As a start, each of us needs to ask when he or she last sat down to think about a problem from the perspective of a Soviet planner, a black African guerrilla, a PLO spokesmen and so on. We all tend to fit new information into our preconceptions, and tend to avoid the discomforting possibility that there are different versions of truth about the same situation. There are no magical solutions to our problems, only better habits. But even better habits are not easily achieved, or we would not need New Year resolutions. However, we can talk about more hopeful directions and, without expecting confidence in complete success, we should hope to be able to reduce the probabilities of error. The prize is important: strategic theory would better fit strategic reality. Universities, as unique and independent centres of learning, have a peculiar opportunity and responsibility in developing these better habits.

There are many research problems for those who would make strategic studies less culture-bound. Inevitably it will be difficult for the student of strategy to travel in and do research upon military matters in countries which may be in an adversary relationship with his own. Military subjects are often sensitive: one's own government and armed forces tend to be prickly enough towards interested outsiders. For those wanting to specialise on foreign countries, there are nearly always language problems involved, and this is a deterrent even to the most well-meaning. This in turn further intensifies the inbred character of the subject: just as the mathematically inclined social scientist is drawn into narrow areas which are quantifiable, so the budding strategist is drawn into studying that which is said in his own language. Progress is further obstructed by administrative constraints, caused by teachers and their students having too much to do and too little time in which to do it. There are additional problems arising from the uncongenial nature of military affairs, which has meant that they have attracted little interest on the part of area studies specialists. In short, in most respects there are easier paths to glory for the young scholar. But the task is not hopeless: there are helpful steps we all can take.

Some reforms could be started with existing resources. Improvements can be made simply by reorganising what already exists. Reading material on strategy courses might include more material on foreign countries, and there might be much more encouragement that it be read. We live in an age of tokenism. It is not only necessary to get more books about foreign countries onto reading lists: it is also important that they be read. To the extent that works about foreign countries are included, they are presently accorded a low priority. Improvement means that the teacher should raise his/her own consciousness and show more awareness of the problem of strategy in a multicultural world. And if the teacher cannot manage to extend his own efforts in new directions, he can at least encourage others to do so. This in itself is an effortless but potentially significant contribution. In this way the inertia might be overcome which implicitly or explicitly determines that the American nuclear theologists of the massive retaliation/flexible response years are what the subject is all about. Students should avoid becoming prisoners of the gilded theorists of the golden age.

Students can hardly be blamed for being culture-bound if their teachers are, and if they are not encouraged to adopt a wider approach. Teaching by example is still perhaps the most effective pedagogical technique. An effective teacher should aim to awaken the curiosity of his students before the incuriosity of the profession sets in. Time will be a problem, but much can be done within existing courses. It is possible to encourage students to read books on alternative approaches, to give space in lectures for alternative views, to propound different philosophies of war, to start to become an area specialist, to go back into strategic history, and to be more sensitive to different perspectives on 'truth'. In the teaching context, strategic studies need broadening rather than deepening.

Within the inevitable time constraints in teaching, the question is: what should go if strategic studies are broadened? If it is hard to say what is the right kind of strategy teaching, it is easier to see what the wrong kind is. What must go is the notion that a course on 'national security policy' constitutes a satisfactory programme of strategic studies. Organising a course around the problems of one's own country is relatively easy, both for the teacher giving it and the students seeking to understand it. But a course on strategic studies should do more than that. Instead of concentrating on the defence problems of one's own country, teachers should try to explain how strategy is conceived from different national standpoints, how different philosophies of war have evolved and relate to each other, and they should examine different historical experiences and a range of national styles of thought about strategic doctrine. If this broader approach is done well, it will be eye-opening for students, and they will not forget it; on the other hand, commentary on current defence problems may be quickly forgotten as new issues arise. Universities are not training grounds for current-affairs commentators. The aim of strategy teaching should be to move students towards a deeper understanding of the nature of strategy and the character of strategic activity. The aim is trained minds, not minds trained in a rapidly obsolescent and fairly narrow range of literature.

If strategic studies are to escape the grip of ethnocentrism and its partner megalogic, and if they are to escape inertia and its partner in-breeding, then the subject needs extending in at least the following dimensions: (i) strategic history, (ii) culture and war, (iii) social psychology, and (iv) area studies. At its bedrock should be the study of international politics, conceived widely and based in the humanities. What this basically entails is a commitment to integrate a wider range of approaches and ideas into strategy courses.

Strategic History

The single most valuable step for the improvement of strategic studies is to introduce students to the subject via strategic history. Being systematically led through the relevant literature is an invaluable starting point for a student; it provides a unique and varied opportunity for the development of strategic judgement. There already exists a substantial and well-established (but certainly improvable) literature. There are general synoptic works,[7] works on national traditions[8] and monographs on specific episodes.[9] With more detailed knowledge of the historical evolution of the strategic hopes and fears, policies and processes, problems and styles, and successes and failures of a range of countries over a number of periods of history, the student will temper the worst effects of ethnocentrism and megalogic and will have the raw material for endless mental exercise.

The advantages of approaching the subject via the strategic history of a variety of countries are manifold. The history of strategy gives the student an understanding of national traditions and idiosyncracies in strategic thinking; it gives an idea of the complexity of causation and the significance of the dynamism of events; it adds perspective, by indicating the source of ideas and movements; it adds understanding and knowledge about foreign countries; it gives a feel for what is enduring and what is transient, and what is important and what is unimportant; it provides material to assist in the development of analytical criteria for assessing strategy, strategists and their concepts; it gives an appreciation of what being an 'expert' entails, by showing what is involved in going into a subject in depth; it helps in the use and the criticism of analogies; it helps to focus thinking in terms of national outlooks; within the limitations of the concept, it assists the characterisation of national 'styles'; it shows the role of the contingent and the unforeseen, and their effects on successes and failures, and is thereby a warning against complacency on matters of theory in human affairs; it should warn one against any tendency to exaggerate the degree of control which statesmen have over their environment; it provides perspective for forecasting; it develops research skills and analytical criteria which can be useful when attention is turned to the modern period; it provides the opportunity for the exercise of judgement over a very wide variety of circumstances, national outlooks, and technologies; it should sensitise students to the importance and variety of individual psychological realities which affect political affairs; it will provide the basis of an understanding of why different national answers may arise to the same strategic problems; it is a corrective for those who believe that the only good idea is a new idea; and it helps break down stereotypes. In short, if approached in a sophisticated manner, history not only provides a good liberal education, but is also the best single introduction to strategic studies. Eschewing the lessons approach, facile analogies, simple extrapolation and the other dangers of (crude) historical studies, the student will find strategic history a healthy breeding ground for scepticism and judgement. History will not give us answers to our present predicaments, but it is a poor student whose judgement will not be sharpened and deepened and who will not be able to ask better questions about contemporary problems as a result of a good course in the history of strategy. In studying strategic history we participate in a time-transcending dialogue with a fascinating variety of theorists and practitioners.

Culture and War

War is a cultural phenomenon (some would say a cultural disease). Unless we attempt to understand the character of different cultures, it will be impossible to appreciate the mainsprings of national strategies. Without knowing about the 'pride, prestige or prejudice, moral outrage, insistence on survival, vanity and vengeance' of different societies,[10] how can we begin to appreciate the roles which such important peoples as the Arabs, black and white Africans, Israelis and Vietnamese might play in contemporary and future military problems? Cultural relativism is one of the 'nails' for the want of which our subject may not hold together. Personality, society and culture form a continuous whole. Society and culture affect perceptual interpretation, motivation, behavioural norms and the structure of man's expectations; man organises his cognition and perception of reality in terms of cultural meanings and values.[11] This is true of war and strategy, as it is of other areas of life: it is therefore an important approach for those who want to understand strategy.

Strategy, society and culture cannot be divorced unless strategy is to be understood as a mere technique. Clausewitz recognised that strategy was a reflection of society, but this dimension was ignored by most later writers. Words and actions have meaning not in themselves but in the meaning given to them by their particular culture. Cultures need to be recognised as morally and intellectually distinct orders; the forces which give authenticity and continuity to their thoughtways need to be isolated; and comparative studies of societies, institutions, processes and ideas should not proceed on the assumption that a word, however common its usage, has unequivocal connotations in all areas of the world. The diversity of thoughtways in the world results in a great diversity of attitudes to those phenomena we understand as 'war', 'violence' and 'strategy'.[12] This point has further implications. In particular, it suggests that the Western definition of 'war' is too narrow if we wish to appreciate the meaning of organised military violence in a comprehensive fashion. It is too narrow from several viewpoints: (1) By equating the concept of war with the political philosophy of

Clausewitz, we overlook both the diversity and changeability of philo-sophies of war. We fail to recognise the extent to which the Clause-witzian philosophy is rooted in the European nation-state idea, an idea which itself is mutable. If society is moving out of the classical age of European chauvinism, in which the nation-state was seen as the embodi-ment of most ideals, the possibility arises that the philosophy of war which accompanied that period of history may also change. (2) By con-centrating on the strategy of conflict — the 'game' of manipulating force — we limit our attention only to the overt phase of the activity.[13] We therefore tend to avoid thinking about the day-to-day conflict which sometimes intensifies in the direction of war. To know about strategy but not about conflict is as possible and as dangerous as to know about surgery but not about medicine. (3) The prevailing Euro-centric definition of war results in our overlooking a considerable amount of human violence. Western strategists have sometimes argued that communal wars are ignorable because they do not disturb inter-national order; they are said to be 'domestic'. The last fifteen years have demonstrated how regional violence has proliferated in scale and importance. Often it is difficult to know in advance which local conflicts will have a wider impact, especially as there seems to be an increasing possibility that outside powers might be dragged into them. But the names of Angola, Eritrea, the Ogaden and Shaba Province in recent years have symbolised both the propensity of some 'local' conflicts to have wide impact, and the risks of involvement by extra-regional nations — and not only the superpowers, but also such paladins of ideological and national advancement as the Cubans and, embryonically, the French.[14] Furthermore, if we ignore the multitude of lesser conflicts which take place, we will underestimate the extent of social conflict throughout the world, and so tend to exaggerate the degree of order which exists. Vietnam is a good example. There has been fighting in that country for nearly forty years, but since the withdrawal of the United States there has been a flight of attention on the part of Western observers which has been at least as hasty and massive as was that of the final American forces. But fighting goes on, now against Cambodia. Historians of the future might characterise this present phase as a 'forgotten war', but for contemporaries there are really no such things. If it is 'forgotten', it is not a 'war': it is merely regarded as a way of life.

In a physically shrinking world, all outbreaks of violence are of con-cern, even when they are ostensibly 'domestic'. They should not be defined out of the strategist's area of enquiry. There was a time when an incipient conflict in Vietnam appeared to be an internal matter. In the late 1950s most outsiders knew little about it, and could not have cared less: by the early 1960s others imagined they knew a great deal about it, and could not have cared more.

Social Psychology

If strategic studies is to take on a human face, it is necessary for the subject to break out of what Brian Porter has called the 'state-jacketed' approach which characterises academic international politics, and instead embrace more levels of analysis. In examining these other levels social psychology can be a source of useful insights, especially if associated with a decision-making approach.

If strategic analysis is to penetrate more deeply into its subject matter, the psychological dimension cannot be ignored. As an approach to 'the essence of decision', the conceptual models discussed by Graham Allison are enormously useful but, as the author himself admitted, his work did not go far enough.[15] Amongst the missing links is the study of the psychological dimension in decision-making. Why men as individuals and groups behave in the manner in which they do may be a matter of individual and group psychology as well as of reason and politics. Military decisions are therefore amenable to psychological as well as 'normal' political science interpretations. Whether or not one agrees in detail with Norman Dixon's analysis, he has certainly established the relevance of psychological factors for an understanding of military incompetence.[16]

In strategy, as in all human behaviour, image and reality are inextricably mixed. The facts of a battle, like the Rorschach ink blot, are objectively the same, but our minds give them different meanings. The examination of this problem is generally an unattended part of the strategic puzzle: this is hardly surprising, for psychology is a subject which is fraught with difficulties, even for its own professionals. It is unrealistic therefore to expect too much from strategists. Social psychology is concerned with topics such as language, stereotypes, perception, memory, motivation, communication, attitude change, influence between people and reference groups, behaviour under stress, socialisation, group structure and dynamics and prejudice.[17] This range of topics is of evident relevance for any study of decision-making. Strategists can make much more use of the findings and insights which do exist, especially from those who have tried to bridge the fields of psychology and international politics.[18] Robert Jervis for example has demonstrated most successfully how the two fields can be brought together to improve our understanding of the causes and consequences of misperception, characteristic perceptual errors in decision-making, and the organisation and use of knowledge. Strategists cannot fail to sharpen their insights by the scientific study of 'mental processes [and behaviour] in so far as these are determined by past or present interaction with other persons'. The study of social psychology should make the amateur psychologist (who inhabits all our heads) slightly less so.

Area Studies

Strategic studies divorced from area studies is largely thinking in a void. The general neglect of area studies is one of the biggest criticisms which can be levelled against strategists. The *process* of strategic thinking apart from the study of particular countries is little better than prejudice. What matters here is not the quality of the end-product, but the process. It makes all the difference to the validity of an idea whether it is based on evidence and systematic study or upon hearsay and preconceived notions. Unfortunately, much so-called strategic thinking is based on a most superficial attempt to understand different national outlooks.

The expansion of the area studies dimension must be an important ingredient in any development in strategic studies. Knowing the enemy is a central activity in strategy, but it has been notoriously badly done, and the chronic incuriousness of strategists remains. There should have been a close relationship, but there has not been. The role of the area-studies specialist has been both small and neglected.

The 1960s showed up the poverty of the relationship between area studies and the theory and practice of strategy in Western thinking. Vietnam was the saddest example. There were few area experts in the West and those who existed were badly used. To point to this neglect is not to assert that a better outcome would inevitably have occurred had they been better used: strategy is more complex than that, and area specialists have honest (and prejudiced) differences of opinion. But one can say, for better or worse, that the guesses on which policy was made would have been educated guesses. The void would have been filled with knowledge and ideas, not left free for logic and ethnocentric pre-dispositions. The war showed the dangers of strategic thinking which is not based on a thorough knowledge of the nations concerned. This is all the more lamentable in wars which are overtly 'political', involving the the winning of hearts and minds, as well as success on the battlefield. Decisive military superiority can bring victories on battlefields, but strategy is also about creating the conditions for winning the peace, and the latter will not be possible in limited or revolutionary wars without a thorough understanding of the area concerned. Such an understanding is a necessary but not sufficient condition for victory. In Vietnam US policy was flawed because it was based on an unsatisfactory knowledge of the enemy (and its determination to fight) and of the client (and its limited ability to build a viable state). Even worse, it was also flawed because some important US policy-makers seemed not to understand the mood and working of their own country.

The strangest neglect by the strategic studies community has been of Soviet military affairs. Incredibly, given its real-world significance, Soviet foreign and military policy has attracted a derisory number of Western scholars. The steady growth of Soviet studies in the 1950s and 1960s did not help as much as it might, for the emphasis was always on domestic affairs.[19] The situation has improved markedly, but the neglect and incuriousness of mainstream strategists about the Soviet Union remains a remarkable feature of contemporary strategic studies. It is the more remarkable since the Soviet Union has been the only state able to pose a devastating threat to the US heartland and in the light of the fact that the Soviet arms build-up since the mid-1960s has posed the single most important empirical strategic question of the period. But how many of the 'community' have seriously tried to answer it? It remains a relatively unexplored question although one's assumptions about it help determine one's ideas about the validity of arms control, deterrence, detente and many other major issues. Strategic theory rests on empirical foundations, but to the extent that one's assumptions about these foundations are based on stereotypes, newspaper headlines and half-remembered fragments from the few half-forgotten books of one's student days, then clearly one's theory will rest on sand. Soviet strategy is the most important strategic problem of the day: nevertheless, the roll-call of specialists in the subject remains remarkably small.[20] The specialists' impact on mainstream strategists is even smaller.

Significantly, neglecting to study one's adversary is not just a Western phenomenon. The study of the United States by Soviet analysts has generally been even more backward. Until recently the studies which have emerged have been unsophisticated and rigid. Only recently does it appear that the higher authorities have become concerned about encouraging serious studies of the United States.[21] Soviet studies of China have been beset by many of the same problems and attitudes. Although Soviet Sinology has developed since Stalin's death, it has not been on a scale commensurate with Soviet involvement with China or of a quality to cope with the complex requirements of that relationship.[22] Clearly, the big three have not made every effort to know each other, and they are only belatedly trying to catch up. In the business of strategy, strange as it may seem, contempt has not bred familiarity.

But familiarity with one's adversaries is a prerequisite for sophisticated strategic thinking. It is important for the successful (and efficient) manipulation of military power. It is liberating because it gives us a different way of looking at the world. And it is useful because it should tell us something about our own thinking and behaviour: it should help us approach our own problems with fresh eyes, give us new insights into our predicaments, and help us to minimise our fallacies. They do not know American strategy who only American strategy know.

To an outsider to the profession this tale of incuriosity must seem incredible. It is an aspect of the subject in which strategists can rightly be criticised for complacency, arrogance and less than professional competence. The mainstream strategist is keen to trace the lineage of nuclear theory in immense detail, but he often assumes that his under-standing of adversaries and allies is something which can be picked up on the side. This conceit is not edifying: it is all the more bizarre given the demands for sophistication in other areas of the subject. But what is the sense in tracing the intellectual history of something like limited war theory but avoiding the nature of Soviet strategic policy? Due to the unsystematic approach to studying the strategy of other nations, there is a tendency for what is picked up to be out of perspective. Strategists are predisposed to look for the worst, and their rolling stone approach to information-gathering means that only moss of the most prickly variety has any chance of sticking. The image of Soviet society held by the mainstream strategist is usually very different from that portrayed by specialists in Soviet domestic politics, or even Soviet diplomacy. The various images touch all too infrequently, for Western scholarship about the Soviet Union is badly compartmentalised. 'Expert shall speak unto expert' is not a powerful maxim in Soviet and strategic studies.[23]

If the study of Soviet strategy has been under-intellectualised, it is hardly surprising that other areas have been even more neglected. There has long been a shortage of specialists on security problems in many significant regions of the world. In the 1960s only a handful of people could make any contribution to our understanding of China or the Middle East. At the present moment, with Africa thrust to the front of the stage, the absence of Africanists is as obvious as it will be important. As the quotations by Kissinger and Johnson at the head of this chapter indicate, there are still plenty of far-away countries about which we know little. Until 1977-8 how many of us were aware of the existence, let alone the problems, of the Ogaden, or Shaba Province? Africa is still a dark continent, even to the most important policy-makers. In this respect James Callaghan, the British Prime Minister, felt compelled to tell the US Administration in mid-1978 that 'There seem to be a number of Christopher Columbuses setting out from the United States to discover Africa for the first time. It's been there a long time.'[24] The sarcasm was well-directed. But it was also insufferably smug, coming from the leader of a country whose actions in the distant past had spawned many of the current problems, and whose government had evaded positive action in the recent past. Furthermore, despite its long involvement with Africa, Britain has only a very small body of expertise. Throughout the West, there may well be fewer African specialists in the late 1970s than there were Indo-China specialists in the early 1960s, although widespread violence in Southern Africa has been forecast for so long. The end of white minority rule in Africa is as predictable as was the end of slavery: the idea that one race can and should dominate another has nearly run its life-span. It is no longer a question of whether change will take place, but rather of *how* and *when, who* will dominate *whom,* and *which* outside power will take the advantage. Trouble has been forecast for so long, but our knowledge has not increased. The lid has been held down while rapid evolution has been taking place below. In southern Africa, the more things have stayed the same, the more they have changed.

As is often the case, we start to learn about the geology of an area only when the volcano makes threatening noises. Clearly, it would be sensible for long-term planners to think about areas of possible eruption in the foreseeable future and to build up banks of expertise. In trying to identify the shatter zones of international relations the involvement of area experts will be vital, for one thing is clear. No area specialist is unimportant in an interdependent world where local identities are being asserted, where numerous old causes of conflict exist, where new stresses are being created, and in which superpower competition is not being reduced.

The area studies input into strategic thinking has been neglected and is presently not satisfactory, but it has been improving. The last ten years have seen a small but steady accumulation of more respectable literature. The Soviet Union has been the main focus of attention, but there has been a trickle in other areas. We now have translations of some of the military classics of other countries;[25] we have much more translation of recent Soviet military writing;[26] we have a growing number of serious analyses of aspects of Soviet military policy[27] and Chinese defence policy;[28] and we have at least the start of a flow of some relevant materials on Third World problems.[29] Finally, there has been a growing body of writing which has sought to explain the ideas and images which different nations have of their interests, concepts and adversaries.[30] This has been one of the most promising trends of recent years: clarifying such images is one of the most useful tasks which area studies specialists can perform for strategists in particular but also for political scientists and policy-makers as a whole.

The fusion of area-studies specialists and strategists is not a panacea for the ills of strategic studies, however. Take language learning for example. It goes without saying that language is an important tool for those keen to understand other societies. But a foreign language is only one of the relevant languages for the aspiring analyst. Strategic studies itself has its own language (and dialects), which requires its own dictionaries and books of grammar. One must guard against the assumption that the area specialist knows what he is talking about, especially if he moves into the military field. Benjamin Franklin's dig at linguists is apposite: we all remember characters who, like Tim, were 'so learned that he could name a horse in nine languages; so ignorant that he bought a cow to ride on'.[31] Similarly, we all probably know area specialists who are sucked into strategic discussions because of their scarcity value, but who interpret evidence idiosyncratically because they have no military frame of reference. They know the meaning of the words of strategy in foreign lands in a lexicographical sense, but not in a strategic one.

Just as language is no panacea, neither is travel. The idea that it broadens the mind is one of the prevailing myths of the twentieth century. It can only broaden minds capable of being broadened. Thomas Fuller put it well: if an ass goes travelling, it will not come home a horse. At least as often as broadening the mind, or giving 'feel' or insight, travel merely confirms prejudices. Appropriately, it was a strategist who said that travel merely proved that 'abroad is worse'. Travelling can be broadening, but it can also give a spurious air of authority to the dilettante. Students must be on guard. People in general see only what they want to see, and most travellers are nothing fancier than moving people.

Strategy is about muddling through. There are no golden roads, only better senses of direction. Strategy will never be an exact science, but that is no reason why it should remain a primitive art. The better use of historians and area specialists should minimise some of the sources of error and help the framing of better questions. There are many problems involved in implementing such an evidently sensible recommendation, however. Financial constraints are but one.[32] Area studies specialists themselves are not final authorities. Area specialists can give different perspectives and knowledge, but they are neither objective nor unbiased. Area specialists fall into all the familiar camps of prejudice, including ethnocentrism. The fact is that there can be no 'final' authorities in this subject. One must therefore choose one's area specialists with all the care with which one would choose one's historian,[33] and then assess what is said with one's best judgement. What usually happens in practice, however, is that one chooses the area specialist who has a view of the adversary which conforms with one's own. Nevertheless, whatever their foibles, area studies specialists should have information, insights and skills (especially linguistic) which strategists do not have. In addition, strategists themselves might consider developing in this direction, both for its own sake and to improve their critical abilities. If mainstream strategy has presently reached the infertile plateau which many have claimed in recent years, then the law of diminishing returns suggests that strategists move into other areas, where richer soil may await them. Strategists should accept, in deed as well as word, that they live in a multi-cultural world.

Towards Strategic Relativism

If the simple notion of Strategic Man is at least to be replaced by the notion of national strategic man, then our images of other nations need to be built up by imagination as well as knowledge. Earlier chapters have shown that important problems in strategy have arisen not from an absence of facts about an adversary, or negligence in conventional thinking patterns ('vertical thinking'), or even any dereliction of professional duty in any narrow sense. What has been missing, and what has caused failure, has often been a lack of understanding in a deeper imaginative sense, that is, an inability to construct accurate images of how another perceives 'reality', how he sees himself and wants to be seen, and how he feels about his hopes and fears. If achieved, such intimate understanding is called empathy. Some, especially the technically oriented, may well cringe at the intrusion of such a word as empathy into strategic terminology, but as a direction it is an imperative, even if as a goal it may not be attainable.

A good example of the gulf between factual knowledge and 'feel' (ultimately becoming empathy) has been the Englishman's congenital inability to understand nationalism. This failure has often resulted in bewilderment when faced by groups who prefer self-government (and from the English viewpoint, inevitably 'worse' government) to than British government. Significantly, this bewilderment does not increase with distance from England itself. In fact, it has often been the case that the nearer the nationalist movement has been to England, the more difficult it has been for the average Englishman to understand that others should feel and think differently from himself, especially if they live on the same group of islands. Many Englishmen have shown an appalling arrogance and crass lack of intelligence in this regard. Other nations have usually had a better grasp of the English, or at least of their weaknesses. Since the time the English gave up using the big stick this has meant that nationalists have been able to exploit this knowledge to their own advantage, for knowledge is a source of power.

The pursuit of cultural relativism is liberating. The attempt to break out of one's cultural strait jacket is a challenging and exciting intellectual experience. To varying degrees we are all prisoners of time and place, and will always be so, but even to recognise this situation is to begin to put oneself in a position to try and counteract the distortions which ethnocentrism causes. Furthermore, deeper awareness of other viewpoints, problems and fallacies should help to equip us to approach our own problems with more perspective and insight. It is exciting to realise that philosophies of war are as ethnocentric as much narrower strategic concepts, and that there is nothing 'innate' or 'natural' about them. Another important and liberating experience is to realise and to feel the well-verified belief that all societies believe that they are the most peaceful. But at the same time one should also realise that there are many different ideas surrounding the conception of peace. The Middle Eastern imbroglio is instructive. In that war-ridden region the Israelis are thinking about peace and security while the Palestinians are thinking about peace and justice; the Western Europeans are thinking about peace and prosperity while the Soviet leaders are thinking about peace and ill-will. Not surprisingly, being most distant but having most external responsibility, the Americans want peace and quiet. The poor man-in-the-street, everywhere, hopeful and unheard, simply and naively wants peace and goodwill.

Looking at problems 'from the other side of the hill' involves imaginative attempts to internalise the hopes and fears of the adversaries concerned. This involves several difficult exercises. In particular, we tend to be unaware of the impact of our own actions on others, and we tend not to see the 'foreign-policy' events of other countries in terms of their domestic setting. We also find it difficult to try and erase the image of our own forces as inherently 'defensive', and instead see them as a threat. Some find this a disturbing and frankly impossible exercise, but those who achieve it experience an intellectual revelation. Attempting a relativist problem also involves overcoming the sort of blind-spot which could see as perfectly proper the idea of defending San Francisco beyond the Mekong, but could not appreciate the legitimacy of the Chinese desire to defend Peking beyond the Yalu. Dag Hammarskjold was aware of these difficulties when he looked at the problem of meditation. 'You can only hope to find a lasting solution to a conflict', he wrote, 'if you have learned to see the other objectively, but, at the same time, to experience his difficulties subjectively.'[34] War graves are evocative of these problems. How different war must seem — how much less an *adventure* and how much more a matter of physical *survival* — if one's border-lands are scarred with cemeteries for the dead of the country's wars. War can never have been conceived as such an ominous business by those nations for whom the fighting has always been 'over there', as with the salt-water strategies of Britain and the United States. For France, Russsia and Germany, on the other hand, war has invariably begun, or ended, by enemy invasion of national territory. It is not so much distance which cuts us off from other nations but our own historical memories, experiences and national ways of looking at things.

The desirability of empathy may be asserted, but one may well question whether it is really possible to experience another's difficulties 'subjectively'. One can possibly identify what somebody from another nation is thinking, or what a particular range of attitudes is, but can one really *become* one of that nation? Knowing by in-dwelling, to use Michael Polanyi's phrase,[35] is theoretically possible, but difficult in practice. But at least enough is knowable, for the diligent person, to perceive 'the other' in his own terms. The problem about going very far in this direction is that a man is more than the sum of his attitudes. The proverbs and literature of the nations attest to the difficulty of 'getting under somebody's skin', understanding his problems, feeling his fears and so on: 'The tears of strangers are only water', as a Russian proverb has it. Achieving empathy is difficult, among other reasons, because it normally requires us to see 'double', which goes against the tendency to dissonance reduction. It requires us 'to hold in suspension two interpretations of the same facts, the other fellow's and one's own'. Seeking certainty, the mind tends to rebel, and empathy is choked off.[36] However unsatisfactory the result, none the less the attempt to take on the 'internal frame of reference' of another self does have some benefits. It is one thing to note another's feeling intellectually, and add it as a 'factor' in some analysis, but it is more important still to recognise that such feelings suffuse the whole thinking of the other person. Such feelings may be strategically important because they affect such matters as the determination with which beliefs are held or the ability to change attitudes. Recognising and giving credit to the psychological realities of 'the other' is at least as important as recognising and giving credit to his weapons inventory, if security is to become the life-long companion of peace. Deepening understanding and sharpening imagination are amongst the most difficult educational tasks. Whether success is achieved may well depend more on temperament than training. All can agree that developing imagination should be a major aim in education, but agreeing upon the nature of imagination is another matter entirely. Imagination is 'that which creates mental images', but where do we go from there? This is no place to discuss the nature of imagination, but what is of relevance in the present discussion is that theory which sees imagination as lying within our control.[37] Imagination is seen as peculiar to rational beings, whose intellectual capacities transcend the fixation with the immediate which is characteristic of merely animal existence. Imagination can also be seen as an active force in understanding, drawing together the observed and hidden aspects of an object and crystallising them into a relatively coherent perception. In this way imagination is essential to comprehending the world, as opposed to merely looking at it. Imagination has a role in shaping our perceptions, in recreating images of things once experienced or perceived, and in producing the insight which separates the gifted from the merely workmanlike, or even the disastrous. Those decision-makers who are weak in imagination are often callous. Lest anyone dismiss the significance of imagination one has only to think of some recent examples from British history: Haig and the battle of the Somme, and Eden and the Foreign Office officials dealing with 'the victims of Yalta'. These men planned but they did not comprehend; they reasoned but they did not imagine. It has been said that all animals perceive, but only some imagine.[38] The same could be said about some strategists.

What can be done to help encourage student imagination in strategy? A variety of ideas come to mind. (1) The provision of knowledge itself should not be underestimated, for it helps to humanise our images of other countries, and it feeds imagination. One of the advantages of area studies is that it enables microanalysis: the concentration on the large scale is a barrier to rapport. (2) The attitudes of teachers themselves often need changing. As a profession teachers should try to avoid strategic groupthink. The sociology of a student's knowledge is interesting. How do students of strategy know what they know? It appears that students of strategy tend to become socialised very quickly, and rapidly take on the 'conventional convictions' of the profession. Typically anybody will pick up the conventional convictions of the middle-of-the-road exponent of the subculture into which he or she has moved. To change thinking it is necessary to encourage thinking in the first place, because the 'opinions that men hold are commonly not a result of any thinking on their personal part at all. Rather, they are the reflection in their minds of other men's reflections.'[39] The example which teachers give is therefore a matter of some importance. (3) It is also helpful to try to break out of the monocultural experience. In a sense it does not matter which other culture one adopts; the likelihood is that having once done it, one will then be more sensitive and receptive to any other different way of looking at reality. (4) Encouraging ways of seeing different points of view can take several forms, and can be attempted without the trouble of moving from one's own base. One such idea is 'the Rapoport debate',[40] in which the objective is not to prove that one's own position is correct, but to seek to understand the other's position. The approach adopted is that in a discussion each proponent should be required to state the opponent's position to the latter's complete satisfaction before advocating his own: this should minimise those aspects of the conflict based on misunderstanding. By adopting such a technique it is hoped that the student would look at a subject with fresh eyes. (5) In order to assist the cause of greater awareness, some experimental work has been done in international relations designed to provide students with cross-cultural and inter-disciplinary perspectives on social, economic and political life. Role-playing in simulation exercises is one example. The stress here is on doing rather than teaching, in accordance with such maxims as 'to do is to learn' (Japanese) or 'experience is the best teacher' (American). Some of these examples of 'active learning' are somewhat self-conscious, but they might help. A similar inspiration has led to some dissatisfaction with the 'detached' character of international relations as presently taught, and has resulted in some teachers worrying about introducing more of 'the human dimension' into the subject.[41] The basis is there: already a long list of potential contributions originating from anthropology, psychology and sociology, and applicable to international studies could be set forth.[42] New blood in the profession might also help. It would at least be interesting if more women were involved in strategic studies, though like all newcomers into a profession they have so far tended to overcome their insecurity by embracing the profession's conventional convictions. But if strategy is to be made to take on a human face, it would seem inappropriate to exclude one sex from the effort.

As anthropological literature stresses, the only antidote to ethnocentric prejudice is comparative knowledge of many cultures. But this is not easy to acquire. It is immensely difficult to translate oneself into a different culture, attempt to understand it, and then return and explain it to one's original culture in the words of the original culture. Strategists can hardly be expected to do better than professional anthropologists, but they are involved in only a small sector of life, and they can at least try. Transcending our ethnocentric outlooks and education is not an easy task. The problems facing the strategist in attempting to achieve cultural relativism are enormous. The strategist is fallible, with his own idiosyncracies and weaknesses. Being a product of a particular society (and subgroup) at a particular time, he is also likely to reflect the prejudices and preoccupations of that group and that time. The setting in which he works will affect the data he selects and how he chooses to interpret them, as will his own needs, experience, taste and interests. His knowledge and understanding will be imperfect. Strategists, like other scholars, are men of time and place, as well as of individual psychology and professional conditioning. The difficulties are great, but academics are too prone to allow the best to become the enemy of *as good as possible*.

With luck, we might minimise some of the grosser distortions, but we should have no false hopes about how far we can go, for men often do not know why they do things. The 'essence of decision', as Kennedy said, will always remain obscure.[43] But in clearing away the mists, and in identifying the fundamental problems, one thing at least is increasingly clear, namely that traditional (human) approaches are preferable to quantitative ones. Statistics are of obvious importance in strategy, but quantitative approaches have little relevance. The attempt to understand strategic processes and their manifestation in power and influence relationships between nations is not seriously amenable to quantification. Mathematical approaches have not proved themselves. The exploration of quantitative methods has been a laudable effort, but the actual contribution has been disappointing, bearing no relationship to the ingenuity deployed, the pages covered or the claims made. 'The intellectual is constantly betrayed by his vanity,' wrote Ann Morrow Lindberg, 'God-like, he blandly assumes that he can express everything in words, whereas the things he loves, lives, and dies for are not, in the last analysis, completely expressable in words.'[44] The collective madness in the summer of 1914, Hitler's accelerating ambitions and his willing following, Khrushchev's 'quick-fixes', the hopes of the 'best and brightest' in the United States in the early 1960s — these strategically important phenomena are not completely amenable to the words we have. If they are not completely expressable in words, they are certainly not expressable in numbers.

Another dimension is required in strategic thinking. As in life in general, much strategic behaviour is not a matter simply of reasoning ability. Perhaps, as Bertrand Russell said, 'We know too much and feel too little.' [45] Bernard Brodie, for example, has rightly pointed to the importance of thinking more explicitly about feelings when we are engaged in prediction. [46] Important account has to be taken of such factors as hopes and fears, which require something other than factual knowledge and logic if the observer is to understand them (feel them subjectively) and then communicate that understanding to others. In the future, as in the past, the seminal elements of strategic life may well elude our analysis unless we begin to accept that to understand is to feel, as well as to know and to reason. The concept of the strategist needs expanding to match the changed concept of strategy, which itself has expanded greatly over the last two hundred years. We need saving from strategists who know the capability of everything but the value of nothing, and strategists with first-class minds but second-class hearts. As Clausewitz rightly pointed out, the good strategist needs a 'natural talent' or genius, as well as knowledge based on study or experience. [47] The aim, in modern parlance, is to develop 'trained intuition' and 'sophisticated realism', a judicious mixture of theory and practice based on intuition, experience, observation, contemplation, reasoning, imagination, reading and feel.[48] These qualities cannot be acquired by rote. Clausewitz created a book, *On War*, but a book on war could never of itself create a Clausewitz.

Self-Awareness in Policy Processes

The study of strategy is concerned with understanding the military world. The profession of strategy, on the other hand, is concerned with maintaining or changing it. Practitioners of strategy should presumably be interested in ways in which academic strategic studies might contribute to better policy prescriptions, and in ways in which their own processes may be improved.

Good strategic studies does not necessarily lead to good policy prescriptions any more than excellence in pure science is bound to lead to a thriving industrial nation. But if strategic studies is to make a contribution there are two immediate requirements: relevance and transmission belts. To be relevant (or rather to be seen as relevant) academics need to be acquainted with the problems facing policy-makers and need to 'speak the same language'. And there must be channels by which academic thinking about strategic problems can be communicated in a usable form to those who might want it. Meeting these requirements is more difficult than one might think.

Academic strategists have probably found it easier to achieve relevance than communication. Over the past twenty-five years the interests of academic strategists have tended to ebb and flow with changes in the interests of policy-makers in the world outside. Naturally, some strategists have properly gone off in esoteric directions, following their own interests rather than the call of relevance. For the most part, however, mainstream strategic studies has shared the same power-political outlook and interests as policy-makers. Those individuals who have not shared the same assumptions or language have been ignored. This is understandable, especially in relation to those branches of conflict resolution and peace research which are meaningful only to their own exponents. But a loss is also involved. By generally avoiding all but the mainstream, some valuable critiques of strategy, strategies, strategists and strategic theories have been neglected by the 'defence community', and not so much because of *what* was said, but because of the *person* saying it. Most policy-makers find it hard to accept criticism, but they find it doubly hard to accept from those they characterise as 'idealists'.

The problem of communication has generally been more serious than that of relevance. Transmission belts have been few. This is true of many other subjects. History is one major academic resource which has been wasted by policy-makers.[49] US administrations have sometimes neglected their own in-house historical expertise. Ernest May has described how some analysts in the CIA and the State Department's Bureau of Intelligence and Research had followed Vietnamese affairs for years. As it happens, they had usually been pessimistic in their estimates of the prospects for either South Vietnamese success or the effective US coercion of North Vietnam. But these specialists were not consulted by the incoming Kennedy Administration. Except for a few journalists, no one attempted to educate high-level officials about what had gone before. With unwarranted understatement, May wrote 'Looking back now, one was entitled to feel that this was at least an oversight.'[50] May also recalls how Dean Rusk, Kennedy's Secretary of

State, was both more knowledgeable about South-East Asian affairs and more sceptical than his colleagues in the Administration. However, despite his early caution about a large US military commitment he came to join the other members of Kennedy's inner circle favouring such a commitment.[51] It was a classic example of specialist knowledge being disregarded, and then of an erstwhile sceptic succumbing to groupthink. US policy in Vietnam was certainly not a unique experience in the way area experts have been disregarded. George Kennan has recorded his slight amazement, tinged with hurt pride, at the fact that nobody in Washington seemed to be interested in his views of conditions in the Soviet Union, although it was a country which he 'had just left and about which ... [he] was supposed to know something'.[52] It was also a country against which the United States was then engaged in a dangerous Cold War.

Improving the policy process therefore requires that experts — insiders as well as outsiders — be used more effectively. Occasionally there are bright spots. After the Carter Administration's initial misreading of the Soviet Union, marked by the latter's abrupt rejection of Carter's SALT proposals, Marshall Shulman was persuaded to join the State Department full time.[53] Shulman is a highly respected scholar in Soviet foreign-policy studies. Although academics have had their fingers burnt and reputations tarnished in Washington many times in the past, one cannot but agree with the rationality of trying to draw into government those who are thought to be amongst the very best foreign-policy analysts in their own areas. It is all very well to have specialists, but policy-makers should also have the processes and spirit to use them. Avoidable mistakes have frequently occurred for the want of shared information and ideas.

In contrast with the general overlooking of area specialists, a small but significant example of how much can be done occurred in World War II. In order to assist policy-makers the British Government set up a group to try and get inside the minds of their German opponents: at the outset, the group was appropriately called Future Operations (Enemy) Section (FOES). It was made up of German specialists and they did well at predicting the positions taken by various parts of the German bureaucracy. The experiment also showed the limits within which such forecasters operate. They failed to predict when Hitler would side with a particular faction, or when he would devise his own solution. But faced with a dictator such as Hitler, the experiment was evidently conducted under the most difficult circumstances, and surely what was impressive was the extent of what was achieved rather than what was not. Typically, 'back in the ministries' there was a good deal of fun poked at this effort to think like the enemy.[54] Such imagination is usually not part of the clay out of which bureaucrats are moulded.

Better policy prescriptions are not the point of strategic studies in a university environment, nor are they a necessary outcome, but neither are they an impossibility or a trivial by-product. On the contrary, the academic study of the subject can be helpful in providing different perspectives as well as basic research, and while the results of study in a university are not 'objective' they should be free from pressures of vested interest and immediate decision. For the academic study of the subject to have any effect, communication channels are needed, and so is an attitude of mutual responsiveness. This is not the place to discuss details of administrative change, because these will be greatly affected by the size, character and responsibilities of the organisations concerned. However, it is pertinent to highlight some of the dangers which competent and lively policy-makers and analysts might guard against. Self-awareness is particularly needed in relation to the following dangers:

The Danger of Ethnocentrism

This has been the main theme of this book. Ethnocentrism inevitably distorts the analysis which is at the basis of all strategic thinking and practice. In particular it distorts threat assessment, which theoretically at least is the main determinant of a nation's strategy. Ethnocentrism can be minimised by liberal education and by attempting to ensure that authoritarian personalities are avoided in posts where it matters. Increased contact with a multicultural and multiassertive world also argues for a more variegated recruitment policy for foreign ministries. In Britain, for example, the archetypal climber in the civil service is unlikely to have the social and political affinities which make for easy rapport with those foreign groups and nations which are insecure, unsuccessful, extremist and disadvantaged. Individuals can markedly affect policies. In view of the tale of incuriosity about foreign affairs exhibited by strategists, or policy-makers acting as strategists, it is no surprise to hear of odd appointments to positions of power. Selwyn Lloyd's posthumous book on Suez confirms this argument.[55] Lloyd records how astonished he was in 1951 at being made Secretary of State for Foreign Affairs. He told Churchill, the Prime Minister, that he had not been abroad except in the army and that he spoke no foreign language. He also added that he did not like foreigners (whether this strengthened Churchill's support of him as Foreign Secretary is not recorded). Most significantly, he said that he had never attended a foreign-policy debate. 'Churchill grandly waved all this aside.' Was this the experience and outlook which would equip a foreign secretary to see the faults of, let alone stand up to, a dogmatic and wrong-headed prime minister such as Anthony Eden in 1956? As it happens Eden himself had all the regular qualifications for dealing with foreign policy. He had travelled widely and had studied foreign languages; his experience at the Foreign Office was long and his interest in foreign affairs was deep. In the event, however, all this counted for little because of his anachronistic attitudes and personal weaknesses. He lacked imagination and empathy, and he was also ethnocentric. Together, his human failings overrode his more formal qualifications, and he engineered the biggest failure in British foreign policy since before World War II.

The Danger of Stereotypes

Friends and enemies cannot be 'known' if they are stereotyped. Overcoming this demands an open mind, a willingness to listen to those who have different views from the prevailing norm, and the accumulation of knowledge (which tends to humanise). A policy based on stereotypes is out of tune with the reality principle. Because of the prevalence of stereotyping in all areas of government it is perhaps even desirable that one's own diplomats do become 'captured' by that state to which they are accredited. Those who can effectively argue that the other country has a strong case are not being disloyal; they are doing a valuable service. Their analysis is important, though any recommendations which follow are not necessarily valid, because the policy-makers of the home country have a wider set of interests to consider. But for all involved, since stereotypes are such a potent feature in our thinking, self-awareness about one's prejudices is at a premium.

The Danger of Psycho-Logic

Psycho-logic substitutes emotional consistency for rational consistency. It involves carrying around in our heads certain basic concepts that are 'goods' or 'bads' emotionally, and which involve the striving to force a complicated world into an oversimplified mould. In Ralph Waldo Emerson's words, it is the 'foolish consistency' which is the 'hobgoblin of little minds'. And as Charles E. Osgood has suggested, the same hobgoblin rides in both big minds and high places.[56] Rather than maintain foolish consistency, a wise leader will tend to resist internal pressures towards a consistent mental picture: he will try to keep 'negative information' alive.[57] This is never easy, because of tendencies towards self-justification and rationalising behaviour. However, it can be countered somewhat if a decision-maker is willing to include in his group people with different temperaments and outlooks, though it obviously takes a man with a strong ego to encourage others to tell him 'not what he wants to hear, but what he ought to know'.[58] No system has ever been conceived which will ensure the adoption of such wise leaders. If countries get the leaders they deserve, hope can only lie in developing the worthy character of the society in which decision-makers are nurtured. It is not only leaders who need open minds: according to the 'creed' of the intelligence profession, an open mind to all new evidence must be one of their attributes (as must be a closed mind to all outside pressures to favour those interpretations that suit the political needs of the policy-makers).[59] In face of entreaties by policy-makers, the pressures of psycho-logic, and all the dynamics of group life, open minds perforce have a low life-expectancy. Against such odds, it is surprising how many of the intelligence community do survive so long, so well and so impressively.

The Danger of False Analogies

Many writers have stressed the dangerous pull which historical analogies can have on the thought patterns of decision-makers.[60] Since analysis and policy-making cannot be undertaken apart from history, it is imperative that better use be made of historical resources and that policy-makers become sensitive to historical argument. One of the current fashions for those who recommend changes in policy-making arrangements is for the encouragement of economic literacy, and preferably technical expertise. These skills are certainly desirable, but their usefulness will be undermined if the overall direction of policy is misconceived as a result of false premises about trends and situations. These false premises are often the consequence of misconceived historical analogies. What price strategic (or economic) expertise in a situation which has been falsely defined?

The Danger of Inertia

The easiest thing in life is to do today what was done yesterday. The belief that policy-makers may be lazy or have closed minds is not just a prejudice on the part of disillusioned voters: it is sometimes valid. One recalls a British prime minister, on being shown a report which indicated that he was wrong, declaring: 'Oh, for God's sake, take that stuff away. If I read it I shan't sleep.'[61] Sparing himself psychological difficulty in the short term, he contributed to the accumulation of every sort of difficulty for himself and his nation in the longer term. Inertia is especially powerful in the realm of ideas. Although it involves less physical effort than almost anything else, changing ideas is never easy. Bureaucracies in particular are notable for their resistance to change. Admittedly, the problems involved in major attitude change can be enormous,[62] but as the 'operational environment' changes, so should the perceptions of those charged with framing policy. Unfortunately, as Stoessinger found in his ten case studies, 'men do not easily abandon misperceptions through rational analysis but primarily through trauma and catastrophe . . . Man, in short, learns and grows largely through suffering.'[63] Adopting new administrative procedures might help,[64] but most important of all is the development of an attitude of individual self-awareness on the part of the policy-makers towards all the problems involved. Strategists and policy-makers often give the impression of being too certain. Their overly professional air sometimes appears to be a version of whistling in the dark, while their great confidence appears to be a manifestation of faith rather than reason. Doubting Thomas may not have been a New Testament hero; neither would he have made a great decision-maker or a congenial bureaucrat; however, he was the only one in his group temperamentally suited to be a social scientist and policy analyst.

The Danger of Groupthink

Strategy is made (if that is not too coherent a word) by groups: it is therefore vulnerable to the pressures of group dynamics. A sophisticated policy group will be aware of these dynamics, but often their excitement about an issue together with the rush of events overwhelms the ideas and hopes developed in periods of quiet and sober calculation. Even in normally busy times the pressures for conformity of viewpoint with respect to adversary images is high, in intelligence agencies for example. The bureaucratic and intragroup environment within which intelligence estimators work makes it hard to change adversary images, especially when there is ambiguity in the evidence,[65] which of course there nearly always is.

Various suggestions have been made towards identifying the symptoms of groupthink and of guarding against them.[66] One regular idea is the creation of devil's advocates. This sometimes works. We have recently seen in the PRM-10 exercise, which challenged some of the existing ideas about US strategy in Europe, the contribution which devil's advocates (and a few highly intelligent women) can make to the strategic debate.[67] In 1976, in order to test the allegedly 'soft' CIA estimates, the notion of a 'competitive estimate' was accepted, and two teams were created, one being the official CIA team while the other was made up of well-known 'hard-liners'.[68] Devil's advocates can be useful if policy-makers are willing to take their arguments seriously: not only do they present different arguments, but they also present fresh evidence. Their alternative mind-sets encourage them to cast their ideas in directions which would otherwise be ignored. It is interesting in this respect that Henry Kissinger promoted divisions within the intelligence community in order to generate data as well as alternative interpretations of the evidence.[69]

But the problem with devil's advocates is that they may well be regarded as no more than tokens. Their ideas may be disregarded *precisely because* they are propounded by people categorised as devil's advocates. Whom decision-makers wish to ignore, they first give the reputation of devil's advocate.

The ideas just identified may well strike the reader as platitudes. However, the dangers referred to are all related to important and interrelated mechanisms in the thinking of individuals and groups, mechanisms which risk undermining the rationality and realism of strategic thinking. Given the costs of strategic failure, it is surely not mistaken to repeat the obvious, especially when the 'obvious' in this case has so often been overlooked. The dangers need stressing, and the antidotes, even if those to whom the remarks are directed may not appreciate them for the very reason that they need to. The obstacles are evident.

One recognises the difficulties of asking a busy and ethnocentric profession to change, but change can take place. As has been shown in this book, devil's advocates have been created, groups have been formed to 'think like the enemy', there has been more education in military affairs, strategic studies have developed somewhat, official windows have been slightly opened to outsiders, stereotyping has been seen to be mistaken, more interest has been shown in the problems of perception and misperception in international politics, and area studies and strategy have occasionally moved together. The problems and the approaches to meeting them all underline the diversity of the world and the value of a diversity of methods directed towards understanding the world and dealing with it. But at the end of the day, even if improvements are made in policy processes, highly pinpointed prediction will remain impossible, and honest differences of opinion may remain both about one's proper aims and about what is rational for their pursuit.

The press of political affairs — such things as surprises, uncertainties and mistakes — is inexorable. As somebody said about life in general, strategy is 'simply one damned thing after another'.

The Greening of Academic Strategists

If bad anthropology makes for bad strategic studies, and if an interdisciplinary approach is necessary to eradicate bad anthropology, then it is evident that the concept of the mainstream academic strategist as it has developed since the late 1950s should be altered. So many security issues today are not amenable to the conventional strategic outlook that academic strategists — brokers in conflict, technique and capabilities — are not fully equipped to deal with them. What is required is a reinvigoration and a new consciousness in the profession. In this regard the strategic mode of thinking should never be allowed to trespass on the major part of an academic strategist's time. If it be argued that this would deprive him of the opportunity to read all that was being produced, then refuge can be taken in the thought that much of what is being produced is of marginal utility. If an interdisciplinary outlook is the bedrock of reform, the existing conception of the academic strategist will be diluted out of existence. By abolishing the idea of the professional academic strategist, we might move to *better* strategic studies.

Better strategic studies would be no small achievement, for it is a subject which focuses on the great issues of peace and war. For those who want 'relevance' from their universities, what could be more significant? So far the study of international politics since 1945 has largely concentrated on matters of high politics, especially military security, though as time has passed there has come a realisation that newer and less dramatic developments are also important. But military security and hence strategy remain of very special significance. Over the long term there may be equally great dangers to life as we know it, but the nuclear threat remains unique because of its destructive potential and immediacy. Even so-called conventional wars are extremely destructive. At this minute there are thousands of babies being born around the world; tons of pollution are being discharged; valuable non-renewable resources are being eaten up; and pressures are growing on renewable resources. Each of these developments threatens our existing way of life. But not yet. Only the thermonuclear threat could turn the world upside down in the time it takes to read this book. To extrapolate Heidegger, such an outcome is the possibility which cancels all our other possibilities.

The threat of nuclear war is one about which most of us have become resigned, although it is hard to imagine anything worse befalling the world. We have become *blasé* because we think it 'unthinkable', although we daily plan it and pay taxes to provision it. In the past it was possible for strategists to learn much from defeat, but at the highest levels of military violence this is a teacher which nobody can now afford. The peacetime study of strategy and the avoidance of strategic incompetence therefore take on a new urgency. We cannot afford failure, because a mistake can mean a unique form of disaster. Even success has its own dangers. In the past strategic success has often bred complacency. The same is true in the nuclear age. One of our fears for the future must be that as the 'success' of deterrence extends, so our sense of urgency and dread will subside. Already, the gap between the lower reaches of nuclear war and increasingly deadly 'conventional war' is visibly closing in front of our eyes: how long will it be before strategists confront the new problem of unthinking the thinkable? The insidious danger, in Marshall McLuhan's words, is that 'The price of eternal vigilance is indifference.'

Because of its evident importance, strategy is an area of public life which is too important to be left in the hands or minds of any narrow professional group or subgroup, with its own inertia, conventional convictions, parochial priorities, biases and limited horizons. Sixty years ago we learned in a most terrible way that war was too serious to be left to the generals. In the last fifteen years strategists have come to believe that peace is too precious to be left to the peace-researchers. It is now well past the time that they realised that strategy is too significant to be left to the strategists.

Notes

1. Ken Booth, 'The Evolution of Strategic Thinking' in Baylis *et al.*, *Contemporary Strategy: Theories and Politics* (London: Croom Helm, 1975), pp. 34-45.

2. Colin S. Gray, 'Across the Nuclear Divide – Strategic Studies, Past and Present', *International Security*, vol. 2(1), (Summer 1977), pp. 24-66. In earlier writing, Gray called this the 'second wave'; in this later reformulation the first and second-wave theorists belong to 1945-6 and 1955-65 respectively.

3. Stanley Hoffmann, *Gulliver's Troubles: Or, The Setting of American Foreign Policy* (New York: McGraw-Hill, 1968), pp. 148-61.

4. Yehezkel Dror, *Crazy States. A Counter Conventional Strategic Problem* (Lexington, Mass.: Heath-Lexington Books, 1971), Ch. 4.

5. See Ken Booth, 'American Strategy: The Myths Revisited", Ch. 1 in Ken Booth and Moorhead Wright (eds.), *American Thinking about Peace and War* (Brighton, Sussex: Harvester Press, 1978), pp. 6-7.

6. John Garnett, 'Strategic Studies and its Assumptions' in Baylis *et al.*, pp. 16-20.

7. E.g. E. M. Earle (ed.) *Makers of Modern Strategy*, 1st ed. (Princeton, N.J.: Princeton University Press, 1941); Theodore Ropp, *War in the Modern World*

168   *Strategy with a Human Face*

(New York: Collier, 1962).

8. E.g. Russell Weigley, *The American Way of War* (New York: Macmillan Co., 1973); Walter Gorlitz, *The German General Staff, Its History and Structure, 1657-1945* (London: Hollis and Carter, 1953).

9. E.g. G. Ritter, *The Schlieffen Plan, Critique of a Myth* (Horsham, Sussex: Riband Books, n.d. [first published in German in 1956].

10. Adda B. Bozeman, 'War and the Clash of Ideas', *Orbis,* vol. 20 (Spring 1976), p. 70.

11. Rudolph J. Rummel, *Understanding Conflict and War,* vol. 1: *The Dynamic Psychological Field* (New York: John Wiley and Sons, 1975), part V.

12. The relationship between local thoughtways and political concepts pervades the work of Adda B. Bozeman: see, inter alia, *Politics and Culture in International History* (Princeton, N.J.: Princeton University Press, 1960) and *Conflict in Africa* (Princeton, N.J.: Princeton University Press, 1976).

13. Bozeman, 'War and the Clash of Ideas, pp. 67-8.

14. The paladin idea is suggested by Edward Gonzalez, 'Complexities of Cuban Foreign Policy', *Problems of Communism,* vol. XXVIC Nov.–Dec. 1977), pp. 1-15.

15. Graham T. Allison, *Essence of Decision: Explaining the Cuban Missile Crisis* (Boston: Little, Brown & Co., 1971), p. 277.

16. See Norman Dixon, *On the Psychology of Military Incompetence* (New York: Basic Books Inc., 1976).

17. Roger W. Brown, *Social Psychology* (New York, Free Press, 1965), Introduction.

18. E.g. Irving L. Janis, *Victims of Groupthink. A Psychological Study of Foreign-Policy Decisions and Fiascos* (Boston: Houghton Mifflin Co., 1972); Robert Jervis, *Perception and Misperception in International Politics* (Princeton, N.J.: Princeton University Press, 1976); Otto Klineberg, *The Human Dimension in International Relations* (New York: Holt, Rinehart and Winston, 1964); Joseph DeRivera, *The Psychological Dimensions of Foreign Policy* (Columbus, Ohio: C. E. Merill Publishing Co., 1969).

19. Of the membership of the National Association for Soviet and East European Studies, only just over 1 per cent claim a special interest in military matters, and only 6 per cent in foreign policy in general.

20. For a long time the subject seemed to be the academic preserve of John Erickson, e.g. *Soviet Military Power* (London: Royal United Services Institute, 1971); Raymond L. Garthoff, e.g. *Soviet Military Policy: A Historical Analysis* (London: Faber and Faber, 1966); J.M. Mackintosh, e.g. *Juggernaut: A History of the Soviet Armed Forces* (London: Secker and Warburg, 1967); and Thomas W. Wolfe, e.g. *Soviet Strategy at the Crossroads* (Cambridge, Mass.: Harvard University Press, 1964).

21. Richard M. Mills, 'Soviet Views of the United States', *Problems of Communism,* vol. XXV(3) (May–June 1976).

22. E. Stuart Kirby, *Russian Studies of China: Progress and Problems of Soviet Sinology* (London: Macmillan, 1975).

23. 'A unique day in British academic life' was the way in which a leading specialist in Soviet military studies described a short conference in April 1977 at which academic specialists on Soviet military studies discussed matters of common interest with British officials. As ever, mainstream academic strategists were significant by their absence.

24. *Time,* 12 June 1978.

25. E.g. S. B. Griffith, *Sun Tzu: The Art of War* (Oxford: Oxford University Press, 1963).

26. E.g. the 'standard' text of Marshal V. D. Sokolovsky, *Soviet Military Strategy,* 3rd ed., trans. and ed. Harriet F. Scott (New York: Crane, Russak and

Co., 1975); a series of books prepared for the Soviet officer corps ('Soviet Military Thought') have been translated under the auspices of the US Air Force, and a series of books on aspects of Soviet strategy, with considerable Soviet material, have been compiled by the Center for Advanced International Studies at the University of Miami. A useful guide to Soviet literature is William F. Scott, *Soviet Sources of Military Doctrine and Strategy* (New York: Crane, Russak and Co., 1975).

27. In addition to the extensive work of the authors in note 19 above, see e.g. the range of contributions in Michael MccGwire, *Soviet Naval Developments* (New York: Praeger Publishers, 1973); Michael MccGwire, *et al., Soviet Naval Policy: Objectives and Constraints* (New York: Praeger Publishers, 1975); and Michael MccGwire and John McDonnell, *Soviet Naval Influence. Domestic and Foreign Dimensions* (New York: Praeger Publishers, 1977).

28. E.g. Arthur Huck, *The Security of China* (London: Chatto and Windus, 1970); Allen S. Whiting, *The Chinese Calculus of Deterrence* (Ann Arbor, Mich.: University of Michigan Press, 1975).

29. E.g. Bozeman's works cited above or, in a different vein, Frantz Fanon, *The Wretched of the Earth* (New York: Grove Press Inc., 1968). In addition, an extensive literature has built up on the role of military establishments in Third World politics; see the useful bibliography in S. E. Finer, *The Man on Horseback. The Role of the Military in Politics* (Harmondsworth, Middx: Penguin Books, 1976), pp. 277-91. The International Institute for Strategic Studies has reflected the need for the strategic community to concern itself with affairs outside the main East–West conflict. This can be seen in the growth of attention to regional security matters in the Institute's annual *Strategic Survey* and in the titles of *Adelphi Papers*.

30. E.g. Stephen P. Gilbert, *Soviet Images of America* (New York: Crane, Russak and Co., 1977); Peter Vigor, *The Soviet View of War, Peace, and Neutrality* (London: Routledge and Kegan Paul, 1975); William Welsh, *American Images of Soviet Foreign Policy* (New Haven, Conn.: Yale University Press, 1970); William Zimmerman, *Soviet Perspectives on International Relations 1956-1967* (Princeton, N.J.: Princeton University Press, 1969).

31. Bernard Brodie's comments about General Maxwell Taylor (Chairman of the Joint Chiefs of Staff, Ambassador to Saigon, and informal adviser in the 1960s) come to mind in this respect: 'urbane, a dedicated acquirer of languages . . . unable to understand why the North Vietnamese launched the Tet offensive . . . [and] totally lacking any comprehension of, let alone dedication to, the qualities and requirements of democracy in his own country'. *War and Politics* (London: Cassell, 1973), pp. 191-3.

32. In Britain, for example, the Political Science and International Relations Committee of the Social Science Research Council considered 92 applications for research grants within their field between April 1972 and March 1974. Of these under one-third could be classified as area studies (over one-third dealt with Western Europe). Of the 16 awards finally granted for area studies research, eight were for research on Western Europe and North America. There was one for research on the Soviet Union and Eastern Europe, and four for work on Asia. *SSRC Newsletter*, no. 28 (June 1975), p. 11.

33. E. H. Carr, *What Is History?* (Harmondsworth, Middx: Penguin Books, 1970), Ch. 1.

34. Quoted from Dag Hammarskjold, *Markings,* 11.9-20.55, by Brian Urquhart, *Hammarskjold* (New York: Knopf, 1972), p. 32.

35. Quoted by Adda B. Bozeman, *The Future of Law in a Multicultural World* (Princeton, N.J.: Princeton University Press, 1971), p. ix.

36. Ralph K. White, *Nobody Wanted War: Misperception in Vietnam and Other Wars* (Garden City, N.Y.: Doubleday, 1968), p. 284.

170   Strategy with a Human Face

37. Roger Scruton, 'Realities and Unrealities', *Times Literary Supplement,* 15 Oct. 1976.

38. Ibid.

39. See C.A.W. Manning, *The Nature of International Society* (London: Macmillan, 1975), pp. 88-90.

40. Anatol Rapoport, *Fights, Games and Debates* (Ann Arbor, Mich.: University of Michigan Press, 1960), part III and pp. 313-15.

41. Note the discussion in 'Human Approaches to the Teaching of International Relations', *International Studies Notes,* vol. 4, issue 2 (Summer 1977), pp. 31-7.

42. E.g. Charles A. McClelland, *Theory and the International System* (New York: Macmillan Co., 1960), pp. 120-37.

43. Quoted by Allison, *Essense of Decision,* Preface.

44. Ann Morrow Lindberg, *The Wave of the Future. A Confession of Faith* (New York: Harcourt, Brace and Co., 1940), p. 6.

45. Bertrand Russell, 'The Role of the Individual', *Authority and the Individual* (London: Allen and Unwin, 1949), pp. 61-2.

46. Note the interesting discussion on the notion of vital interests in Brodie, *War and Politics,* Ch. 8.

47. Carl von Clausewitz, *On War,* trans. by Michael Howard and Peter Paret (Princeton, N.J.: Princeton University Press, 1976), Book III, Ch. 2, pp. 146-7.

48. Manning, *International Society,* p. 137.

49. Ernest R. May, *'Lessons' Of The Past. The Use and Misuse of History in American Foreign Policy* (New York: Oxford University Press, 1973).

50. Ibid., p. 174.

51. Ibid., pp. 88-97.

52. George F. Kennan, *Memoirs 1950-1963,* vol. II (Boston: Little, Brown and Co., 1972), p. 172.

53. *Time,* 24 Apr..1978.

54. Donald McLachan, *Room 39* (New York: Atheneum, 1968), pp. 251-60.

55. Discussed by Keith Kyle, 'Interpretations of Suez', *Listener,* 22 June 1978.

56. Charles E. Osgood, *An Alternative to War or Surrender* (Urbana, Ill.: University of Illinois Press, 1962), pp. 26-27.

57. DeRivera, *Psychological Dimensions,* pp. 61-2, 77-8, 103-4; John Stoessinger, *Nations in Darkness – China, Russia, and America* (New York: Random House, 1975), p. 196.

58. Stoessinger, *Nations in Darkness,* p. 196.

59. An interesting discussion of these problems can be found in Lawrence Freedman, *US Intelligence and the Soviet Strategic Threat* (London: Macmillan, 1977), pp. 184ff.

60. Esp. May, *passim.*

61. Quoted by Jervis, *Perception and Misperception,* pp. 172-3. The Prime Minister quoted was Stanley Baldwin, and the subject-matter was German re-armament.

62. Ibid., Ch. 7.

63. Stoessinger, *Nations in Darkness,* p. 194.

64. See DeRivera's summary, *Psychological Dimensions,* p. 434.

65. Freedman, *U.S. Intelligence,* p. 185.

66. Janis, *Victims of Groupthink,* pp. 191ff.; DeRivera, *Psychological Dimensions,* pp. 432-4.

67. Phillip A. Petersen, 'American Perceptions of Soviet Military Power', *Parameters,* vol. VII, no. 4, pp. 71-82 gives part of the picture.

68. Freedman, *US Intelligence,* pp. 197-8.

69. Ibid., pp. 188-9.

8 STRATEGIC THINKING AND SECURITY IN A LIBERAL SOCIETY

> You're all the same, you intellectuals: everything is cracking and collapsing, the guns are on the point of going off, and you stand there calmly claiming the right to be convinced. *Brunet* (Jean-Paul Sartre, *The Age of Reason*)

> It's a good thing to have people size ye up wrong, whin they've got ye'er measure ye'er in danger. *Mr Dooley* (Finley Peter Dunne, *Mr. Dooley On Making a Will*)

The subject of this book has moved far beyond the problems caused by ethnocentric distortion in particular episodes in strategic affairs. The implications of ethnocentrism are now seen to spread into most questions relating to the security of nations. This final chapter will briefly consider some of the peculiar and complex problems facing liberal societies in trying to maintain their security in a world where potential adversaries have more traditional attitudes to the use of force, together with ideologically distorted or crude conceptions of the outside world. In most respects already the problems of defence policy-making are generally more confusing for the relatively liberal members of international society. Problems such as decisive leadership, military morale, public education in foreign affairs, deciding 'how much is enough?' (or 'what do we want to afford?'), the political guidance of military force — are all difficult and sometimes contentious issues for societies which allow individual freedom, uncensored debate and the democratic interplay of groups. Furthermore, because liberal societies are more likely than authoritarian societies to be sensitive to the attitudes of other nations, the former will be confronted by additional and different dilemmas: one problem arises out of the possibility that any sense of cultural relativism may risk subverting self-confidence.

Sentiment and Security

Interest in ethnocentrism generally begins with the belief that it is a major cause of international conflict. However, if it is assumed that there will always be irreducible suspicion between groups, and ensuing conflicts of interest, then it can be argued that the minimising of ethnocentrism in a particular society may well have risky implications for the security of that society. What might the effects be of minimising ethnocentrism and reducing adversary stereotypes for the running of the armed forces?

When does tolerance become dangerous? Is an 'understanding' society an unsafe society? Is sensitivity synonymous with indecision?

If the arguments in Chapter 5 were valid regarding the utility of ethnocentrism in the running of a military machine, then the disadvantages of freeing military life from 'hate education' are obvious. This is especially so if some well-known maxims and aphorisms about 'understanding' are valid. If it is true that to start to understand is to start to approve, and if to understand is to forgive, then the armed forces of a society free from ethnocentrism are on a slippery slope as far as morale and motivation are concerned. Rumours about the present state of morale in some of NATO's armed forces are relevant in this respect. They show that it is difficult enough to motivate troops in a democracy even in a period of shaky detente. If this is so in countries which by no means approve of their Soviet adversary, how much more difficult would it be if they 'understood' and 'forgave', even if they did not actually want to be part of that system? This type of problem will always be a serious one for relatively tolerant and open societies living in a world where fear and ambition are present, and where military force is seen by some as having a relatively high utility. It is sad, but historically true, that when well-meaning liberal societies have valued peace at almost any price, and have abjured the use of the military instrument, international politics have fallen under the sway of those countries willing to manipulate and use force, and willing to take risks to change the status quo.

This problem leads to the question of national leadership and public opinion. Are tolerant and understanding leaders necessarily the best leaders in terms of a country's security interest? One immediate possibility is that of the Hamlet syndrome: if an individual thinks too deeply about an adversary, and the unpleasant actions which he might have to take, then the momentum for action may be dissipated. An interesting illustration of the impact of such sentiment has been British attitudes towards the complex problems of the 'Muddle East' (as some Foreign Office wags called it). In that region political perplexity was the natural corollary of the British belief that both the Arabs and the Jews had rightful causes. The confusion has been compounded by guilt feelings towards both parties which have lasted from World War I down to the present day. Another good (or bad) illustration of the impact of sentiment, indeed national tolerance, occurred in British relations with Germany in the inter-war years. On this occasion appeasement was the natural corollary of the recognition by leading circles in Britain that Germany had a reasonable case against the Treaty of Versailles. Guilt

Appeasement was a tactic which in some circumstances might have worked, but it was almost inevitably a disaster when tried against Nazi Germany. In the sporting language so much used by British diplomats, Neville Chamberlain backed the wrong horse, forgetting the dictum 'horses for courses'. Neville Chamberlain and his closest advisers fell down badly in this respect. Not only were they self-proclaimed 'men of peace', but they also had a lamentable lack of understanding of the world outside.[1] Statesmen can only appease the appeasable.

Chamberlain believed that he knew and understood Hitler. He believed that he could do a deal with the German Chancellor, and that Hitler could be expected to abide by the deal, like any regular business-man. The consequence of Chamberlain's assumption that Hitler operated within the same framework of norms nearly brought complete disaster to Britain, not to mention the rest of Europe. But the British political community as a whole was no better attuned to international realities than its Prime Minister. Public opinion has often been described as the Achilles heel of democracies: 'foreign policy must rest upon the support of those who cannot be expected to understand what at bottom it is all about – the support, that is, not of the sophisticated few, but of the gullible many'.[2] But when the ostensibly sophisticated few are also not attuned to international realities, such a country is in trouble. This was Britain's position in the late 1930s.

Chamberlain, the man who hoped that others would be as reason-able as himself, lost. He did not know his enemy. Twentieth-century history is not unfamiliar with well-meaning people whose wish to see the best in others, allied to a profound ignorance of foreign affairs, has encouraged conquest or tyranny. The attitude of many Western liberals towards Stalin in the 1930s was the worst example of such credulousness. Hitler was not so gullible: he had a much better understanding of those with whom he was dealing. He understood their fear of war and their desire for peace at almost any price. The British and French leaders projected their own peaceful ambitions onto Hitler, but Hitler did not make the mistake of transferring his ambitions onto them: in this one area at least he was able to compartmentalise his obsessive and evil ethnocentrism. He used his understanding of the British and French leaders not to live in harmony with them, but to exploit their weakness, and to try to dominate them.

Then, as now, many liberal thinkers in the West have underestimated the readiness with which other societies will use their armed force. Neither have they readily appreciated, with their own preference for 'peace' (the status quo), the demands and preference of other societies for *justice* rather than *peace*. This is pertinent today, when in many parts of the world there is a much greater willingness to resort to force than in the industrialised West. If ethnocentrism results in a failure to understand this, important inputs into forecasting will be lost.

If 'men of peace' have a low sensitivity to threat, and if liberal societies have sometimes had to be rescued by a harder breed, it does not necessarily follow that liberal societies will be more secure with self-professed 'men of war' at the helm. Security is more than military power and the ability to manipulate it. As Chapters 5 and 6 showed, an overly militarised policy can provoke the very problems it was designed to ameliorate, and an overly strategic outlook can result in the over-looking of opportunities for constructing a more positive type of peace. Men of war and men of peace need not be mutually exclusive beings, although they often seem to be. E. H. Carr recognised, though not all his readers noted sufficiently, that 'Any sound political thought must be based on elements of both utopia and reality.'[3]

The inter-war period showed that when nation A did not understand B, but B understood A, then the latter was made seriously vulnerable to manipulation and threat. Mutual ethnocentric distortion can cause problems and tension in strategic relations, but so can being understood too well. Knowledge can be used to assist coercion, as Hitler showed. It can also be used to further one's interests in a more seductive fashion, however. This was vividly brought out in a short scene in the film *Lawrence of Arabia*. At one point Prince Faisal was criticising a British military adviser for trying to impose on the Arabs a set of conventional European ideas about fighting. Faisal claimed that these ideas were not transferable. More important, he showed that the narrow Western concept of 'interest' was not appropriate. Lawrence adopted a different approach, and quickly won over the Arab leader to join in the attack on Aqaba. Lawrence appealed not to Prince Faisal's love of money or his anti-Turkish sentiments, but instead stressed that it would be the Prince's *pleasure* to take Aqaba. The Prince was won over. The art of diplomacy-as-seduction has also been attributed to Henry Kissinger. His skill as a 'consummate negotiator' has been explained in terms of his empathetic skill, which enabled him to persuade others that he understood and sympathised with their point of view.[4] His ability to identify with his opponent enabled him to make others believe in his sincerity. This ability permitted tactics of both ingratiation and flattery. But such an approach can also bring risks, if, as has been alleged about Kissinger, the negotiator actually identifies with his opponents more than he realises.[5] The question then becomes: *who* manipulates *whom*?

The not unfamiliar phenomenon in diplomatic history of the psychological 'capturing' of ambassadors is one manifestation of this risk.[6] Although knowledge and understanding can be forms of power, over-identification with the opponent may result in an inner confusion about one's interests and role, with a consequent weakening of one's effectiveness in presenting the case of one's own nation.

Pseudocorollaries and Indecision

Strategists have to make stands. Even if they do not always recognise it, they are in the business of promoting or at least preserving one set of values against another. Unlike philosophers, they are paid not just to think, but also to advise and to decide: and often enough this activity has to take place in the most difficult of circumstances, with inadequate information and limited time. Only the significance of the issues is more than enough. But making decisions is not usually the strategist's main problem. As numerous illustrations in this book have suggested, strategists have often had less trouble in deciding than in conceptualising, less anxiety in dealing out answers than in asking the right questions, and less difficulty in talking than in thinking.

If the strategist is to be directly relevant for policy-makers, he must offer ethnocentric advice:[7] his advice must be conceived in terms of the interest of his own group. This means, ideally, that the analyst must reduce ethnocentric thinking to the minimum if he is to know his enemy, but when it comes to giving advice as to what to do next, his own value preferences must be allowed to surface. Unfortunately, as in the study of other areas of human behaviour, the 'is' and the 'ought' become jumbled. This degrades the process of description, which is at the basis of effective prescription. When he moves beyond analysis to prescription, the strategist has to leave cultural relativism behind, but if he is a good strategist his prescription will have been informed by a sense of strategic relativity.

Academic strategists may have the privilege of thinking free from problems of relevance or practicality, but practising strategists do not. The latter have to establish priorities, and choose courses of action. One implication of this is that the practising strategist, unlike the independent researcher, cannot assume that all cultural values, including political philosophies, are equal, and that one's own is not to be preferred. Policies have to be formulated on the basis of value preference, and often enough in ambiguous and complex circumstances. (Few people are lucky enough to have the choice between simple good and simple evil: usually, those who think they are so lucky need watching carefully.) There invariably comes a point in international politics at which the actor, however minor, must take an ethnocentric stand if he is acting on behalf of a government. Cultural relativism may be viewed as 'an ideal postulate of liberal culture which is tolerant of all other cultures',[8] but it is not a postulate which the practising strategist can follow very far in his everyday life. For the strategic decision-maker relativism is not an option.

For the practising strategist (and for the academic strategist *as citizen*) ethnocentric-free thinking is desirable as long as it does not lead to the 'pseudocorollaries' of cultural relativism when it comes to decision-making. Some of these pseudocorollaries arise out of the concept of mirror images. They are not necessarily implicit in the concept itself, but have been said to have emerged by 'a process of insinuation'.[9]

James Dougherty and Robert Pfaltzgraff have listed a number of illogical inferences which have arisen from mirror-image theory and which also stand as the potential pseudocorollaries of strategic relativism. It may be a pseudocorollary to assume (i) that the social and political vaules of two sides are scarcely distinguishable from each other; (ii) that neither party can properly be cast in the role of aggressor or defender; (iii) that both sides are equally right, equally wrong or equally responsible for pursuing policies that produce international tension; (iv) that the strategic behaviour of the two sides springs from thought processes that are essentially similar; and (v) that the reduction of image distortion can be accomplished with equal ease on both sides. An attitude of strategic relativism is an appropriate one to adopt in analysis and explanation, but its potential pseudocorollaries must be abjured in the process of prescription and decision.

The analyst as strategic anthropologist should be a cultural relativist; he should not seek to pass judgement, or he will risk confusing description and prescription. The strategist as policy adviser, however, must let his own preference intrude. An inability or unwillingness to make judgements will be a discouragement from acting. In some circumstances that may be desirable, but not in all. If an adviser's desire to avoid ethnocentrism results in a preference against making any judgements, he will be in a strategist's nightmare: he will portray all Hamlet's indecisiveness, but he will not have an audience to which to play.

The strategic decision-maker has therefore to walk a difficult path. He has to see the other's viewpoint accurately if he is to base his policy on the real world, but he has to avoid losing his own sense of identity, and the interests of his own community. It was noted earlier that some observers thought that Kissinger had sometimes gone too far in seeing the other's point of view, especially in the Middle East. Kissinger himself was aware of the danger. At one point he warned that 'too often the laudable tendency to see the other point of view is carried to the extreme of refusing to make any moral distinctions'. His admirers, however, believed that he had managed to walk this intellectual, political and temperamental tightrope very successfully. They argued that Kissinger 'always retains a large conceptual framework, never losing sight of his central objectives. . .and that this ability goes hand in hand with his empathetic approach'.[10]

Strategists have to decide, but from what posture? If a label has to be attached, the most useful is that of Charles Manning which was used earlier, namely 'sophisticated realism'. A strategist whose thinking is grounded in the study of mankind as a whole in its global dimension (Manning's 'social cosmology') and is sensitive to cultural relativism will understand both the significance of the human dimension in its many forms and the systemic pressure of the 'absolute predicament and irreducible dilemma'. If this is done successfully the strategist will avoid, in Manning's words,

the stultifications of fanaticism on the one hand and of a pale non-alignment on the other. And so will be vindicated, if only by implication, the virtue, secularly speaking, in an age of evaporating values, of sophisticated realism as an attitude to life.[11]

Such a posture would not guarantee strategic success, but it should avoid the excesses or weakness of other standpoints, such as the inhumanity of militarism on the one hand and what Adam Ulam has called 'the immorality of unrealism'[12] on the other.

It is obviously easier to proclaim sophisticated realism rather than precisely define it. However, its chief characteristics include a knowledgeable, educated and dispassionate mind, clarity about one's own interests and sensitivity to those of others, an appreciation of one's own assumptions, an awareness of the sources of misperception, a sense of what is practical and achievable, and an ability and a willingness to try to look at questions from the perspectives of other nations. Anyone who purports to undertake the task of achieving such self and other-awareness may well be accused of *hubris*, but the greening of strategists is none the less to be encouraged. Andrew Jackson's comment about generals is also relevant for strategists: they cannot guarantee success; they can only conduct themselves so as to deserve it.

Strategists for All Seasons

This book has largely been about failure and fault within the strategic community. This focus has been deliberate, although it entails the risk of spreading an overly jaundiced opinion of strategists. However, this concentration on failure and fault should not obscure either the value of or need for strategists in a world of independent sovereign states. Indeed, given the problems we face, it is very important to have both better strategists and a clearer global vision on strategic affairs. In particular, free and tolerant societies need skilful strategists, for there are no signs that states are going to eschew the use of force to settle some conflicts, and there are no signs that such conflicts are getting fewer in a world which is becoming not a 'global village' but a 'global city', in which a succession of Towers of Babel are set against the dark skyline.

A 'good society', however defined, must show a tough and cunning side if its good qualities are to survive in a brutish world. The tension between man's desire to be good and his need to keep alive and effective was the dilemma which Brecht juggled with so brilliantly in the *Good Woman of Setzuan*. Tolerance and social justice cannot flourish without security. Brecht's message was more universalist than socialist. What price liberal values if the directing of international politics falls into the hands of societies with more ambition and less horror of violence?

Strategy is an overly maligned activity. It is ghastly, grim and grisly. But it is more important than that, for it is also about the survival of cherished human values. The values of liberal societies are protected by their armed forces, as well as threatened by them. The enemy might be *us*, but it might also be *them*. Liberal societies need soldiers, and soldiers need to be 'professional', with all that that entails. In harsh times, their peacetime vices become virtues. Where would freedom and tolerance be in Western Europe today, but for terrible deeds which erased a doctrine that no amount of tolerance could have overcome? But in peace, their wartime virtues become vices. Armed forces cannot be maintained without a baggage train of political as well as economic problems for liberal societies. As professionals with 'the blindness of involvement' they will favour their own instrumentality, and they will find threats to guard against. They should: that is their function. If politicians always believe them, that is their incompetence, and their people's ill fortune. Societies need armed forces like many individuals need a god: they do not want to be troubled when things are going well, but they need a force to appeal to when life gets tough. Such inconsistencies and hypocrisies are part of the 'absolute predicament'.

Politicians are relatively comfortable when operating in such a messy environment, but most other professions are not. For their different reasons, both soldiers and intellectuals look for consistency, but in a world which defies both the black-and-white thinking of the former and the megalogic of the latter, the drive for consistency can be the curse of the military and intellectual classes.

If values are worth having, they are presumably worth preserving. We have to live with the world as it is (or as it seems to be), a world in which it is easier and pleasanter to think up beguiling futures than to see and live with and attempt to improve the existing 'realities'. Benevolent change may or may not come, but if it does it will not come quickly. In the meantime, governments have to attend to the military aspect of security. A balance has to be struck. If one wishes to develop a moderate and well-integrated international society, it is necessary that foreign policy analysts do their utmost to try to understand the real hopes and fears of those who challenge them. But this does not mean that lines do not have to be drawn or that stands do not have to be taken. Nor does it mean that one must abjure the use of force to define those lines or to support those stands. As General Curtis LeMay once put it, in his own inimitable style: 'you don't have to roll over and play dead just because somebody challenges you'.[13]

If the very few societies in the world which are relatively free and tolerant do not take risks to protect their values, there is a possibility that those values will disappear altogether. If the relatively free societies do not continue to flourish, what future is there for the better fulfilment of individual human potential on a wider scale? And what future is there for dealing with the creeping threats to world society as a whole? Western liberal societies, for all their many failings and with all their scope for improvement, do uniquely represent the best hopes for the preservation and furthering of the most cherished human aspirations. Ultimately, there is no need to apologise for some ethnocentric values.

Conclusion

The aim of this book has been to bring together the concepts of ethnocentrism and strategy more explicitly than has so far been the case and to point out the major contours of the relationship. This exercise in consciousness-raising leads to three broad conclusions.

Ethnocentrism Is a Pervasive Feature Throughout the Theory and Practice of Strategy

Strategists and all those concerned with what strategists think and do should recognise ethnocentrism for what it is. It is not simply a matter of national traditions in strategic thinking, but is rather one of the important and pervasive sources of misjudgement which have so often affected the theory and practice of strategy. It should also have become clear that its implications run more widely than strategy: they extend to the study of all aspects of international relationships. There is therefore an important need to raise the level of consciousness about the phenomenon: action is needed in bureaucratic as well as teaching processes. Ethnocentrism plays an important role, together with other distorting mechanisms, in the many processes of misperception in international politics: it is therefore a variable which can only be neglected at somebody's peril. Those who are not aware of the problem need to be made aware, and some of those who say they are aware need to be encouraged to behave as if they are.

Overcoming Ethnocentrism Is Not the Key to Peace

The submerging of ethnocentrism is not synonymous with peace, although interest in ethnocentrism is invariably sparked by the belief that it is. Ethnocentric perceptions may cause, complicate or exacerbate international conflicts, but they are by no means the only or main factors which have these effects. Conflicts of interest do exist, even when seen by the most objective eye. Some conflicts appear irreducible, no matter how much one understands the other's viewpoint. There are some conflicts which, if they cannot be lived with or compromised, have only two solutions; surrender or force. Overcoming ethnocentrism might increase the possibility that nations will look for positive and co-operative solutions to their differences, but it will not remove all conflicts.

Ethnocentrism is not synonymous with peace in another sense. This arises out of the two impulses behind attempts to improve the understanding of other nations. The first impulse is the desire of 'idealists' to minimise *mutual* misunderstanding in order to lessen the sources of international conflict. The second impulse, however, is the professional strategist's hope of maximising his own government's *unilateral* understanding ('knowing the enemy' in military parlance) in order to beat the other nation or at least to deter it successfully. This dichotomy is evident when status quo countries contemplate their adversaries. On the one hand, they would wish their adversaries to reduce their ethnocentric attitudes so that they would understand that no aggressive threat was intended. On the other hand, they would not want their potential adversaries to use any better understanding in order to exploit weaknesses and take advantages (and open societies will always be at a potential disadvantage here, because they inevitably expose more of themselves than their adversaries).

The truth is that 'better' strategies can be used for any purpose. Like all types of knowledge, improved strategic knowledge, unbefuddled by ethnocentrism, can be used on the side of the devil as well as the angels.

Better Strategy Requires that Ethnocentrism and Incuriosity Be Replaced by Sophisticated Realism and Strategic Relativism

As the twentieth century has stumbled along its increasingly crumbly cliff-edge, the need for better strategies and strategists has become self-evident. The Great War was the great lesson. The 'strategic community' in the West has partly developed in response to this need, and has certainly met some of the challenges of our age. But there is plenty left to do if it is fully to conduct itself in such a way as to deserve success for the foreseeable future. While some strategists think they are doing the best job in the best possible world, other people see them as an important part of the problem.

In thinking about the theory and practice of strategy, universities have a special role – some would say a duty. Academic strategists, unlike their professional counterparts, have the opportunity to think in the longer term and take hold of problems which policy-makers hardly have a chance to think about. Academics can try to help by attempting to think of new things (or the old things in a relevant way) and by enlarging our understanding of strategy in an environment of constant political, economic, social and technical change. Academics can attempt to remove the worst faults of the profession and try to set an improved tone. Better habits, if they can be achieved, cannot in themselves assure success, but they can help minimise the possibility of failure. And every single failure in strategy is costly.

In many of the episodes discussed in this book, what has been at fault has not been the effort or professional competence of the analysts, or their rationality or strategic logic, or even their basic factual knowledge. Instead, what has been missing has been a shortage of real understanding of other nations, including a subjective feeling of how other societies see themselves and would wish to be seen. Imagination, feel and empathy are not characteristics normally associated with the hard-nosed strategic community. Nevertheless, is is evident from the illustrations discussed that these qualities are professionally relevant. Existing knowledge informed by ethnocentric perceptions is not enough, whether one's objective is better strategic thinking for national or for international purposes.

enough, whether one's objective is better strategic thinking for national or for international purposes.

Many of the important things which happen in life are not the products of logic or rationality. This is certainly so in the case of strategy, an activity which helps to determine not only whether nations win or lose in war, but how well or badly they live in 'peace'. To attempt to comprehend strategy requires cultural relativism as well as basic knowledge; it requires an understanding of the humanities as well as of technology and economic styles of thinking; and it requires imagination as well as reasoning ability. Strategy is a subject which has its roots in a sort of military logic, set by the constraints of time, space and capability, but its branches reach out far into history, culture and philosophy. This is its nature, and this is only how it can begin to be understood. Any alternative approach is too narrow. Those who conceive strategy too narrowly or too theoretically should take warning from Samuel Butler's words: 'Logic is like the sword – those who appeal to it shall perish by it.'[14]

Notes

1. See, inter alia, Alfred L. Rowse, *Appeasement* (New York: Norton, 1961), pp. 18-19.

2. C.A.W. Manning, *The Nature of International Society* (London: Macmillan, 1975), p. 191.

3. E. H. Carr, *The Twenty Years' Crisis, 1919-1939: An Introduction to the Study of International Relations* (London: Macmillan, 1940), pp. 89, 94.

4. Bruce Mazlish, *Kissinger. The European Mind in American Policy* (New York: Basic Books Inc., 1976), pp. 202-7.

5. Ibid., p. 204.

6. Robert Jervis, *Perception and Misperception in International Politics* (Princeton, N.J.: Princeton University Press, 1976), pp. 332-3; Fred Charles Ilke, *How Nations Negotiate* (New York: Harper and Row, 1964), pp. 143-50.

7. This is so for foreign policy analysts in general. See Colin S. Gray, 'The Practice of Theory in International Relations', *Political Studies*, Vol. XXII, No. 2, June 1974, pp. 130-1.

8. David Bindey 'Cultural Relativism' in *International Encyclopedia of The Social Sciences*, vol. 3, (New York: Macmillan Co. and Free Press, 1968), pp. 546-7.

9. James E. Dougherty and Robert L. Pfaltzgraff, *Contending Theories of International Relations* (Philadelphia: J. B. Lippincott Co., 1971), p. 226.

10. Mazlish, *Kissinger*, pp. 204-5.

11. Manning, *International Society*, p. 216.

12. Adam B. Ulam, *The Rivals. America and Russia since World War II* (New York: Viking Press, 1971), pp. 383-95.

13. Quoted by Andrew Wilson, *War Gaming* (Harmondsworth, Middx: Penguin Books, 1970), p. 125.

14. Samuel Butler, 'First Principles', *The Note-Books of Samuel Butler*, (London: A.C. Fifield, 1918), p. 330.

INDEX

Prepared by Jane Davies